Berlitz® speaking your language

German
in 30 days
Course Book

by Angelika G. Beck

30

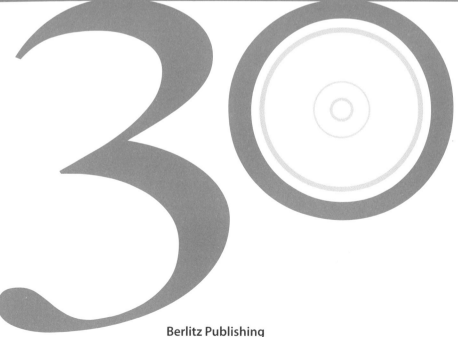

Berlitz Publishing
New York London Singapore

Contacting the Editors

Every effort has been made to provide accurate information in this publication, but changes are inevitable. The publisher cannot be responsible for any resulting loss, inconvenience or injury. We would appreciate it if readers would call our attention to any errors or outdated information. Please contact us at: comments@berlitzpublishing.com

Second edition
Printed in China, October 2014

Original edition: 2003 by Langenscheidt KG, Berlin and Munich

Senior Commissioning Editor: Kate Drynan
Design: Beverley Speight
Picture research: Beverley Speight
German editor: Dr Vincent Docherty

Cover photos: © All APA/Jon Santa-Cruz except for 'A sign' shot APA/Glyn Genin
Interior photos: © istockphotos p62, 71, 80, 102, 116, 124, 142, 151, 159, 182, 189, 195, 203, 211, 239, 258; APA Peter Stuckings p15; APA Jon Santa-Cruz p22, 30, 53, 134, 173, 221, 231; APA Bev Speight p108, 245; APA Mina Patria p252; APA Nowitz p91, 165; APA Britta Jaschinski p40

Distribution

Worldwide
APA Publications GmbH & Co. Verlag KG
(Singapore branch)
7030 Ang Mo Kio Ave 5
08-65 Northstar @ AMK, Singapore 569880
Email: apasin@singnet.com.sg

UK and Ireland
Dorling Kindersley Ltd
(a Penguin Company)
80 Strand, London, WC2R 0RL, UK
Email: sales@uk.dk.com

US
Ingram Publisher Services
One Ingram Blvd, PO Box 3006
La Vergne, TN 37086-1986
Email: ips@ingramcontent.com

Australia
Woodslane
10 Apollo St
Warriewood, NSW 2102
Email: info@woodslane.com.au

German
in 30 days

Course Book
by Angelika G. Beck

Contents

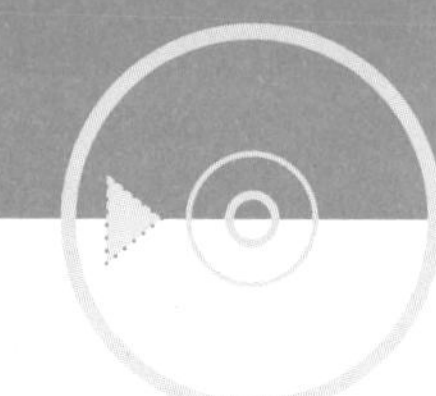

How to Use this Book

German in 30 Days is a self-study course which will provide you with a basic knowledge of everyday German in a very short time. The course is divided into 30 short, manageable daily lessons. This book will familiarize you with the main grammatical structures of German and provide you with a good command of essential vocabulary. In 30 days you will acquire both an active and a passive understanding of the language, enabling you to function effectively in day-to-day life.

Each chapter is an episode in a journey that takes place over 30 days, from your arrival to your final departure, with the main focus on typical, day-to-day situations. Each day has the same pattern: first, there is a short intro into what you will learn as well as some country and culture information about Germany. You will then have a text in German – generally a dialogue – followed by a grammar section and a number of exercises to help reinforce what you have learned. At the end of each lesson you will find a list of vocabulary. The quick grammar and vocabulary tests, together with the answer key at the back of the book, will enable you to check your progress.

The audio CD contains all the dialogues from the book. These are marked by a CD symbol. Days 1 to 10 are spoken twice: the first time, quickly and fluently so that you get used to hearing everyday German and, the second time, slowly and more clearly. From day 11 onwards you'll be advanced enough to follow the German text, which will now be spoken only once, in the faster speech of everyday language.

Pronunciation

1. Spelling

Use of capital letters

In German the following words are written with a capital letter:

– the first word in a sentence

Ich komme aus Japan.	I come from Japan.

– all nouns

Tee, Computer, Foto...	tea, computer, photo...

– nominalized verbs

das Lesen, das Schwimmen...	reading, swimming...

– nominalized adjectives

etwas Gutes,	something good,
das Schönste...	the most beautiful thing...

– pronouns (polite forms only)

Sie, Ihnen, Ihr:	
Wie heißen Sie?	What's your name?
Wie geht es Ihnen?	How are you?
Ist das Ihr Gepäck?	Is this your luggage?

Use of lower case letters

The following words are written with a lower case letter:

– verbs

heißen, trinken, kommen...	to be called, to drink, to come...

–	adjectives	
	groß, klein…	large, small…
–	pronouns	
	ich, du, er… mein, dein…	I, you, he… my, your…
–	conjunctions	
	und, oder, aber…	and, or, but…
–	adverbs	
	schnell, dort, bald…	quickly, there, soon…
–	prepositions	
	für, auf, unter, in…	for, on, under, in…

ß and ss

ß is found

–	after long vowels:	
	Straße, Spaß, grüßen…	street, fun, to greet…

ss is found

–	after short vowels:	
	Kuss, muss, dass…	kiss, must, that…

2. Pronunciation

Long vowels

–	a doubled vowel is long:	
	Tee, Zoo…	tea, zoo…
–	a vowel followed by an **h** is long:	
	Jahr, fahren, ihr…	year, to drive, her…

– a vowel is long when it is followed by a consonant and then by a vowel:

fragen, hören, Rose… ask, to hear, rose…

– when an **e** follows an **i**, the **i** is long:

Sie, wie, viel… you, how, much…

Short vowels

– a vowel at the end of a word is short:

Taxi, Katze, lese… taxi, cat, read ...

– a vowel is usually short when two or more consonants follow:

offen, morgens, Herbst… to open, in the morning, autumn…

Consonants

Specific characteristics

-ch:

After **i** and **e**, after **l**, **r**, **n** and with the ending **-ig**, **ch** is formed at the front of the mouth:

ich, sprechen… I, to speak…

After **a**, **o** and **u**, **ch** is formed at the back of the mouth:

machen, noch, Buch, auch… to make, still, book, also…

st and **sp**

St- or **sp-** at the beginning of a word or syllable is pronounced **sch**: ***stehen, Gespräch…*** to stand, conversation…

Plurals

To indicate the plural of a noun, the following conventions are used in the vocabulary list at the end of each day:

– singular and plural are identical

Example:

Zimmer, das, – room ***Zimmer*** rooms

– + letter add that letter to the end of the word

Example:

Rose, die, –n rose ***Rosen*** roses

–¨ replace the **a**, **o**, or **u** closest to the end of the word with that letter's umlaut (**ä**, **ö**, **ü**)

Example:

Bruder, der, –¨ brother ***Brüder*** brothers

Exception: an **au** construction becomes **äu**

Example:

Maus, die, –¨e mouse ***Mäuse*** mice

–¨ + letter(s) replace the final **a**, **o**, or **u** with its umlaut, and add the letter(s) to the end of the word

Example:

Wort, das, –¨er word ***Wörter*** words

The Alphabet

A	ah
B	bay
C	tsay
D	day
E	ay
F	eff
G	gay
H	haa
I	eeh
J	yot
K	kah
L	ell
M	em
N	en
O	oh
P	pay
Q	koo
R	er
S	es
ß	esszet
T	tay
U	ooh
V	fow
W	vay
X	ix
Y	uep-siilohn
Z	tset

The ¨ is an accent called an **umlaut**. It can appear on **ä**, **ö** and **ü**. Note that the **umlaut** changes the sound of the vowel.

Numbers

0	**null** *nool*
1	**eins** *iens*
2	**zwei** *tsvie*
3	**drei** *drie*
4	**vier** *feer*
5	**fünf** *fewnf*
6	**sechs** *zehks*
7	**sieben** *zeeb•uhn*
8	**acht** *ahkht*
9	**neun** *noyn*
10	**zehn** *tsehn*
11	**elf** *ehlf*
12	**zwölf** *tsverlf*
13	**dreizehn** *driet•sehn*
14	**vierzehn** *feert•sehn*
15	**fünfzehn** *fewnf•tsehn*
16	**sechszehn** *zehk•tsehn*
17	**siebzehn** *zeep•tsehn*
18	**achtzehn** *ahkht•tsehn*
19	**neunzehn** *noyn•tsehn*
20	**zwanzig** *tsvahnt•seek*
21	**einundzwanzig** *ien•oond•tsvahn•tseek*
22	**zweiundzwanzig** *tsvie•oond•tsvahn•tseek*

30	**dreißig** *drie•seekh*
31	**einunddreißig** *ien•oont•drie•seekh*
40	**vierzig** *feert•seek*
50	**fünfzig** *fewnf•tseeg*
60	**sechzig** *zehkht•seeg*
70	**siebzig** *zeeb•tseeg*
80	**achtzig** *ahkht•tseeg*
90	**neunzig** *noynt•seek*
100	**einhundert** *ien•hoon•dehrt*
101	**einhunderteins** *ien•hoon•dehr•tiens*
200	**zweihundert** *tsvie•hoon•dehrt*
500	**fünfhundert** *fewnf•hoon•dehrt*
1,000	**eintausend** *ien•tow•zuhnt*
10,000	**zehntausend** *tsehn•tow•zuhnt*
1,000,000	**eine Million** *ien•uh mihl•yohn*

Days

Monday **Montag** *mohn•tahk*

Tuesday **Dienstag** *deens•tahk*

Wednesday **Mittwoch** *miht•vohkh*

Thursday **Donnerstag** *dohn•ehrs•tahk*

Friday **Freitag** *frie•tahk*

Saturday **Samstag** *zahms•tahk*

Sunday **Sonntag** *zohn•tahk*

Months

January **Januar** *yahn•ooahr*

February **Februar** *fehb•rooahr*

March **März** *mehrts*

April **April** *ah•prihl*

May **Mai** *mai*

June **Juni** *yoo•nee*

July **Juli** *yoo•lee*

August **August** *ow•goost*

September **September** *zehp•tehm•berr*

October **Oktober** *ohk•toh•berr*

November **November** *noh•vehm•berr*

December **Dezember** *deh•tsehm•berr*

day: 1

At the Airport

Welcome to Germany! Day 1 introduces you to the present tense of verbs such as *wohnen* (to live) and the essential *sein* (to be) and *haben* (to have). You will learn how to talk about yourself and ask basic questions. You will also start to build your vocabulary, and pick up some important language and cultural tips.

FORMS OF ADDRESS…

Sie *is the polite form of address to use when speaking to a stranger:* ***Wie heißen Sie?*** *(What's your name?);* ***Wo wohnen Sie, Frau Müller?*** *(Where do you live, Mrs Müller?).* ***Du*** *is the form of address to use for friends and relatives as well as for children and young people up to about 16:* ***Wie heißt du?*** *(What's your name?);* ***Wo wohnst du, Franz?*** *(Where do you live, Franz?).*

Dialogue: Im Flugzeug

Yuki is now in Munich. Munich is in southern Germany and is the capital of Bavaria. At the beginning Yuki had some difficulty understanding people who spoke Bavarian. In Germany, each town and region has its own dialect.

Flugbegleiterin:	**Etwas zu trinken?**
Yuki:	**Ja, bitte.**
Flugbegleiterin:	**Kaffee oder Tee?**
Yuki:	**Kaffee, bitte.**
Flugbegleiterin:	**Mit Milch und Zucker?**
Yuki:	**Mit Milch.**
Theresa:	**Entschuldigung, wann sind wir in München?**
Flugbegleiterin:	**In zwei Stunden.**
Yuki:	**Kommen Sie aus Deutschland?**
Theresa:	**Nein, ich komme aus Luxemburg. Und Sie?**
Yuki:	**Ich komme aus Japan.**
Theresa:	**Aus Tokio?**
Yuki:	**Nein, aus Sapporo. Und wo wohnen Sie?**
Theresa:	**In Augsburg.**
Yuki:	**Und ich, ich wohne in München bei Frau Glück.**
Theresa:	**Sie haben aber Glück!**

English conversation: On the plane

Flight attendant:	**Something to drink?**
Yuki:	**Yes, please.**
Flight attendant:	**Coffee or tea?**
Yuki:	**Coffee, please.**
Flight attendant:	**With milk and sugar?**
Yuki:	**Just with milk.**
Theresa:	**Excuse me, when do we arrive in Munich?**
Flight attendant:	**In two hours' time.**
Yuki:	**Do you come from Germany?**
Theresa:	**No, I come from Luxembourg. And you?**
Yuki:	**I come from Japan.**
Theresa:	**From Tokyo?**
Yuki:	**No, from Sapporo. And where do you live?**
Theresa:	**In Augsburg.**
Yuki:	**I live in Munich at Mrs. Glück's.**
Theresa:	**You're really lucky.**

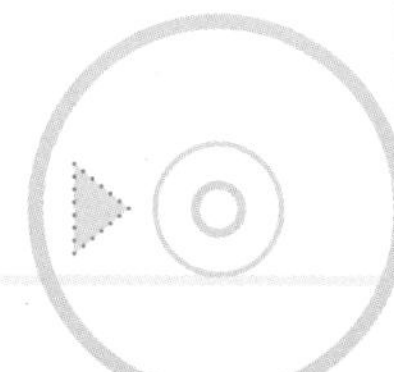

Grammar

Personal pronouns

singular		
1st person	ich	I
2nd person	du *(infml)*/Sie *(fml)*	you
3rd person	er/sie/es	he/she/it

plural		
1st person	wir	we
2nd person	ihr *(infml)*/Sie *(fml)*	you
3rd person	sie	they

There are three personal pronouns for the 3rd person singular.

masculine	er	he	*(e.g.* **der** *Mann/man)*
feminine	sie	she	*(e.g.* **die** *Frau/woman)*
neuter	es	it	*(e.g.* **das** *Kind/child)*

infml = informal *fml = formal* *pl = plural*

Note that the polite form **Sie** is used for both the 2nd person singular and plural.

Wohnen **Sie** in München? *(Frau Glück)*	Do you live in Munich?
Wohnen **Sie** in München? *(Frau Glück and Herr Mayer)*	Do you live in Munich?

Present tense: regular verbs

wohnen	**to live**				
singular			*plural*		
ich	wohn**e**	I live	wir	wohn**en**	we live
du	wohn**st**	you live *(infml)*	ihr	wohn**t**	you (pl) live
Sie	wohn**en**	you live *(fml)*	Sie	wohn**en**	you live *(fml)*
er/sie/es	wohn**t**	he/she/it lives	sie	wohn**en**	they live

Note that the forms of the 1st and 3rd person plural (**wir** and **sie**) and the polite forms of the 2nd person singular and plural (**Sie**) have the same ending as the infinitive: **-en**.
The forms of the 3rd person singular (**er/sie/es**) and 2nd person plural (**ihr**) have the same ending: **-t**.

Present tense: sein and haben

sein	to be		
singular		*plural*	
ich	bin	wir	sind
du	bist	ihr	seid
Sie	sind	Sie	sind
er/sie/es	ist	sie	sind

haben	to have		
singular		*plural*	
ich	habe	wir	haben
du	hast	ihr	habt
Sie	haben	Sie	haben
er/sie/es	hat	sie	haben

Affirmative statements

Ich	komme	aus Luxemburg.	I come from Luxembourg.
1	2	3	
subject	*verb*		

In statements the subject is in position 1 and the verb in position 2.

Questions: with a question word

Wo	wohnen	Sie?	Where do you live?
1	2	3	
	verb	*subject*	

With question words (**wann**, **wo**...) the verb is in position 2 and the subject in position 3.

Questions: without a question word

Kommen	Sie	aus Deutschland?	Do you come from Germany?
1	2	3	
verb	*subject*		

Without a question word, the verb is in position 1 and the subject in position 2.

Exercises

Exercise 1

Complete the sentences using the correct personal pronouns.

1 ....wohnt in Deutschland. (feminine)

2 ....trinkst Bier.

3 .... /....................... kommen aus Amerika.

4 .... trinkt Tee. (masculine)

5 .... kommt aus Mexiko. (feminine)

Exercise 2

Complete the sentences using the correct form of the verb.

1 Ihr (lernen) ....Deutsch.

2 Wir (wohnen) ....in Berlin.

3 Er (kommen) ....aus China.

4 Sie (trinken) ....Kaffee.
(Yuki)

5 Ich (lernen) ....Französisch.

Exercise 3

Fill in the correct form of *sein*.

1 Du ....in Nürnberg.

2 Ihr ....in München.

3 Sie ....aus Köln.
(Michaela and Peter)

4 Wann .... wir in München?

Exercise 4

Fill in the correct form of *haben*.

1 Sie .... /..........................Glück.

2 Wir ....Pech.

3 Ich ....Hunger.

4 Es ....Durst.

Exercise 5

Match the following sentences, based on the dialogue on page 16.

1 Wo wohnt Yuki?

2 Kommt Yuki aus Tokio?

3 Wo wohnt Theresa?

4 Was trinkt Yuki?

a Sie trinkt Kaffee mit Milch.

b Sie wohnt bei Frau Glück.

c Sie wohnt in Luxemburg.

d Nein, sie kommt aus Sapporo.

1 .... **2** .... **3** .... **4** ....

Vocabulary

Below is a list of vocabulary encountered in this chapter.

aber *in:* **Sie haben aber Glück!**	*really*
aus	*from*
Amerika	*America*
Augsburg	*Augsburg*
bei *in:* **bei Frau Glück**	*at*
bitte	*please*
China	*China*
Deutschland	*Germany*
Deutsch	*German*
Durst *in:* **Durst haben**	*to be thirsty*
Entschuldigung	*excuse me*
etwas zu trinken	*something to drink*
Flugbegleiterin, die	*flight attendant*
Französisch	*French*
Frau, die	*woman*
Glück, das *in:* **Glück haben**	*to be lucky*
haben	*to have*
heißen *in:* **wie heißen Sie?**	*to be called*
Hunger, der *in:* **Hunger haben**	*to be hungry*
ich	*I*
in	*in*
ja	*yes*
Japan	*Japan*
Kaffee, der	*coffee*
Kind, das	*child*
Köln	*Cologne*
kommen	*to come*
lernen	*to learn*
Luxemburg	*Luxembourg*
Mann, der	*man*
Mexiko	*Mexico*
Milch, die	*milk*
mit	*with*
München	*Munich*
nein	*no*
Nürnberg	*Nuremberg*
oder	*or*
Österreich	*Austria*
Pech, das *in:* **Pech haben**	*to be unlucky*
Sapporo	*Sapporo*
sein	*to be*
Sie	*you (fml)*
Stunden, die *(pl)*	*hours*
Tee, der	*tea*
Tokio	*Tokyo*
trinken	*to drink*
und	*and*
wann?	*when?*
Wien	*Vienna*
wir	*we*
wo?	*where?*
wohnen	*to live*
Zucker, der	*sugar*
zwei	*two*

day: 2

At home

Day 2 sees you settling into your new home. You will learn about the gender of nouns, as well as definite and indefinite articles and how to ask questions. You will learn the nouns that take the nominative and accusative case, as well as how the verbs you need to say you know *(können)*, may *(dürfen)* and would like to *(mögen)*.

HALLO ...

At any time of the day you can greet someone formally with ***Guten Tag!*** *(Good day!) and by shaking hands. Up until about 10:00 a.m. you can also greet each other with* ***Guten Morgen!*** *(Good morning!). Then from 6:00 p.m. you use* ***Guten Abend!*** *(Good evening!). When leaving, all you have to say is* ***Auf Wiedersehen!*** *(Goodbye!), and shake hands again.*
More informally, you can just say ***Hallo!*** *or* ***Grüß dich!*** *(only used with friends) and a simple* ***Tschüs*** *on leaving.*

German conversation: Ankunft bei Frau Glück

Yuki:	Guten Tag, Frau Glück! Ich bin Yuki.
Frau Glück:	Guten Tag! Willkommen in Deutschland! Bitte kommen Sie herein.
Yuki:	Danke!
Frau Glück:	Hier ist das Wohnzimmer. Bitte, nehmen Sie Platz! Sie sind sicher durstig. Möchten Sie ein Wasser, einen Kaffee oder eine Cola?
Yuki:	Eine Cola bitte.
Frau Glück:	Hier ist die Küche. Hier essen wir. Das ist das Schlafzimmer. Das ist das Bad. Da können Sie duschen. Und das Zimmer ist für Sie.
Yuki:	Oh! Das Zimmer ist groß und hell. Da habe ich viel Platz. Es gibt auch einen Fernseher!
Frau Glück:	Ja, Sie können hier fernsehen oder im Wohnzimmer.
Yuki:	Und wer ist das?
Frau Glück:	Das ist Mainzel, die Katze. Sie dürfen Mainzel ruhig streicheln.
Yuki:	Ich liebe Tiere. Ich habe zu Hause einen Hund. Er heißt Männchen.

English conversation: Arriving at Mrs. Glück's

Yuki:	Hello, Mrs. Glück. I'm Yuki.
Mrs. Glück:	Hello, welcome to Germany. Please, come in.
Yuki:	Thank you.
Mrs. Glück:	Here is the living room. Please, have a seat. I'm sure you must be thirsty. Would you like a glass of water, a coffee or a cola?
Yuki:	A cola, please.
Mrs. Glück:	Here is the kitchen. We eat in here. That's the bedroom. That's the bathroom. You can have a shower there. And this room is for you.
Yuki:	Oh, the room is big and light. There's lots of space. There's a TV, too.
Mrs. Glück:	Yes, you can watch television here or in the living room.
Yuki:	And who is that?
Mrs. Glück:	That's Mainzel, the cat. You can pet Mainzel if you want.
Yuki:	I love animals. I've got a dog at home. His name is Männchen.

Grammar

Nouns: gender

Each noun has a gender. The definite article shows the gender: **der** masculine, **das** neuter, **die** feminine.

singular		
masculine	*neuter*	*feminine*
der Mann	**das** Kind	**die** Frau
der Fernseher	**das** Bad	**die** Flugbegleiterin
der Kaffee	**das** Wasser	**die** Stunde

Tip: always learn nouns with the article:
der Fernseher, **das Wasser**, **die Stunde**.

There are some rules which help you to recognize gender, i.e. female persons are normally feminine, and male persons are usually masculine. However, nouns ending in **-chen** e.g. **das Mädchen**, **das Brötchen**, **das Kätzchen** are always neuter and take the article **das**.

Gender rules	
feminine	
female persons, animals and professions	**die Mutter, die Oma, die Katze, die Lehrerin, die Kellnerin** mother, grandma, cat, teacher, waitress
masculine	
male persons, animals and professions	**der Vater, der Opa, der Kater, der Lehrer, der Kellner** father, granddad, tomcat, teacher, waiter
days of the week	**der Montag, der Dienstag, der Mittwoch, der Donnerstag, der Freitag, der Samstag, der Sonntag** Monday, Tuesday, Wednesday, Thursday, Friday, Saturday, Sunday
neuter	
nouns with the ending **-chen** and **-o**	**das Mädchen, das Kätzchen, das Auto, das Büro** girl, kitten, car, office

Definite and indefinite articles

masculine	*neuter*	*feminine*
der/ein Mann	**das/ein** Kind	**die/eine** Frau
der/ein Kaffee	**das/ein** Wasser	**die/eine** Stunde

Indefinite article: **ein**, **ein**, **eine** is used when something is unknown or new in the text.
Definite article: **der**, **die**, **das** is used when something is known or not new.
e.g.: **Das ist ein Zimmer**. **Das Zimmer ist groß und hell**. *(That is **a** room. **The** room is big and light.)*

Nominative and accusative

Nouns can be in four different cases: nominative, accusative, dative or genitive. Most verbs take the accusative (see the list below). Only two verbs, **sein** and **werden**, take the nominative.
The verb determines which case the noun and article take.

verbs with the nominative	**sein, werden**	to be, to become, to get
	Das ist **die Küche.**	That is the kitchen.
verbs with the accusative	**haben, kaufen, brauchen, trinken, nehmen, mögen**	to have, to buy, to need, to drink, to take, to like
	(infinitive of: **ich möchte***)*	
	Ich habe **eine Katze.**	I have a cat.
	Ich möchte **einen Kaffee.**	I'd like a coffee.

Definite and indefinite articles: nominative and accusative

singular	*masculine*	*neuter*	*feminine*
nominative	der ein Kaffee	das/ein Wasser	die/eine Cola
accusative	den/ein**en** Kaffee	das/ein Wasser	die/eine Cola

Question words for persons and things: nominative and accusative

Person(s)

nominative		
Das ist Yuki.	**Wer** ist das?	Who is that?
Das sind Yuki und Frau Glück.	**Wer** sind die Frauen?	Who are the women?
accusative		
Ich sehe Yuki.	**Wen** sehen Sie?	Who(m) do you see?
Ich sehe Yuki und Frau Glück.	**Wen** sehen Sie?	Who(m) do you see?

Thing(s)		
nominative		
Das ist ein Fernseher.	Was ist das?	What is that?
Das sind zwei Fernseher.	Was sind das?	What are these?
accusative		
Ich sehe einen Fernseher.	Was sehen Sie?	What do you see?
Ich sehe zwei Fernseher.	Was sehen Sie?	What do you see?

Modal verbs

können	can		
singular		*plural*	
ich	kann	wir	können
du	kannst	ihr	könnt
Sie	können	Sie	können
er/sie/es	kann	sie	können

dürfen	may		
singular		*plural*	
ich	darf	wir	dürfen
du	darfst	ihr	dürft
Sie	dürfen	Sie	dürfen
er/sie/es	darf	sie	dürfen

mögen*	would like		
singular		*plural*	
ich	möchte	wir	möchten
du	möchtest	ihr	möchtet
Sie	möchten	Sie	möchten
er / sie / es	möchte	sie	möchten

***Note that mögen here is in the subjunctive tense (*would* like).**

Mögen in the present tense can also mean, to like, e.g.:

ich mag, du magst, er/sie/es mag, wir mögen , ihr mögt, Sie/sie mögen

Exercises

Exercise 1

Complete the sentences using der, die, or das.

1 ....Hund heißt Männchen.

2 ....Baby schreit.

3 ....Zimmer ist für Sie.

4 ....Bad ist groß.

5 ....Fernseher ist im Wohnzimmer.

Exercise 2

Complete the sentences using the correct article.

1 Das ist .... Frau. .... Frau heißt Yuki.

2 Das ist .... Hund. .... Hund heißt Männchen.

3 Das ist .... Katze. .... Katze heißt Mainzel.

Exercise 3

Complete the sentences using ein, eine or einen.

1 Ich möchte .... Tee und .... Wasser.

2 Ich nehme .... Kaffee mit Milch.

3 Yuki trinkt .... Cola.

4 Yuki hat .... Hund.

5 Frau Glück hat .... Katze.

6 Er kauft .... Auto.

Exercise 4

Complete the sentences using wer, wen or was.

1 .... ist das? Das ist Frau Glück.

2 .... ist das? Ein Fernseher.

3 Ich sehe die Lehrerin. .... sehen Sie?

4 Ich nehme einen Kaffee.

.... nehmen Sie?

5 Wir sehen Yuki. .... sehen Sie?

Exercise 5

Fill in the correct form of können, dürfen or mögen.

1 Was (mögen) .... du trinken?

2 Wir (dürfen) .... hier nicht parken.

3 Yuki (können) .... im Wohnzimmer fernsehen.

4 Ihr (können) .... im Bad duschen.

5 Du (dürfen) .... hier rauchen.

Vocabulary

Below is a list of vocabulary encountered in this chapter.

Ankunft, die, -¨e*	*arrival*
auch	*too*
Auto, das, -s	*car*
Baby, das, -s	*baby*
Bad, das, -¨er	*bathroom*
brauchen	*to need*
Brötchen, das, -	*roll*
Büro, das, -s	*office*
Cola, die, -	*coke*
da	*then*
danke	*thank you*
Dienstag, der, -e	*Tuesday*
Donnerstag, der, -e	*Thursday*
dürfen	*may*
durstig	*thirsty*

duschen (sich)	*to take a shower*
es gibt	*there is/there are*
essen	*to eat*
fernsehen	*to watch TV*
Fernseher, der, -	*television (set)*
Flugbegleiter, die, -s	*flight attendant*
Freitag, der, -e	*Friday*
für	*for*
groß	*big*
guten Tag!	*hello*
hell	*light*
herein *in:* **kommen Sie herein**	*in*
hier	*here*
Hund, der, -e	*dog*
Kater, der, -	*tomcat*
Kätzchen, das, -	*kitten*
Katze, die, -n	*cat*
kaufen	*to buy*
können	*can, to be able to*
Küche, die, -n	*kitchen*
Lehrer, der, -	*teacher*
Lehrerin, die, -nen	*teacher*
lieben	*to like; to love*
Mädchen, das, -	*girl*
Mittwoch, der, -e	*Wednesday*
(ich) möchte	*(I) would like*
mögen	*to like*
Montag, der, -e	*Monday*
Mutter, die, -¨er	*mother*
nehmen	*to take*
nehmen Sie Platz!	*take a seat*
nicht	*not*
Oma, die, -s	*grandma*
Opa, der, -s	*granddad*
parken	*to park*
Platz, der, -¨e	*room*
Radio, das, -s	*radio*
rauchen	*to smoke*
ruhig in: ruhig streicheln	*if you want*
Samstag, der, -e	*Saturday*
Schlafzimmer, das, -	*bedroom*
schreien	*to cry*
sehen	*to see*
sicher	*sure*
Sonntag, der, -e	*Sunday*
streicheln	*to stroke/to pet*
Tier, das, -e	*animal*
trinken	*to drink*
Vater, der, -¨er	*father*
viel	*a lot of*
was?	*what?*
Wasser, das, -	*water*
wer?	*who?*
willkommen	*welcome*
Wohnzimmer, das, -	*living room*
zeigen	*to show*
zu Hause	*at home*
Zimmer, das, -	*room*

day: 3

Downtown

Day 3 talks about irregular verbs, modal verbs (*wollen* - to want, *sollen* - should, and *müssen* - must), word order, how to use the pronoun *man*, negation (how to say no using *nicht*). You'll also pick up some new vocabulary and learn a little about public transport.

LOCAL TRANSPORT...

There is a good public transport system in all the major cities. You can usually use the same ticket on buses, trams, the subway and suburban trains. You can get tickets at the kiosks in the station, from ticket machines and directly from the driver on the bus. Most ticket machines take coins and notes and give change. If you travel on the subway or suburban trains, you must stamp your ticket before going on the platform or boarding.

German conversation: Yuki möchte in die Stadt fahren

Yuki: **Ich möchte in die Stadt fahren.**
Frau Glück: **Da nehmen Sie am besten die U-Bahn.**
Yuki: **Wo ist denn die Haltestelle?**
Frau Glück: **Gleich um die Ecke.**
Yuki: **Wohin fährt die U-Bahn?**
Frau Glück: **Direkt ins Zentrum.**
Yuki: **Wie viele Stationen muss ich denn fahren?**
Frau Glück: **Vier Stationen bis ins Zentrum.**
Yuki: **Wo kann ich eine Fahrkarte für die U-Bahn kaufen?**
Frau Glück: **Am Automaten oder am Kiosk. Kaufen Sie am besten eine Streifenkarte.**

(Am Kiosk)

Yuki: **Guten Morgen! Eine Streifenkarte, bitte.**
Herr Schmidt: **Bitte schön! 9 Euro.**
Yuki: **Ich will in die Stadt. Wie viele Streifen muss ich stempeln?**
Herr Schmidt: **Zwei Streifen. Auf Wiedersehen!**

English conversation: Yuki wants to go to town

Yuki: **I want to go into town.**
Mrs. Glück: **Then the best thing to do is to take the subway.**
Yuki: **Where is the station?**
Mrs. Glück: **Just round the corner.**
Yuki: **Where does the subway go?**
Mrs. Glück: **Right into the city centre.**
Yuki: **How many stops are there?**
Mrs. Glück: **Four stops to the centre.**
Yuki: **Where can I buy a ticket for the subway?**
Mrs. Glück: **From the ticket machine or at a kiosk. The best thing to do is to buy a strip ticket.**

(At a kiosk)

Yuki: **Good morning. A strip ticket, please.**
Mr. Schmidt: **Here you are. 9 euros, please.**
Yuki: **I want to go to the city centre. How many strips should I stamp?**
Mr. Schmidt: **Two strips. Goodbye.**

Grammar

The particle denn

Wo ist denn die Haltestelle?
Where is the station *(then)*?
Denn is used only in questions. Denn makes the question sound less direct.

Present tense: irregular verbs

nehmen	**to take**		
singular		*plural*	
ich	nehme	wir	nehmen
du	nimmst	ihr	nehmt
Sie	nehmen	Sie	nehmen
er/sie/es	nimmt	sie	nehmen

fahren	**to go**		
singular		*plural*	
ich	fahre	wir	fahren
du	fährst	ihr	fahrt
Sie	fahren	Sie	fahren
er /sie /es	fährt	sie	fahren

sprechen	**to speak**		
singular		*plural*	
ich	spreche	wir	sprechen
du	sprichst	ihr	sprecht
Sie	sprechen	Sie	sprechen
er/sie/es	spricht	sie	sprechen

Modal verbs

wollen	**to want**		
singular		*plural*	
ich	will	wir	wollen
du	willst	ihr	wollt
Sie	wollen	Sie	wollen
er/sie/es	will	sie	wollen

sollen	should		
singular		*plural*	
ich	soll	wir	sollen
du	sollst	ihr	sollt
Sie	sollen	Sie	sollen
er/sie/es	soll	sie	sollen

müssen	to have to, must		
singular		*plural*	
ich	muss	wir	müssen
du	musst	ihr	müsst
Sie	müssen	Sie	müssen
er/sie/es	muss	sie	müssen

Modal verb + main verb: word order

Note the position of the modal verb and the main verb in the infinitive in the following sentences. The infinitive always comes at the end of the sentence.

statement:			
Yuki	kann	im Wohnzimmer	fernsehen.
Yuki	will	in die Stadt	fahren.

question word:			
Wo	kann	ich eine Fahrkarte	kaufen?
Wie viele Stationen	muss	ich denn	fahren?

question:		
Darf	ich Mainzel	streicheln?
modal verb		infinitive

When the context is clear, it is possible to omit the infinitive:

Ich möchte einen Kaffee. *(trinken)*	I'd like a cup of coffee.
Yuki will in die Stadt. *(fahren)*	I want to go into town.

The meaning of the modal verbs

wollen	
Yuki will in die Stadt fahren.	Yuki wants to go into town.

Wollen expresses an intention or a wish. Children use this word a lot: Ich will ein Eis. *(I want an ice cream.)* When adults want something, they generally use the following of mögen:
Ich möchte einen Kaffee. *(I would like a coffee.)*

sollen

Sie **sollen** nicht rauchen.	You shouldn't smoke.

Sollen expresses a piece of advice or a recommendation.

müssen

Yuki **muss** zwei Streifen stempeln.	Yuki has to stamp two strips.

Müssen expresses a necessity or compulsion.

können

Yuki **kann** am Kiosk eine Fahrkarte kaufen.	Yuki can buy a ticket at the kiosk.
Yuki **kann** Deutsch sprechen.	Yuki can speak German.
Yuki **kann** im Wohnzimmer fernsehen.	Yuki can watch TV in the living room.

Können expresses possibility, ability or permission.

dürfen

Hier **darf** man rauchen.	You are allowed to smoke here.
Hier **darf** man nicht rauchen.	Smoking is not allowed here.
Darf ich die Katze streicheln?	May I pet the cat?

Dürfen expresses permission, or is used in polite questions.

The pronoun man

Man *(one, you)* is used in generalisations.

Hier darf man parken.	Parking is allowed here.
Hier darf man nicht rauchen.	Smoking is not allowed here.

Negation

Verbs can be made negative using **nicht**. It comes after the verb.

Kommen Sie aus Deutschland?	Do you come from Germany?
Nein, ich komme **nicht** aus Deutschland.	No, I don't come from Germany.
Das Zimmer ist klein.	The room is small.
Nein, das Zimmer ist **nicht** klein.	No, the room isn't small.

In a sentence with a modal verb and an infinitive, **nicht** comes between the two verbs as in English.

Ich kann **nicht** kommen.	I can't come.
Du sollst **nicht** rauchen.	You shouldn't smoke.

Prepositions with the accusative

Prepositions are normally found before a noun and require a particular case (accusative, dative or genitive). Prepositions that take the accusative only are: **bis, durch, für, gegen, ohne** and **um**.

Das Flugzeug fliegt **bis München.**	The plane is flying to Munich.
Der Zug fährt **durch den Tunnel.**	The train goes through the tunnel.
Das Medikament ist **für das Kind.**	The medicine is for the child.
Das Auto fährt **gegen den Baum.**	The car drives into the tree.
Wir reisen **ohne ihre Kinder um die Welt**.	We are traveling around the world without our children.

Prepositions

In is used with the accusative when you can ask the question **Wohin?** *(Where... to?)*

Yuki fährt **in** die Stadt.	Yuki is going into town.
Wohin fährt Yuki?	Where is Yuki going?
Die U-Bahn fährt **ins** Zentrum.	The subway goes to the town centre.
Wohin fährt die U-Bahn?	Where does the subway go to?

(ins = in das)

Exercises

Exercise 1

Make questions using the Sie form.

1 Was möchtest du trinken? ....

2 Wohin willst du fahren? ....

3 Wohin fährst du? ....

4 Was nimmst du? ....

Excerise 2

Complete the sentences using the correct form of wollen.

1 Das Kind .... Schokolade.

2 Wir .... in die Stadt fahren.

3 Yuki .... eine Fahrkarte kaufen.

4 Frau Glück und Yuki .... Kaffee trinken.

5 Du .... Deutsch lernen.

Exercise 3

Form sentences using a modal verb + an infinitive.

1 Yuki spricht Deutsch. (können)

....

2 Yuki fährt in die Stadt. (wollen)

....

3 Sie kauft eine Fahrkarte. (müssen)

....

4 Sie stempelt die Fahrkarte. (müssen)

....

Exercise 4

Complete the sentences with the correct forms of können, dürfen, müssen or sollen.

1 .... ich Ihnen das Zimmer zeigen?

2 Du .... die Schoko-lade essen.

3 Yuki .... zwei Streifen stempeln.

4 Ihr .... nicht streiten.

Exercise 5

You see the following signs below. Complete the sentences with the correct forms of können, dürfen or müssen.

Parking	**1** Hier .... / .... man parken.
No Parking	**2** Hier .... man nicht parken.
Right Turn Only	**3** Hier .... man rechts abbiegen.
No Smoking	**4** Hier .... man nicht rauchen.
Café	**5** Hier .... man Kaffee trinken.

Exercise 6

Form sentences with nicht.

1 Ich gehe in die Stadt.

....

2 Wir fahren nach Paris.

....

3 Ich möchte fernsehen.

....

4 Die U-Bahn fährt ins Zentrum.

....

Exercise 7

Complete the sentences using wohin, wie viele, wo or was.

1 .... lernt Yuki?

2 .... kann Yuki eine Fahrkarte kaufen?

3 .... ist die Haltestelle?

4 .... will Yuki fahren?

5 .... wohnt Yuki?

6 .... Streifen muss Yuki stempeln?

7 .... fährt die U-Bahn?

Exercise 8

Complete the sentences with durch, für, gegen, ohne, um, bis or in.

1. Yuki fährt ..../... die Stadt.

2. Ihr geht.. /.. den Wald.

3 .... Geld kann man nichts kaufen.

4 Der Zug fährt .... Frankfurt.

5 Die Blumen sind .... Frau Glück.

6 Das Auto fährt .... die Ecke.

7 Der FC Bayern München spielt .... Real Madrid.

Vocabulary

Below is a list of vocabulary encountered in this chapter.

abbiegen	*to turn*
am (= an dem) *in:* **am Kiosk**	*at the*
am besten	*the best thing*
auf Wiedersehen	*goodbye*
Automat, der, -en	*ticket machine*
Baum, der, -¨e	*tree*
Bitte schön.	*Here you are.*
bis *in*: **bis ins Zentrum**	*to*
Blume, die, -n	*flower*
Buch, das, -¨er	*book*
denn	*then*
direkt *in:* **direkt ins Zentrum**	*right*
durch	*through*
Ecke, die, -n	*corner*
Eis, das	*ice cream*
fahren	*to go*
Fahrkarte, die, -n	*ticket*
Flugzeug, das, -e	*plane*
gegen *in:* **gegen den Baum**	*into*
Geld, das, -er	*money*
gleich	*just*
Haltestelle, die, -n	*station*
ins (= in das)	*into the*
Kiosk, der, -e	*kiosk*
klein	*small*
man	*one*
Medikament, das, -e	*medicine*
müssen	*must*
nach *in:*	*to*

nach Paris

ohne *without*

parken *to park*

rechts *to the right*

reisen *to travel*

Schokolade, die, -n *chocolate*

sollen *should*

Sprache, die, -n *language*

sprechen *to speak*

Stadt, die, -¨e *town*

Station, die, -en *stop*

stempeln *to stamp*

Streifen, der, - *strip*

Streifenkarte, die, -n *strip ticket*

streiten *to quarrel*

Student, der, -en *student*

Taxi, das, -s *taxi*

Tunnel, der, - *tunnel*

U-Bahn, die, -en *subway/underground*

um *around*

vier *four*

Wald, der, -¨er *forest*

welche? *which?*

Welt, die, -en *world*

wie viele? *how many?*

wohin? *where to?*

wollen *to want*

Zentrum, das; die Zentren *(Pl.)* *centre*

Zug, der, -¨e *train*

day: 4

Making Friends

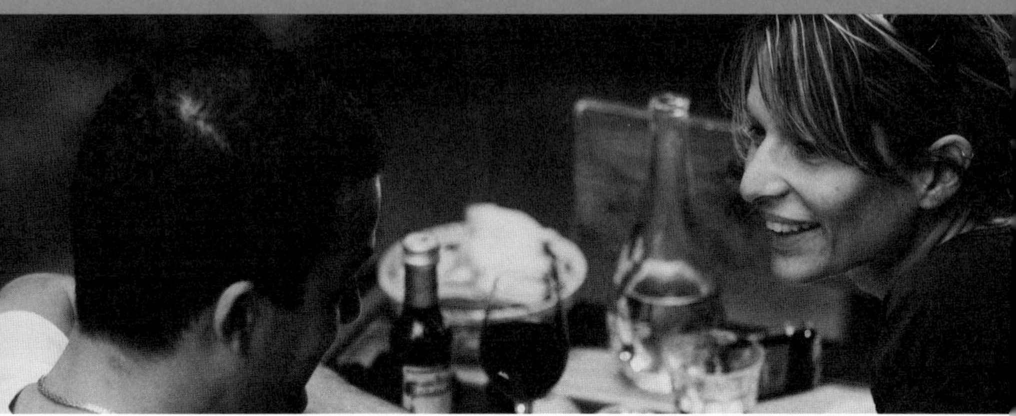

Day 4 sees you become more comfortable talking to groups of people and talking about yourself and other nationalities. You will learn compound words, how to tell the time, numbers and the days of the week.

OPENING HOURS...

Department stores and most of the large shops in big cities are open from Monday to Saturday until 8:00 p.m. Specialty shops usually don't open until 9:00 a.m. or 10:00 a.m. Small shops and shops in small towns usually close at around 6:00 p.m. On Sundays, only a few bakers and florists are open in the morning; some bakeries also open in the afternoon. At other times you can buy drinks, newspapers and a limited selection of food at filling stations and main railway stations.

German conversation: Der Deutschkurs

Heute Morgen geht Yuki in die Schule. Der Deutschunterricht beginnt. Die Kursteilnehmer kommen aus Frankreich, England, Italien, Spanien, Polen, China, Bolivien, den USA und Afghanistan. Alle wollen Deutsch lernen.

Frau Holzer:	**Guten Morgen! Herzlich willkommen in der Schule. Ich heiße Frau Holzer. Ich komme aus Deutschland und wohne in München. Ich möchte Sie gerne kennen lernen. Woher kommen Sie?**
Yuki:	**Ich komme aus Japan, aus Sapporo.**
Frau Holzer:	**Und wie heißen Sie?**
Yuki:	**Ich heiße Yuki Naito.**
Frau Holzer:	**Und wer sind Sie?**
Jean-Luc:	**Mein Name ist Jean-Luc Mathieu. Ich komme aus Frankreich, aus Toulouse.**
Frau Holzer:	**Und woher kommen Sie?**
Olivia:	**Ich komme aus Bolivien, aus La Paz.**
Frau Holzer:	**Ich habe Bücher und einen Stundenplan für Sie. Bitte schön! Der Unterricht beginnt morgens um 8.00 Uhr. Von 10.15 bis 10.45 Uhr machen wir eine Pause.**
Yuki:	**Können wir etwas zu trinken kaufen?**
Frau Holzer:	**Ja. Sie können in die Cafeteria gehen. Die Mittagspause beginnt um 12.30 Uhr. Nachmittags beginnt der Unterricht um 13.30 Uhr. Er dauert bis 16.00 Uhr.**
Yuki:	**Was können wir danach noch machen?**
Frau Holzer:	**Danach können Sie noch eine Stunde in die Bibliothek gehen. Sie schließt um 17.00 Uhr. Montags, mittwochs und freitags sind wir nachmittags im Sprachlabor. Es ist im Raum 7 im Erdgeschoss. Jeden Dienstag und Donnerstag sind wir nachmittags im Videoraum. Heute endet der Unterricht um 15.00 Uhr. Heute Abend feiern wir eine Begrüßungsparty. Sie dürfen gerne Freunde mitbringen.**
Yuki:	**Wie lange haben denn die Geschäfte auf? Ich muss noch in ein Blumengeschäft.**
Frau Holzer:	**Sie haben noch Zeit. Die Geschäfte schließen werktags um 20.00 Uhr.**

English conversation: The German Course

This morning Yuki is going to the language school. Her German language course is starting. The other members of the course come from France, England, Italy, Spain, Poland, China, Bolivia, the USA and Afghanistan. They all want to learn German.

Mrs. Holzer:	**Good morning. Welcome to the school. My name is Mrs. Holzer. I'm from Germany and live in Munich. I'd like to get to know you all. Where do you come from?**
Yuki:	**I'm from Japan, from Sapporo.**
Mrs. Holzer:	**And what's your name?**
Yuki:	**My name's Yuki Naito.**
Mrs. Holzer:	**And who are you?**
Jean-Luc:	**My name's Jean-Luc Mathieu. I come from France, from Toulouse.**
Mrs. Holzer:	**Where do you come from?**
Olivia:	**I come from Bolivia, from La Paz.**
Mrs. Holzer:	**I've got books and a timetable for you. Here you are. Lessons start at 8 o'clock in the morning. There's a break from 10:15 to 10:45.**
Yuki:	**Can we buy something to drink?**
Mrs. Holzer:	**Yes, you can go to the cafeteria. Lunch break starts at 12:30. Lessons start again at 1:30 in the afternoon and go on till 4 o'clock.**
Yuki:	**What can we do afterwards?**
Mrs. Holzer:	**After the lessons you can go to the library for another hour. It closes at 5 o'clock. On Monday, Wednesday and Friday afternoons we are in the language lab. It's in room 7 on the ground floor. On Tuesdays and Thursdays we are in the video room in the afternoon. Today the lessons end at 3 o'clock. Tonight we are giving a party to welcome you. You can bring your friends along as well, if you like.**
Yuki:	**How long are the shops open? I've got to go to a flower shop.**
Mrs. Holzer:	**There is plenty of time. Shops close at 8 o'clock on weekdays.**

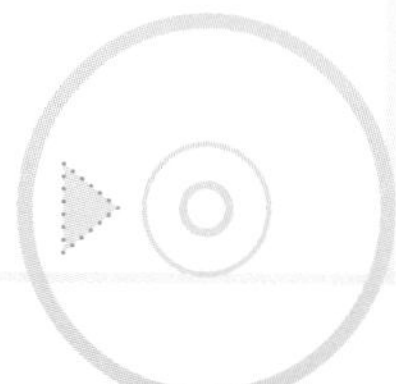

Grammar

Word formation: compounds

New words can be made in German by combining a noun with another noun, e.g.:

das Video	+	der Raum	=	der Videoraum
video		room		video room
die Begrüßung	+	die Party	=	die Begrüßungsparty
welcome		party		welcoming party
die Stunden *(Pl.)*	+	der Plan	=	der Stundenplan
hours		plan		timetable

Numbers

0	null	**22**	zweiundzwanzig	**800**	achthundert
1	eins	**23**	dreiundzwanzig	**900**	neunhundert
2	zwei	**24**	vierundzwanzig	**1000**	(ein)tausend
3	drei	**25**	fünfundzwanzig	**2000**	zweitausend
4	vier	**26**	sechsundzwanzig	**3000**	dreitausend
5	fünf	**27**	siebenundzwanzig	**4000**	viertausend
6	sechs	**28**	achtundzwanzig	**5000**	fünftausend
7	sieben	**29**	neunundzwanzig	**6000**	sechstausend
8	acht	**30**	dreißig	**7000**	siebentausend
9	neun	**40**	vierzig	**8000**	achttausend
10	zehn	**50**	fünfzig	**9000**	neuntausend
11	elf	**60**	sechzig	**10000**	zehntausend
12	zwölf	**70**	siebzig	**20000**	zwanzigtausend
13	dreizehn	**80**	achtzig	**30000**	dreißigtausend
14	vierzehn	**90**	neunzig	**40000**	vierzigtausend
15	fünfzehn	**100**	(ein)hundert	**50000**	fünfzigtausend
16	sechzehn	**200**	zweihundert	**60000**	sechzigtausend
17	siebzehn	**300**	dreihundert	**70000**	siebzigtausend
18	achtzehn	**400**	vierhundert	**80000**	achtzigtausend
19	neunzehn	**500**	fünfhundert	**90000**	neunzigtausend
20	zwanzig	**600**	sechshundert	**100000**	(ein)hunderttausend
21	einundzwanzig	**700**	siebenhundert	**1000000**	eine Million

From number twenty onwards you read the second digit first, then add und followed by the first digit. With three and four digit numbers you read the hundreds and thousands first.

21 einundzwanzig
35 fünfunddreißig
246 zweihundertsechsundvierzig
1397 eintausenddreihundertsiebenundneunzig

Time

Wie spät ist es?/Wie viel Uhr ist es? — What time is it?

Everyday language	On the radio and television
(informal)	*(formal)*
8:00 acht Uhr	acht Uhr
8:15 Viertel nach acht/ fünfzehn Minuten nach acht	acht Uhr fünfzehn
8:20 zwanzig nach acht	acht Uhr zwanzig
8:30 halb neun*	acht Uhr dreißig
8:35 fünf nach halb neun/ fünfundzwanzig	acht Uhr fünfunddreißig
8:45 Viertel vor neun/ fünfzehn Minuten vor neun	acht Uhr fünfundvierzig

You say ein Uhr (1:00 p.m.) but halb eins (*12:30 p.m. - i.e. half an hour before 1:00p.m. This is the same system as used above for 8:30 p.m.) and Viertel vor eins (12:45 p.m.)

Everyday language		On the radio and television	
die Sekunde	second	die Sekunden *(Pl.)*	seconds
die Minute	minute	die Minuten *(Pl.)*	minutes
die Stunde	hour	die Stunden *(Pl.)*	hours

Time of day

Heute Abend feiern wir.	We are giving a party tonight.
Nachmittags beginnt der Unterricht um 13.30 Uhr.	The lessons begin at 1:30 in the afternoon.

am Morgen	in the morning (early)
morgens	every morning (early)
am Vormittag	in the morning
vormittags	every morning
am Nachmittag	in the afternoon
nachmittags	every afternoon
am Abend	in the evening

abends	in the evening
heute Morgen	this morning (early)
heute Vormittag	this morning
heute Nachmittag	this afternoon
heute Abend	this evening

Days of the week

am Montag	on Monday	montags	every Monday
am Dienstag	on Tuesday	dienstags	every Tuesday
am Mittwoch	on Wednesday	mittwochs	every Wednesday
am Donnerstag	on Thursday	donnerstags	every Thursday
am Freitag	on Friday	freitags	every Friday
am Samstag	on Saturday	samstags	every Saturday
am Sonntag	on Sunday	sonntags	every Sunday
morgens = jeden Morgen = immer am Morgen			every morning
freitags = jeden Freitag = immer am Freitag			every Friday

In southern Germany people usually say Samstag and samstags, whereas in northern Germany people usually say Sonnabend and sonnabends for Saturday and on Saturdays.
Days of the week and the time of the day are **masculine**. Exception: die Nacht *(night)*.

Word order with time words

When time words are at the beginning of the sentence, the position of the subject and the verb changes:

1. Um acht Uhr	beginnt	der Unterricht.

When time words are at the end of the sentence, the position of the subject and the verb stays the same:

2. Der Unterricht	beginnt	um acht Uhr.

Countries and nationalities

country		nationality	
		male	*female*
Afghanistan	Afghanistan	der Afghane	die Afghanin
Ägypten	Egypt	der Ägypter	die Ägypterin
Australien	Australia	der Australier	die Australierin
Bolivien	Bolivia	der Bolivianer	die Bolivianerin
China	China	der Chinese	die Chinesin
Dänemark	Denmark	der Däne	die Dänin
Deutschland	Germany	der Deutsche	die Deutsche
England	England	der Engländer	die Engländerin
Finnland	Finland	der Finne	die Finnin
Frankreich	France	der Franzose	die Französin

Griechenland	Greece	der Grieche	die Griechin
Indien	India	der Inder	die Inderin
Irland	Ireland	der Ire	die Irin
Israel	Israel	der Israeli	die Israelin
Italien	Italy	der Italiener	die Italienerin
Japan	Japan	der Japaner	die Japanerin
Kanada	Canada	der Kanadier	die Kanadierin
Mexiko	Mexico	der Mexikaner	die Mexikanerin
Neuseeland	New Zealand	der Neuseeländer	die Neuseeländerin
die Niederlande	the Netherlands	der Niederländer	die Niederländerin
Nordirland	Northern Ireland	der Nordire	die Nordirin
Norwegen	Norway	der Norweger	die Norwegerin
Österreich	Austria	der Österreicher	die Österreichern
Polen	Poland	der Pole	die Polin
Portugal	Portugal	der Portugiese	die Portugiesin
Russland	Russia	der Russe	die Russin
Schottland	Scotland	der Schotte	die Schottin
Schweden	Sweden	der Schwede	die Schwedin
die Schweiz	Switzerland	der Schweizer	die Schweizerin
Spanien	Spain	der Spanier	die Spanierin
die Türkei	Turkey	der Türke	die Türkin
die Vereinigten Staaten *(Pl.)* = die USA	the United States of America	der Amerikaner	die Amerikanerin
Wales	Wales	der Waliser	die Waliserin

The names of countries do not normally take an article.

Except: *feminine:* die Bundesrepublik Deutschland *(the Federal Republic of Germany)*, die Schweiz *(Switzerland)*, die Türkei *(Turkey)*

masculine: der Iran *(Iran)*, der Irak *(Iraq)*

plural: die Niederlande *(the Netherlands)*, die USA (die Vereinigten Staaten von Amerika) *(the United States of America)*

Ich fahre in die Schweiz, in die Türkei. (Wohin?)

I'm travelling to Switzerland, to Turkey. (Where to?)

Ich fahre in die Niederlande, in die USA. (Wohin?)

I'm travelling to the Netherlands, to the USA. (Where to?)

but:

Ich komme aus* der Schweiz, aus der Türkei. (woher?)

I come from Switzerland, from Turkey. (where from?)

Ich komme aus den Niederlanden, aus den USA. (woher?)

I come from the Netherlands, from the USA. (where from?)

*the preposition aus takes the dative case. See page 94 for more on this.

Articles in the nominative: singular and plural

singular	definite article		indefinite article	
masculine	der Fernseher	the television	ein Fernseher	a television
neuter	das Geschäft	the shop	ein Geschäft	a shop
feminine	die Stunde	the hour	eine Stunde	an hour

plural				
masculine	die Fernseher	the televisions	– Fernseher	– televisions
neuter	die Geschäfte	the shops	– Geschäfte	– shops
feminine	die Stunden	he hours	– Stunden	– hours

Articles in the accusative: singular and plural

singular	definite article		indefinite article	
masculine	den Fernseher	the television	einen Fernseher	a television
neuter	das Geschäft	the shop	ein Geschäft	a shop
feminine	die Stunde	the hour	eine Stunde	an hour

plural				
masculine	die Fernseher	the televisions	– Fernseher	– televisions
neuter	die Geschäfte	the shops	– Geschäfte	– shops
feminine	die Stunden	the hours	– Stunden	– hours

Note the plural of the articles. Definite article: die for masculine, feminine, neuter. Indefinite article: no article.

Nouns: singular and plural

As there are no hard and fast rules on how to form the plural of nouns, it is advisable to learn the article and the plural along with the noun: **das Haus**, **die Häuser**.
Note that a, o, u is usually ä, ö, ü in the plural:

Singular		Plural	
der Apfel *(Sg.)*	the apple	die Äpfel *(Pl.)*	the apples
die Mutter *(Sg.)*	the mother	die Mütter *(Pl.)*	the mothers
der Vater *(Sg.)*	the father	die Väter *(Pl.)*	the fathers

singular		plural	
das/ein Zimmer	the/a room	die/– Zimmer	the/– rooms
der/ein Kuchen	the/a cake	die/– Kuchen	the/– cakes
der/ein Apfel	the/an apple	die/– Äpfel	the/– apples
das/ein Mädchen	the/a girl	die/– Mädchen	the/– girls
das/ein Blümlein	the/a little flower	die/– Blümlein	the/– little flowers

Nouns with the ending **-er**, **-en**, **-chen**, **-lein** are the same in the singular and the plural.

singular		plural	
der/ein Brief	the/a letter	die/– Briefe	the/– letters
der/ein Abend	the/an evening	die/– Abende	the/– evenings
das/ein Geschäft	the/a shop	die/– Geschäfte	the/– shops
der/ein Stuhl	the/a chair	die/– Stühle	the/– chairs

Many nouns take the plural ending **-e**.

singular		plural	
das/ein Kind	the/a child	die/– Kinder	the/– children
der/ein Mann	the/a man	die/– Männer	the/– men
das/ein Buch	the/a book	die/– Bücher	the/– books

Many one syllable neuter nouns and some masculine nouns take the plural ending **-er**. Note that there are some common execptions: **das Spiel, die Spiele** (game/games), **das Tier, die Tiere** (animal/animals).

singular		plural	
die/eine Stunde	the/an hour	die/– Stunden	the/– hours
die/eine Pause	the/a break	die/– Pausen	the/– breaks
die/eine Uhr	the/a clock	die/ – Uhren	the/– clocks

Nearly all feminine nouns ending in **-e** take the plural ending **-n**. Nearly all feminine nouns ending with a consonant take the plural ending **-en**.

singular		plural	
die/eine Oma	the/a grandma	die/– Omas	the/– grandmas
das/ein Auto	die/– Autos	the/a car	the/– cars
das/ein Taxi	die/– Taxis	the/a taxi	the/– taxis
das/ein Hotel	die/- Hotels	the/a hotel	the/– hotels

Nouns with the ending **-a**, **-o**, **-i** and many foreign words take the plural ending **-s**.

Exercises

Exercise 1

Form compounds and fill in the articles.

1 die Stadt das Zentrum ....

2 die Bücher *(pl.)* der Schrank ....

3 der Brief die Marke ....

4 der Brief der Umschlag ....

5 der Abend das Essen ....

Exercise 2

Write out the numbers in figures.

1 siebenunddreißig ....

2 zweiundvierzig ....

3 neunundneunzig ....

4 achthundertsiebenundsechzig ....

5 tausendzweihundert ....

Exercise 3

Write out the time of the day in full (informal and formal).

1 9.15 ....

....

2 12.30 ....

....

3 4.45 ....

....

4 8.10 ....

....

5 6.25 ....

....

Exercise 4

Complete the sentences with samstags, morgens, mittags, abends or nachts.

1 .... schläft Peter immer bis 8.00 Uhr.

2 .... macht er immer eine Pause.

3 Nicole geht .... immer früh ins Bett.

4 Sie trinkt .... nie Kaffee.

Sie kann sonst .... nicht schlafen.

5 .... schlafe ich bis 10 Uhr.

Exercise 5

Complete the sentences with the respective nationalities.

1 Gail kommt aus den USA. Sie ist ....

2 Gérard kommt aus Frankreich. Er ist ....

3 Danuta kommt aus Polen. Sie ist ....

4 Ergün kommt aus der Türkei. Er ist ....

Exercise 6

Using the following example, form sentences.

Angelika – Deutschland – England

Angelika kommt aus Deutschland und fährt nach England.

1 Agne – Schweden – USA

....

2 Carlos – Spanien – Polen

....

3 John – England – Schweiz

....

4. David – Israel – Portugal

....

Exercise 7

Put the nouns into the plural.

1 Yuki hat zwei .... (der Koffer).

2 Die Kursteilnehmer lesen .... (das Buch).

3 Am Kiosk kann man .... (die Streifenkarte) kaufen.

4 Yuki kauft .... (der Apfel).

5 München und Köln sind große ....(die Stadt).

Vocabulary

Below is a list of vocabulary encountered in this chapter

Abend, der, -e	*evening*
Abendessen, das	*supper/dinner*
Afghanistan	*Afghanistan*
alle	*all*
Apfel, der, -¨	*apple*
beginnen	*to start*
Begrüßung, die, -en	*greeting*
Begrüßungs-party, die, -s	*(welcoming) party*
Bibliothek, die, -en	*library*
Bild, das, -er	*picture*
Blümlein, das, -	*little flower*
Blumen-geschäft, das, -e	*flower shop*
Bolivien	*Bolivia*
Brief, der, -e	*letter*
Bücherschrank, der, -¨e	*bookcase*
Cafeteria, die, -s	*cafeteria*
danach	*afterwards*
dauern	*to last*
Deutschkurs, der, -e	*German course*
Deutschunter-richt, der	*German language course*
enden	*to finish*
England	*England*
Erdgeschoss, das, -e	*ground floor/ first floor*
Essen, das, - *in:* **das Abendessen**	*meal*
feiern *in:* **Party feiern**	*to give a party*
Foto, das, -s	*photo*
Frankreich	*France*
Freund, der, -e	*friend*
früh	*early*
gehen	*to go*
Geschäft, das, -e	*shop*
gerne *in:* **gerne mitbringen**	*if you like*
Guten Morgen!	*Good morning!*
hängen	*to hang*
heute	*today*

im *(=* **in dem***)*	*in the*
Italien	*Italy*
jeden	*every*
kennenlernen	*to get to know*
Koffer, der, -	*suitcase*
Kuchen, der, -	*cake*
Kursteilnehmer, der, -	*course participant*
machen	*to make*
Marke, die, -n *in:* **Briefmarke, die, -n**	*stamp*
Maschine, die, -n *in:* **Kaffeemaschine**	*machine*
mein Name ist	*my name is*
mitbringen	*to bring (along)*
Mittagspause, die, -n	*lunch break*
Morgen, der, -	*morning*
morgens	*every morning*
Nachmittag, der, -e	*afternoon*
Nacht, die, -¨e	*night*
nachts	*every night*
nachmittags	*every afternoon*
nie	*never*
noch *in:* **noch Zeit haben**	*still*
Pause, die, -n	*break*
Polen	*Poland*
Raum, der, -¨e	*room*
reservieren	*to reserve*
schlafen	*to sleep*
schließen	*to close*
Schule, die, -n	*school*
sonst	*otherwise*
Spanien	*Spain*
Sprachlabor, das, -e	*language lab*
Stadtzentrum, das, Stadtzentren	*city centre*
Stuhl, der, -¨e	*chair*
Stunde, die, -n	*hour*
Stundenplan, der, -¨e	*timetable*
Teilnehmer, der, -	*participant*
Uhr, die, -en	*clock*
um *in:* **um 8 Uhr**	*at*
Umschlag, der, -¨e *in:* **Briefumschlag, der, -¨e**	*envelope*
Unterricht, der	*lessons*
Video, das, -s	*video*
Videoraum, der, -ë	*video room*
Viertel, das, -	*quarter*
von *in:* **von… bis**	*from*
Vormittag, der, -e	*morning*
vormittags	*every morning*
werktags	*on weekdays*
Wie lange?	*How long?*
Wie spät ist es?	*What time is it?*
Wie viel Uhr ist es?	*What time is it?*
woher?	*where from?*
Wort, das, -¨er	*word*
Zeit, die, -en	*time*

day: 5

The Post Office

Day 5 will help you to start speaking more fluently and get you used to using demonstrative and personal pronouns. You will also learn how to write and say numbers and further build your vocabulary. At the end of the chapter you will also get to use the fun Test game to practise what you have learnt so far.

ZIP...

When looking for addresses and when mailing items, remember that German zip codes or postcodes should have five numbers. These are written in front of the place name, e.g. ***81379 München*** *is the zip code for a part of Munich. Every town has a different code so it is easy to instantly recognize places using this system.*

German conversation: Das Postamt

Yuki möchte einen Brief und eine Postkarte aufgeben.

Yuki: **Was kostet dieser Brief nach Japan?**
Beamter: **Per Luftpost?**
Yuki: **Ja bitte.**
Beamter: **Einen Moment. Ich muss ihn wiegen. Der Brief wiegt 60 Gramm. Das macht 5,11 Euro.**
Yuki: **Das ist aber teuer!**
Beamter: **Möchten Sie Sondermarken?**
Yuki: **Ja bitte. Ich möchte zwei Sondermarken zu 3 Euro.**
Beamter: **Tut mir leid. Ich habe nur Sondermarken zu 1,50 Euro.**
Yuki: **Dann nehme ich fünf Sondermarken zu 1,50 Euro. Diese Postkarte möchte ich in die Schweiz schicken.**
Beamter: **Für eine Postkarte in die Schweiz brauchen Sie eine Briefmarke für 51 Cent. Das macht zusammen 8,01 Euro. 10 Euro. Dann bekommen Sie noch 1,99 Euro zurück. Bitte schön.**
Yuki: **Ich möchte noch Geld umtauschen. 100000 Yen in Euro.**
Beamter: **Gerne. 100000 Yen, das macht 793 Euro. Wie möchten Sie das Geld haben? Drei Hunderter, zwei Zweihunderter und einen Fünfziger, vier Zehner, den Rest in Münzen?**
Yuki: **Einen Fünfhunderter und zwei Hunderter, einen Fünfziger, vier Zehner, den Rest in Münzen, bitte.**

English conversation: The post office

Yuki wants to send a letter and a postcard.

Yuki: **How much does it cost to send this letter to Japan?**
Post office clerk: **By airmail?**
Yuki: **Yes, please.**
Post office clerk: **Just a moment, please. I'll have to weigh it. The letter weighs 60 grammes. That's 5 euros and 11 cents.**
Yuki: **That's rather expensive.**
Post office clerk: **Do you want commemorative stamps?**
Yuki: **Yes, please. I'd like two 3-euro commemorative stamps.**
Post office clerk: **I'm sorry. I've only got 1.50-euro commemorative stamps.**
Yuki: **Then I'll take five 1.50-euro commemorative stamps. I want to send this postcard to Switzerland.**

Post office clerk:	**You need a 51-cent stamp for a postcard to Switzerland. That's 8.01 euros altogether. Ten euros. And 1 euro and 99 cents change. Here you are.**
Yuki:	**I also want to change some money. 100 000 yen into euros.**
Post office clerk:	**Yes, of course. 100000 yen, that's 793 euros. How would you like the money? Three 100-euro notes, two 200-euro notes, and one 50-euro note, four 10-euro notes, the rest in coins?**
Yuki:	**One 500-euro note and two 100-euro notes, one 50-euro note, four 10-euro notes, the rest in coins, please.**

Grammar

Aber

The particle **aber** is used to express surprise and astonishment., e.g.:

Das ist aber teuer!	That's rather expensive.
Du hast aber Glück!	You're really lucky.

Demonstrative pronoun: dieser

The demonstrative pronoun **dieser** is used to refer to a particular object.
Demonstrative pronouns are declined in the same way as the definite article.

	singular			plural
	masculine	*neuter*	*feminine*	
nominative	dieser (der)	dieses (das)	diese (die)	diese (die)
accusative	diesen (den)	dieses (das)	diese (die)	diese (die)

Note that in the accusative only the masculine form changes from **dieser** to **diesen**:

Yuki möchte **diesen** Brief, **dieses** Paket und **diese** Postkarte aufgeben. *(accusative singular)*

In the nominative and accusative plural the forms stay the same: **diese**.

Yuki möchte **diese** Briefe, **diese** Pakete und **diese** Postkarten aufgeben. *(accusative plural)*

Most alcoholic drinks are masculine. Exception: **das Bier**

der Wein	wine	**der Cognac**	brandy
der Champagner	champagne	**der Whiskey**	whiskey

Personal pronouns: nominative and accusative

Nehmen Sie diesen Wein?	Ja, ich nehme **ihn.**
Are you taking this wine?	Yes, I am.
Kennen Sie diese Frau?	Ja, ich kenne **sie.**
Do you know this woman?	Yes, I do.
Lesen Sie dieses Buch?	Ja, ich lese **es.**
Are you reading this book?	Yes, I am.

singular		**plural**	
nominative	*accusative*	*nominative*	*accusative*
ich	**mich**	**wir**	**uns**
du	**dich**	**ihr**	**euch**
Sie	**Sie**	**Sie**	**Sie**
er	**ihn**	**sie**	**sie**
sie	**sie**		
es	**es**		

Years

You write:	**2014**	**1812**
You say:	**zweitausendvierzehn** or **zwanzigvierzehn**	**achtzehnhundertzwölf**

Money

You write:	**1,50 €**	**0,50 €**
You say:	**ein Euro fünfzig**	**fünfzig Cent**

For bills you say:

ein Fünfer	or	**ein 5-Euro-Schein**
ein Zehner	or	**ein 10-Euro-Schein**
ein Zwanziger	or	**ein 20-Euro-Schein**
ein Fünfziger	or	**ein 50-Euro-Schein**
ein Hunderter	or	**ein 100-Euro-Schein**
ein Zweihunderter	or	**ein 200-Euro-Schein**
ein Fünfhunderter	or	**ein 500-Euro-Schein**

Telephone numbers and postcodes

You write:	**089/62 30 84 13**
You say:	**null acht neun sechs zwo drei null acht vier eins drei**
or	**null acht neun zwoundsechzig dreißig vierundachtzig dreizehn**
You write:	**80805 München**
You say:	**achtzig achtzig fünf München**

On the telephone you often say **zwo** instead of **zwei** for two.

Exercises

Exercise 1

Yuki goes shopping. Form sentences using the following example.

das Brot: Ich möchte dieses Brot. Was kostet dieses Brot?

1 der Käse: ....

2 die Wurst: ....

3 die Milch: ....

4 das Bier: ....

5 der Honig: ....

Exercise 2

Replace the underlined words by a personal pronoun.

Was kostet diese Schokolade? Was kostet sie?

1 Ich möchte diesen Champagner. ....

2 Wohin geht Frau Glück? ....

3 Yuki trifft Franz. ....

4 Yuki trifft Hans und Franz. ....

5 Wo wohnt Herr Müller? ....

Exercise 3

Look at the example and fill in the sums of money in words.

€ 12,93: zwölf Euro dreiundneunzig Cent

1 € 4,68 ....

2 € 18,17 ....

3 € 127,15 ....

4 € 1345,11 ....

5 € 10699,30 ....

6 € 216222,99 ....

Exercise 4

Which number or numbers are correct?

1 Tel.: 642 66

a sechshundertzweiundvierzigsechsundsechzig

b sechs vier zwo sechs sechs

c sechs zwoundvierzig sechsundsechzig

2 Jahreszahl 1996

a neunzehnhundertsechsundneunzig

b eintausendneunhundertsechsundneunzig

c neunzehnsechsundneunzig

3 € 1275,–

a tausendzweihundertfünfundsiebzig Euro

b eintausendzweihundertfünfundsiebzig Euro

c eintausendzweihundertsiebenundfünfzig Euro

Exercise 5

What is the English translation for the following words? Match the column on the left with those on the right.

1 der Briefträger	**A** The postcard	1....................................
2 die Postkarte	**B** The telephone	2....................................
3 das Telefon	**C** The postman	3....................................
4 die Adresse	**D** The package	4....................................
5 die Briefmarke	**E** The postbox	5....................................
6 der Briefkasten	**F** The stamp	6....................................
7 das Paket	**G** The address	7....................................
8 der Briefumschlag	**H** the envelope	8....................................

Vocabulary

Below is a list of vocabulary encountered in this chapter.

Adresse, die, -n *address*
aufgeben *in:* **eine Postkarte aufgeben** *to send*
bekommen *in:* **Geld zurückbekommen** *to get back*
Bier, das, -e *beer*
Briefkasten, der, -¨ *letter box/mailbox*
Briefträger, der, - *postman/mailman*
Brot, das, -e *bread*
Champagner, der *champagne*
Cognac, der, -s *brandy*
dann *then*
das macht *that's*
dieser, -e, -es *this*
diese *(pl.)* *these*
einkaufen *to buy*
Ende, das, -en *end*
Fall, der, -¨e *fall*
Fünfhunderter, der, - *500-euro note/bill*
Fünfziger, der, - *50-euro note/bill*
Gramm, das, - *gramme*
Honig, der *honey*
Hunderter, der, - *100-euro note/bill*
Jahreszahl, die, -en *year*
Käse, der *cheese*
die Käse (pl.)/ **Käsesorten**
kosten *to cost*
lesen *to read*
Moment, der, -e *moment*
Paket, das, -e *parcel*
per Luftpost *by airmail*
Porto, das, -s *postage*
Post, die *post*
Postamt, das, -¨er *post office*
Postkarte, die, -n *postcard*
Postleitzahl, die, -en *postcode/zip code*
Schein, der, -e *(money) note/bill*
schicken *to send*
Sondermarke, die, -n *commemorative stamp*
Telefon, das, -e *telephone*
Telefonzelle, die, -n *telephone booth*
Telegramm, das, -e *telegram*
teuer *expensive*
tut mir Leid *I'm sorry*
umtauschen *to change*
Wein, der, -e *wine*
Whiskey, der, -s *whiskey*
wiegen *to weigh*
Wurst, die, -¨e *cold meat*
Yen, der, - *yen*
Zehner, der, - *10-euro note/bill*
zurück *back*
zusammen *altogether*
Zwanziger, der, - *20-euro note/bill*
Zweihunderter, der, - *200-euro note/bill*

Test 1

Work your way around the board. Each correct answer will take you to the next question until you have completed the exercise. Enjoy!

1

Choose one of the two possible solutions. Then go to the square showing the number of the solution you think is correct.

2

Er … aus Deutschland.
kommt ▶ 8
kommen ▶ 15

3

Wrong!

Go back to number 5.

8

Correct, continue:
Yuki … die U-Bahn.
nehme ▶ 6
nimmt ▶ 25

9

Wrong!

Go back to number 25.

10

Sorry!

Go back to number 14.

11

Wrong!

Go back to number 29.

16

Good. Carry on:
… Geld kann man nichts kaufen.
Ohne ▶ 22
Mit ▶ 18

17

Wrong!

Go back to number 22.

18

Wrong!

Go back to number 16.

19

Correct!

End of exercise.

24

Wrong!

Go back to number 12.

25

Very good. Go on:
16 = …
sechzehn ▶ 14
sechszehn ▶ 9

26

Wrong!

Go back to number 30.

27

Good. Next one:
München und Berlin sind große …
Stadt ▶ 23
Städte ▶ 12

4

Good, continue:
Yuki trinkt … Tee.
einen ▶ 20
eine ▶ 7

5

Correct, continue:
… ist das? Das ist Yuki.
Was ▶ 3
Wer ▶ 13

6

Wrong!

Go back to number 8.

7

Wrong!

Go back to number 4.

12

Very good, continue:
Was … Sie trinken?
möchten ▶ 16
möchtest ▶ 24

13

Correct! Continue:
Yuki … in die Stadt fahren.
willst ▶ 21
will ▶ 29

14

Very good. Next:
… ist die Haltestelle?
Wohin ▶ 10
Wo ▶ 30

15

Wrong!

Go back to number 2.

20

Well done! Next question:
Was kostet Brot?
dieses ▶ 5
diese ▶ 28

21

Sorry!

Go back to number 13.

22

Correct!
Yuki kauft zwei …
Briefmarke ▶ 17
Briefmarken ▶ 19

23

Wrong!

Go back to number 27.

28

Wrong!

Go back to number 20.

29

Well done, continue:
Ich fahre in … Schweiz.
das ▶ 11
die ▶ 27

30

Correct. Go on: … schlafe ich immer bis acht Uhr.
Mittags ▶ 26
Morgens ▶ 4

day:6

Shopping

Day 6 teaches you about using adjectives in their various forms. You will become more and more used to the nominative and accusative cases, and further increase your vocabulary.

SOUVENIRS...

Each region in Germany has something to offer as a souvenir - cuckoo clocks in the Black Forest; ***Zwetschegenmännle*** *(plum cake men) and gingerbread in Nuremberg;* ***Meissen porcelain*** *from the Dresden area; and* ***marzipan*** *from Lübeck. Other possibilities are pottery, hand-made crystal, blown glass or silverware.* ***Bierkrüge*** *and wooden toys and* ***Steiff teddy bears*** *are also popular gifts.*

German conversation: Im Kaufhaus

Frau Glück und Yuki wollen einen Einkaufsbummel machen. Yuki möchte einen hellen Mantel, ein Paar schwarze Schuhe und vielleicht ein hübsches Kleid kaufen.

Yuki: **Wohin sollen wir gehen?**

Frau Glück: **Am besten gehen wir in ein großes Kaufhaus im Stadtzentrum. Da kann man günstig einkaufen.**

Frau Glück und Yuki sind im Kaufhaus.

Frau Glück: **Gehen wir zuerst in den ersten Stock in die Abteilung für Damenbekleidung. Da finden wir sicher ein hübsches Kleid und einen neuen Mantel für Sie.**

Yuki: **Das ist eine gute Idee.**

Verkäuferin: **Kann ich Ihnen helfen?**

Yuki: **Ja, gerne. Ich suche ein rotes Sommerkleid.**

Verkäuferin: **Welche Größe haben Sie?**

Yuki: **Größe 36.**

Verkäuferin: **In Größe 36 haben wir eine große Auswahl. Bitte kommen Sie.**

Yuki sucht und findet ein hübsches Kleid.

Yuki: **Dieses Kleid ist sehr hübsch. Kann ich es anprobieren?**

Verkäuferin: **Natürlich! Die Umkleidekabine da drüben ist frei.**

Yuki: **Dieses Kleid passt sehr gut. Es ist nicht zu lang und nicht zu eng. Die Farbe ist wunderschön. Ich glaube, ich nehme es.**

Verkäuferin: **Gerne. Brauchen Sie sonst noch etwas?**

Yuki: **Ja. Ich suche noch einen hellen, schicken Sommermantel. Wo finde ich Sommermäntel?**

Verkäuferin: **Gleich da drüben. Kommen Sie, bitte.**

Yuki sucht und findet einen hellen Sommermantel.

Verkäuferin: **Brauchen Sie sonst noch etwas?**

Yuki: **Ja, ich brauche noch ein Paar schwarze Schuhe.**

Verkäuferin: **Gehen Sie in den dritten Stock. Da ist die Schuhabteilung Sie können dann alles im vierten Stock bezahlen. Da ist die Sammelkasse.**

Yuki: **Vielen Dank für Ihre Hilfe!**

An der Sammelkasse.

Kassiererin: **Bezahlen Sie in bar oder mit EC-Karte?**

Yuki: **Kann ich mit Kreditkarte zahlen?**

Kassiererin: **Selbstverständlich.**

English conversation: In a department store

Mrs. Glück and Yuki want to look around the shops. Yuki would like to buy a light-coloured coat, a pair of black shoes and possibly a pretty dress.

Yuki: **Where should we go then?**

Mrs. Glück: **The best thing is for us to go to a large department store in the city centre. Things are reasonably priced there.**

Mrs. Glück and Yuki are in the department store.

Mrs. Glück: **Let's go first to the ladies' department on the 1st (US 2nd) floor. We're sure to find a pretty dress and a new coat for you there.**

Yuki: **That's a good idea.**

Shop assistant: **Can I help you?**

Yuki: **Yes, please. I'm looking for a red summer dress.**

Shop assistant: **What size are you?**

Yuki: **Size 36.**

Shop assistant: **There is a wide selection in size 36. Please, come with me.**

Yuki looks for and finds a pretty dress.

Yuki: **This dress is very pretty. Can I try it on?**

Shop assistant: **Of course. The changing room over there is free.**

Yuki: **This dress fits me perfectly. It's not too long and not too tight. It's a beautiful colour. I think I'll take it.**

Shop assistant: **Certainly. Is there anything else you need?**

Yuki: **Yes, I'm also looking for a smart, light-coloured summer coat. Where can I find summer coats?**

Shop assistant: **Just over there. Come this way, please.**

Yuki looks for and finds a light-coloured summer coat.

Shop assistant: **Is there anything else you need?**

Yuki: **Yes, I also need a pair of black shoes.**

Shop assistant: **Go to the 3rd (US 4th) floor. The shoe department is there. Then you can pay for everything on the 4th (US 5th) floor. The main cash desk is there.**

Yuki: **Thank you very much for your help.**

At the main cash desk.

Cashier: **Are you paying in cash or by EC card?**

Yuki: **Can I use my credit card?**

Cashier: **Of course.**

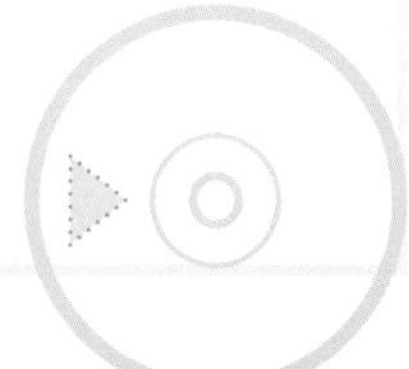

Grammar

Adjectives after sein

Dieses Kleid ist hübsch.	This dress is pretty.

Nouns can be qualified by adjectives.
Note that when the adjective comes after the verb sein, it is not declined.

Adjectives following the definite article: nominative and accusative

singular nominative		
masculine	der helle Mantel	dieser helle Mantel
neuter	das bunte Hemd	dieses bunte Hemd
feminine	die weiße Bluse	diese weiße Bluse

singular accusative		
masculine	den hellen Mantel	diesen hellen Mantel
neuter	das bunte Hemd	dieses bunte Hemd
feminine	die weiße Bluse	diese weiße Bluse

plural nominative		
masculine	die hellen Mäntel	diese hellen Mäntel
neuter	die bunten Hemden	diese bunten Hemden
feminine	die weißen Blusen	diese weißen Blusen

singular accusative		
masculine	die hellen Mäntel	diese hellen Mäntel
neuter	die bunten Hemden	diese bunten Hemden
feminine	die weißen Blusen	diese weißen Blusen

Note that adjectives after der and dieser in the nominative singular always take the ending **-e**. In the masculine accusative singular, these words end in -en, while in the neuter and feminine accusative singular they end in -e. In the plural all the endings are the same: -en.

Adjectives following the indefinite article: nominative and accusative

singular nominative	
masculine	ein/kein heller Mantel (a bright coat)
neuter	ein/kein buntes Hemd (a colorful shirt)
feminine	eine/keine weiße Bluse (a white blouse)

accusative	
masculine	einen/keinen hellen Mäntel
neuter	ein/kein buntes Hemd
feminine	eine/keine weiße Bluse

plural nominative		
masculine	helle Mäntel	keine hellen Mäntel
neuter	bunte Hemden	keine bunten Hemden
feminine	weiße Blusen	keine weißen Blusen

accusative		
masculine	helle Mäntel	keine hellen Mäntel
neuter	bunte Hemden	keine bunten Hemden
feminine	weiße Blusen	keine weißen Blusen

Note that adjectives after the indefinite article **ein** in the nominative singular end in: masculine **-er**, neuter **-es**, feminine **-e**. The adjective endings after **kein** are different from when you have no article. Hence the 2 columns above.

In the accusative singular in both neuter and feminine, adjectives take the same endings as in the nominative, the masculine form only ending in **-en**.

In the plural there is no indefinite article. All adjectives end in **-e**.

The negative of **ein**, **kein**, is also declined like an indefinite article. Unlike **ein**, **kein** also exists in the plural.

Exercises

Exercise 1

Look at the example and make sentences using a suitable adjective.

hell hübsch groß schwer günstig

Kleid Das Kleid ist günstig.

Zimmer **1** ....

Kaufhaus **2** ....

Mantel **3** ....

Brief **4** ....

Exercise 2

Look at the example and make sentences.

ein Kleid (hübsch)

Yuki will ein hübsches Kleid.

1 ein Buch (neu)

Yuki möchte ....

2 ein Fahrrad (günstig)

Yuki braucht ....

3 eine Bluse (weiß)

Yuki sucht ....

4 eine Idee (gut)

Yuki hat ....

5 eine Zeitung (neu)

Yuki braucht ....

Exercise 3

Match the German words to the correct English translation.

der Regenschirm, die Handtasche, der Aktenkoffer, die Bluse, der Rock, die Strumpfhose, die Schuhe, der Hut, das Halstuch, das Hemd, die Hose, das Jackett, die Krawatte

Women's clothing

1 the hat
2 the briefcase
3 the skirt
4 the scarf
5 the tights
6 the handbag
7 the blouse

Men's clothing

1 the shirt
2 the tie
3 the umbrella
4 the tousers
5 the shoes
6 the jacket

1 ....
2 ....
3 ....
4 ....
5 ....
6 ....
7 ....

1 ....
2 ....
3 ....
4 ....
5 ....
6 ....

Exercise 4

Match each question with the appropriate answer.

1 Kann ich Ihnen helfen?
2 Brauchen Sie sonst noch etwas?
3 Welche Größe haben Sie?
4 Wie möchten Sie zahlen?
5 Wo ist eine freie Umkleidekabine?

a Mit Kreditkarte, bitte.
b Gleich da drüben.
c Ja gerne. Ich suche einen Regenschirm.
d Nein danke. Das ist alles.
e Ich habe Größe 38.

1 .... 2 .... 3 .... 4 .... 5 ....

Vocabulary

Below is a list of vocabulary encountered in this chapter.

Abteilung, die, -en	*department*
Aktenkoffer, der, -	*briefcase*
alles	*everything*
anprobieren	*to try on*
Anzug, der, -¨e	*suit*
Auswahl, die	*selection*
bar *in: in* ***bar***	*in cash*
bezahlen	*to pay for*
blau	*blue*
Bluse, die, -n	*blouse*
Brauchen Sie sonst noch etwas?	*Is there anything else you need?*
braun bunt	*brown colored*
da drüben	*over there*
dann	*then*
Damen-bekleidung, die	*ladies' fashions*
EC-Karte, die, -n	*EC card*
Einkaufs-bummel, der	*look around the shops*
eng	*tight*
erster Stock	*1st floor/ 2nd floor*
Fahrrad, das, -¨er	*bike*
Farbe, die, -n	*colour*
finden	*to find*
frei	*free*
gerne *in:* **ja, gerne**	*yes, please*
glauben	*to think*
gleich da drüben	*just over there*
Größe, die, -n	*size*
grün	*green*
günstig	*reasonably priced*
gut	*good*
Halstuch, das, -¨er	*scarf*
Handtasche, die, -n	*handbag/purse*
helfen	*to help*
Hemd, das, -en	*shirt*
Hilfe, die, -n	*help*
Hose, die, -n	*trousers/ pants*
hübsch	*pretty*
Hut, der, -¨e	*hat*
Idee, die, -n	*idea*
Jackett, das, -s	*jacket*
Kann ich Ihnen helfen?	*Can I help you?*
Kaufhaus, das, -¨er	*department store*
Kleid, das, -er	*dress*
Krawatte, die, -n	*tie*
Kreditkarte, die, -n	*credit card*
kurz	*short*
lang	*long*
Mantel, der, -¨	*coat*
natürlich	*of course*

nett	*nice*
neu	*new*
Paar, das, -e	*pair*
passen	*to fit*
Regenschirm, der, -e	*umbrella*
Rock, der, -¨e	*skirt*
rot	*red*
Sammelkasse, die, -n	*main cash desk/ main cash register*
schick	*smart*
Schuh, der, -e	*shoe*
Schuhabteilung, die, -en	*shoe department*
schwarz	*black*
schwer	*heavy*
sehr	*very*
selbstverständlich	*of course*
Sommerkleid, das, -er	*summer dress*
Sommermantel, der, -¨	*summer coat*
sonst *in*: **sonst noch etwas**	*anything else*
Stock, der, Stockwerke *(pl.)*	*floor*
Strumpfhose, die, -n	*tights*
suchen	*to look for*
Umkleidekabine, die, -n	*changing room*
Verkäuferin, die, -nen	*shop assistant*
vielen Dank	*thank you very much*
Vielen Dank für Ihre Hilfe!	*Thank you very much for your help*
vielleicht	*possibly*
vierter Stock	*4th floor/5th floor*
weiß	*white*
Wintermantel, der, -¨	*winter coat*
wunderschön	*beautiful*
zahlen	*to pay*
Zeitung, die, -en	*newspaper*
zuerst	*first*

day: 7

Dining In

Day 7 introduces you to the particles *nur* and *bloß*, separable and inseparable verbs, how to talk about yourself using reflexive verbs, as well as talk about dates and different times of the year. You will also learn more about German culture and eating habits.

EATING HABITS...

Most Germans usually have breakfast at home before they leave for work. It may consist of a cup of coffee or tea and a slice of bread and jam, but it is also common to have orange juice, bread or rolls and a boiled egg, or even muesli, cheese, cold cuts and scrambled eggs. At home early in the evening, people often have bread, cheese and cold cuts and a salad. When Germans dine out, they tend not to dine much later than 9:00 p.m. You may also find that restaurants in some small towns do not serve hot meals after10:00 p.m.

German conversation: Einladung zum Essen

Yuki kommt nach Hause. Frau Glück hat einen Brief für sie. Yuki macht den Brief auf. Sie liest:

Einladung zum Abendessen am Samstag, den 1.April um 19.30 Uhr bei Familie Gebhardt.

U. A. w. g. Gabi und Johannes Gebhardt

Yuki: **Das ist aber nett! Aber wer ist denn die Familie Gebhardt?**

Frau Glück: **Frau Gebhardt ist eine Kollegin. Herrn Gebhardt kenne ich auch. Sie sind ein nettes Ehepaar. Frau Gebhardt ist übrigens eine ausgezeichnete Köchin und Herr Gebhardt ein Weinkenner.**

Yuki: **Das klingt gut. Ich nehme die Einladung an. Aber was ziehe ich bloß an?**

Frau Glück: **Vielleicht das hübsche rote Kleid. Machen Sie sich schick!**

Yuki: **Etwas verstehe ich nicht. Was heißt U.A.w.g.?**

Frau Glück: **Um Antwort wird gebeten. Ich rufe Frau Gebhardt an und sage zu.**

Yuki: **Was bringen wir denn mit?**

Frau Glück: **Wir kaufen am besten einen Blumenstrauß und eine Flasche Wein.**

Am Samstagabend sind Frau Glück und Yuki bei Familie Gebhardt. Herr Gebhardt bietet einen Aperitif an.

Herr Gebhardt: **Möchten Sie einen Sherry?**

Yuki: **Ja, gerne!**

Herr Gebhardt (zu Frau Glück): **Angelika, nimmst du auch einen Sherry?**

Frau Glück: **Ja, bitte.**

Herr Gebhardt erhebt sein Glas.

Herr Gebhardt: **Auf die Gäste. Zum Wohl!**

Yuki: **Ich möchte mich für die freundliche Einladung bedanken.**

Frau Gebhardt: **Das Essen ist fertig. Wollen wir uns an den Tisch setzen?**

Frau Glück: **Was gibt's denn Gutes?**

Frau Gebhardt: **Wiener Schnitzel mit Kartoffelsalat. Bitte bedienen Sie sich!**

Rezept: Wiener Schnitzel

Zutaten für vier Personen: 4 dünne Schnitzel, Salz und Pfeffer, Mehl, 1 Eigelb, Paniermehl, 1 Tasse Öl, 1 Bund Petersilie, ½ Zitrone

Das Fleisch mit Salz und Pfeffer würzen. Zuerst in Mehl, danach in Eigelb und Paniermehl wenden. In heißem Öl knusprig backen. Die Schnitzel gut abtropfen lassen und mit Petersilie und Zitronenscheiben garnieren.

Rezept: Kartoffelsalat

Zutaten für vier Personen: 1 kg Kartoffeln, 1 Tasse Fleischbrühe, 2–4 Esslöffel Öl, 1 Esslöffel Essig, 1 kleine Zwiebel, Salz und Pfeffer

Die gekochten, warmen Kartoffeln schälen und in Scheiben schneiden. Öl, Essig, warme Fleischbrühe und die Gewürze zugeben. Vorsichtig mischen und ziehen lassen.

English conversation: Invitation to dinner

Yuki comes home. Mrs. Glück has a letter for her. She opens the letter and reads it.

The Gebhardt family invites you to dinner on Saturday, April 1st at 7:30 p.m.
R. S. V. P. Gabi and Johannes Gebhardt

Yuki: **That's very nice. But who are the Gebhardts?**

Mrs. Glück: **Mrs. Gebhardt is a colleague from work. I know Mr. Gebhardt, too. They are a nice couple. Mrs. Gebhardt is an excellent cook and Mr. Gebhardt is a wine connoisseur.**

Yuki: **That sounds good. I'll accept the invitation. But what on earth shall I wear?**

Mrs. Glück: **Perhaps the pretty red dress. Wear something really smart!**

Yuki: **There is something I don't understand. What does R. S. V. P. mean?**

Mrs. Glück: **Répondez s'il vous plaît – Please reply. – I'll ring Mrs. Gebhardt and accept the invitation.**

Yuki: **What shall we take with us?**

Mrs. Glück: **I think we should buy a bunch of flowers and a bottle of wine.**

On Saturday evening Mrs. Glück and Yuki are at the Gebhardt's. Mr. Gebhardt offers them a drink.

Mr. Gebhardt: **Would you like a sherry?**

Yuki: **Yes, please.**

Mr. Gebhardt (to Mrs. Glück): **Angelika, would you like a sherry, too?**

Mrs. Glück: **Yes, please.**

Mr. Gebhardt raises his glass.

Mr. Gebhardt: **To our guests. To your health!**

Yuki: **I'd like to thank you very much for the kind invitation.**

Mrs. Gebhardt: **The meal's ready. Shall we sit down at the table?**

Mrs. Glück: **What's on the menu for tonight?**

Mrs. Gebhardt: **Wiener schnitzel and potato salad. Please help yourselves!**

Recipe: Wiener Schnitzel

Ingredients for four persons: Four thin pieces of veal, salt and pepper, flour, one egg yolk, bread crumbs, one cup of oil, a sprig of parsley, half a lemon

Season the meat with salt and pepper, coat in flour, then dip in the egg yolk and in bread crumbs. Fry in hot oil until crisp. Remove excess fat from the schnitzel and garnish with parsley and lemon slices.

Recipe: potato salad

Ingredients for four persons: One kilo of potatoes, 1 cup of stock, 2–4 tablespoons of oil, 1 tablespoon of vinegar, 1 small onion, salt and pepper

Peel the boiled potatoes when warm and cut into slices. Add oil, vinegar, warm stock and seasoning. Mix carefully and let it stand.

Grammar

Particles *nur* and *bloß*

Was ziehe ich bloß an?	What on earth shall I wear?
Was ziehe ich nur an?	What shall I wear then?

The particles bloß and nur in questions mean that the person speaking is not sure of something.

Separable and inseparable verbs

Verbs with prefixes

Prefixes change the meaning of a verb.

kommen:	Yuki kommt aus Japan.
to come:	Yuki comes from Japan.
bekommen:	Yuki bekommt eine Einladung.
to get:	Yuki gets an invitation.
ankommen:	Yuki kommt in Deutschland an.
to arrive:	Yuki arrives in Germany.

There are separable and inseparable verbs. Inseparable prefixes are not stressed. The most important inseparable prefixes are:

be-	bezahlen	to pay
emp-	empfehlen	to recommend
ent-	entscheiden	to decide
er-	erklären	to explain
ge-	gestehen	to admit
ver-	versuchen	to try
zer-	zerstören	to destroy

In statements and questions, the separable prefixes come at the end of the sentence. The most important separable prefixes are:

ab-	abholen	to pick up
an-	anrufen	to telephone/call
auf-	aufmachen	to open
aus-	ausfüllen	to fill in
ein-	einkaufen	to buy
mit-	mitbringen	to bring/take along
vor-	vorbereiten	to prepare
weg-	weggehen	to go away
zu-	zusagen	to accept
zurück-	zurückkommen	to come back

anrufen:	Frau Glück ruft Frau Gebhardt an.	to call
zusagen:	Yuki sagt Familie Gebhardt zu.	to accept the invitation from

In sentences with modal verbs the verb comes at the end. The prefix must not be separated.

Frau Glück will Frau Gebhardt anrufen.

Frau Glück wants to call Frau Gebhardt.

Reflexive verbs

Some verbs can or must take a reflexive pronoun.

sich schick machen:	Machen Sie sich schick!
	Wear something really smart.
sich bedanken:	Ich bedanke mich für die Einladung.
	I'd like to thank you for the invitation.
sich bedienen:	Bitte bedienen Sie sich!
	Please help yourselves.

further examples:	
sich amüsieren	to enjoy oneself
sich freuen	to be pleased
sich ärgern	to get angry
sich setzen	to sit down
sich bewerben	to apply (for)
sich vorstellen	to introduce oneself
sich duschen	to take/have a shower

sich bedanken	to thank someone for				
ich	bedanke	mich	wir	bedanken	uns
du	bedankst	dich	ihr	bedankt	euch
Sie	bedanken	sich	Sie	bedanken	sich
er/sie/es	bedankt	sich	sie	bedanken	sich

Note that the declension of the reflexive pronoun is the same as the personal pronouns in the accusative. Exception: sich is always used in the polite form Sie (singular and plural) as well as in the 3rd person singular er/sie/es and 3rd person plural sie.

Word formation

In German, many nouns can be formed from the verb stem and the ending -ung.
Nouns ending in -ung always take the article die.

bedienen	to serve	die Bedienung	waiter/waitress
begrüßen	to greet	die Begrüßung	greeting

Date

Die Party beginnt am Montag, den 14.Februar um 20.00 Uhr.
The party begins on Monday, February 14th, at 8:00 p.m.

In a letter you write:
Hamburg, den 3.April 2014 **oder** 3.4.2014

Months

der Januar	January	der Juli	July
der Februar	February	der August	August
der März	March	der September	September
der April	April	der Oktober	October
der Mai	May	der November	November
der Juni	June	der Dezember	December

Names of the months take the article der.

Exercises

Exercise 1

Look at the example and make sentences with separable verbs.

den Brief/Yuki/abholen/. Yuki holt den Brief ab.

1 Yuki/ausgehen/heute Abend/.

....

2 diesen/müssen/Sie/Antrag/ausfüllen/.

....

3 was/ich/Abend/heute/anziehen/?

....

4 ich/Ihnen/darf/was/anbieten/?

....

5 Regenschirm/ich/den/mitnehmen/.

....

6 Yuki/Einladung/annehmen/die/ .

....

Exercise 2

Fill in the reflexive pronouns.

1 Yuki macht .... schick.

2 Ich bedanke .... für das Essen.

3 Wir amüsieren ....

4 Bitte bedienen Sie ....

5 Frau Glück und Yuki freuen .... über die Einladung.

Exercise 3

Form nouns.

1 beraten ....

2 einzahlen ....

3 sitzen ....

4 wohnen ....

Vocabulary

Below is a list of vocabulary encountered in this chapter.

abtropfen *in:* **Fett abtropfen**	*to drain off*
am *in:* **am Samstag**	*on Saturday*
amüsieren (sich)	*to enjoy oneself*
an	*at*
anbieten	*to offer*
ankommen	*to arrive*
annehmen	*to accept*
anrufen	*to telephone/call*
Antrag, der, -¨e	*application form*
anziehen	*to wear*
Aperitif, der, -s	*aperitif*
April, der	*April*
ärgern (sich)	*to get annoyed*
auf die Gäste	*to our guests*
aufmachen	*to open*
aufstehen	*to get up*
August, der	*August*
ausfüllen	*to fill in*
ausgezeichnet	*excellent*
backen	*to fry/to bake*
in: **in heißem Öl backen**	

bedanken (sich)	*to say thank you*
bedienen	*to serve*
bedienen (sich)	*to help oneself*
Bedienung, **die, -en**	*waiter/waitress*
begrüßen	*to greet*
bekommen	*to get*
beraten	*to advise*
bewerben (um) (sich)	*to apply (for)*
bloß *in:* **bloß anziehen**	*on earth*
Blumenstrauß, **der, -¨e**	*bunch of flowers*
Bund Petersilie, der, -	*sprig of parsley*
Dezember, der	*December*
dünn	*thin*
Ehepaar, das, -e	*couple*
Eigelb, das, -e	*egg yolk*
Einladung, **die, -en**	*invitation*
einzahlen	*to deposit*
empfehlen	*to recommend*
entscheiden	*to decide*
erklären	*to explain*
Essig, der	*vinegar*
Esslöffel, der, -	*tablespoon*
etwas	*something*
Familie, **die, -n**	*family*
Februar, der	*February*
fertig	*ready*
Flasche, **die**, *-n*	*bottle*
Fleisch, das	*meat*
Fleischbrühe, **die, -n**	*stock*
freuen (sich)	*to be pleased*
freundlich	*kind*
garnieren	*to garnish*
Gast, der, -¨e	*guest*
gekocht	*boiled*
gestehen	*to admit*
Gewürz, **das, -e**	*spice*
Glas, das, -¨er	*glass*
Gutes *in:*	*something good*
Was gibt's denn Gutes?	*What's on the menu?*
Januar, der	*January*
Juli, der	*July*
Juni, der	*June*
Kartoffel, **die, -n**	*potato*
Kartoffelsalat, **der, -e**	*potato salad*
kennen	*to know*
klingen	*to sound*
knusprig	*crisp*
Köchin, **die, -nen**	*cook*
Kollegin, **die, -nen**	*colleague*
Machen Sie sich schick!	*Wear something smart.*
Mai, der	*May*
März, der	*March*
Mehl, das	*flour*
mischen	*to mix*
November, der	*November*
Öl, das, -e	*oil*

Paniermehl, das -	*breadcrumbs*
Person, **die, -en**	*person*
Pfeffer, der	*pepper*
Rezept, das, -e	*recipe*
Salz, das	*salt*
schälen	*to peel*
Scheibe, **die, -n**	*slice*
schneiden	*to cut*
Schnitzel, **das, -**	*piece of veal*
September, der	*September*
setzen (sich)	*to sit down*
Sherry, der, -s	*sherry*
sitzen	*to sit*
sitzung	*meeting*
Tasse, die, -n	*cup*
Tisch, der, -e	*table*
U.A.w.g. = Um Antwort wird gebeten	*Please reply (R.S.V.P. = Répondez s'il vous plaît)*
übrigens	*by the way*
verstehen	*to understand*
versuchen	*to try*
vorbereiten	*to prepare*
vorsichtig	*carefully*
vorstellen (sich)	*to introduce (oneself)*
warm	*warm*
was gibt's *in:*	*is there*
weggehen	*to go away*
Weinkenner, **der, -**	*wine connoisseur*
wenden *in:* **in Paniermehl wenden**	*to dip in breadcrumbs*
Wiener Schnitzel	*Wiener schnitzel*
wohnen	*to live*
wohnung	*flat*
würzen	*to season*
zeichnen	*to draw*
zerstören	*to destroy*
ziehen lassen	*to let something stand*
Zitrone, **die, -n**	*lemon*
Zitronenscheibe, **die, -n**	*slice of lemon*
zu viel	*too much*
zugeben	*to add*
zum = zu dem	*to (the)*
Zum Wohl!	*To your health!*
zurückkommen	*to come back*
zusagen	*to accept an invitation*
Zutat, **die, -en**	*ingredient*
Zwiebel, die, -n	*onion*

day:8

Sightseeing

Day 8 sees you out and about exploring and you will learn how to ask questions and use adverbs, and how to use the imperative to give commands. You will also build up your vocabulary on food and sightseeing.

PALACES, CASTLES AND CHURCHES…

Millions of tourists come to Germany every year to see the romantic palaces and castles, for example the fairy tale castles of Ludwig II in Bavaria, the old castle in Heidelberg, the Hohenzollern castle, the castles along the Rhine, the Charlottenburg and Bellevue palaces in Berlin and Zwinger Palace in Dresden. There are famous cathedrals in Speyer, Worms, Cologne and Ulm. The elaborately-decorated rococo churches in Upper Bavaria are also worth visiting. In the summer months music festivals and concerts are held in many palaces, castles and churches.

German conversation: Stadtbesichtigung

Heute ist Sonntag. Yuki möchte eine Stadtbesichtigung machen. Am Treffpunkt warten viele Touristen.

Stadtführerin: **Willkommen in München! Wir befinden uns mitten im Stadtzentrum am Marienplatz. Hier sehen Sie das Rathaus mit Glockenspiel. Es spielt viermal täglich. Um 11.00 und 12.00 Uhr vormittags, um 17.00 Uhr nachmittags und um 21.00 Uhr abends. Jetzt drehen Sie sich bitte nach links. Sie sehen nun die Frauenkirche. Die zwei Türme sind das Wahrzeichen von München. Nun drehen Sie sich bitte nach rechts und Sie sehen den Alten Peter. Der Alte Peter ist ein interessanter Aussichtsturm. Können Sie die Leute dort oben sehen?**

Yuki: **Ja, dort oben sind Leute! Wie kommt man da hinauf?**

Stadtführerin: **300 Stufen führen nach oben. Sie haben dort einen herrlichen Blick über die ganze Stadt und manchmal können Sie sogar die Alpen sehen.**

Yuki: **Das ist ja toll!**

Stadtführerin: **Nun überqueren wir die Straße und gehen geradeaus weiter. Das ist der Viktualienmarkt. Hier können Sie Obst und Gemüse, aber auch Brot, Fleisch, Wurst, Käse, Blumen sowie Kräuter und Gewürze kaufen.**

Die Gruppe geht weiter.

Stadtführerin: **Hier ist das Hofbräuhaus. Vielleicht möchten Sie hineingehen? Ich warte draußen auf Sie.**

Yuki geht hinein und kommt schnell wieder heraus.

Stadtführerin: **Wie gefällt Ihnen das Hofbräuhaus?**

Yuki: **Sehr schön, aber sehr voll. Darf ich Sie etwas fragen?**

Stadtführerin: **Natürlich. Fragen Sie!**

Yuki: **Die Bedienungen tragen so schöne Kleider mit Blusen und Schürzen. Wo kann man diese Kleider kaufen?**

Stadtführerin: **Das sind Dirndl. Man kann sie in Trachtengeschäften kaufen.**

Yuki: **Wo ist das nächste Trachtengeschäft?**

Stadtführerin: **Hier vorne rechts.**

Yuki: **Vielen Dank für die Auskunft und die interessante Führung!**

English conversation: Guided tour of the city

It's Sunday today. Yuki wants to go on a guided tour of the city. A lot of tourists are waiting at the meeting place.

Tour guide: **Welcome to Munich. We're at Marienplatz in the city centre. You can see the town hall with the glockenspiel. It chimes four times a day. At 11 o'clock and 12 o'clock in the morning, at 5 o'clock in the afternoon and at 9 o'clock in the evening. Now, please turn to the left. Now you can see the Frauenkirche. The two towers are Munich's landmark. Now turn to your right and you can see Der Alte Peter. Der Alte Peter is an interesting observation tower. Can you see the people standing up there?**

Yuki: **Yes, there are people up there. How do you get up there?**

Tour guide: **There are three hundred steps up to the top. From there you have a wonderful view over the whole city and sometimes you can even see the Alps.**

Yuki: **That's great!**

Tour guide: **Now we are going to cross the road. Please walk straight ahead. This is the Viktualienmarkt. Here you can buy fruit and vegetables, bread, cold meats, cheese, flowers as well as herbs and spices.**

The group continue their tour.

Tour guide: **This is the Hofbräuhaus. Perhaps you'd like to go in. I'll wait outside for you.**

Yuki goes inside and comes out again quickly.

Tour guide: **How do you like the Hofbräuhaus?**

Yuki: **It's very nice, but very crowded. Can I ask you something?**

Tour guide: **Of course. Ask me anything you like.**

Yuki: **The waitresses are wearing such beautiful dresses with blouses and aprons. Where can you buy those dresses?**

Tour guide: **You can buy them in a traditional costume shop. They are called dirndl.**

Yuki: **Where's the nearest traditional costume shop?**

Tour guide: **Over there on the right.**

Yuki: **Thank you for the information and the interesting tour.**

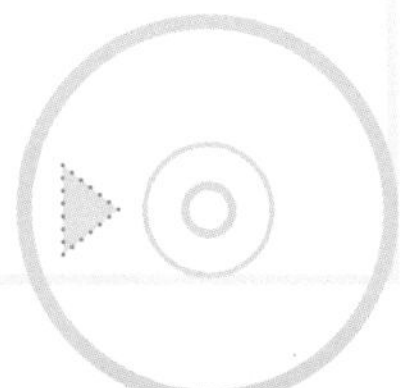

Grammar

The particle *mal*

Vielleicht möchten Sie mal hineingehen?
Perhaps you might like to go inside?
Probieren Sie mal!
Why don't you try it?

Mal is used when you suggest that someone does something, both in statements and in questions.

Adverbs

Wir befinden uns jetzt mitten im Stadtzentrum.
We are now in the middle of the city centre.
Hier vorne rechts ist ein Trachtengeschäft.
There is a traditional costume shop in front of you to your right.

Adverbs are normally not declined. They modify verbs, adjectives, nouns and sometimes even the whole sentence. They can be divided into three groups:

Adverbs of place	
Wo?	Where?
da/dort/hier	there/over there/here
Da/dort/hier sehen Sie das Rathaus.	There/over there/here you can see the town hall.
draußen	outside
Ich warte draußen auf Sie.	I'll wait for you outside.
links/rechts	left/right
Drehen Sie sich nach links/rechts.	Turn to your left/right.
oben/unten	up/down
Dort oben haben Sie einen herrlichen Blick.	You have a wonderful view from up there.
mitten	in the middle of
Wir befinden uns mitten im Stadtzentrum.	We are in the middle of the city centre.
Wohin?	Where to?
hinauf/hinunter	up/down
Hinauf geht es langsam, hinunter ziemlich schnell.	Walking up is slow, walking down is quite fast.
hinein/heraus	in/out
Yuki geht hinein und kommt schnell wieder heraus.	Yuki goes in and comes out again quickly.
geradeaus	straight ahead
Bitte gehen Sie geradeaus weiter.	Please walk straight ahead.

Adverbs of time and frequency	
Wann? - jetzt	When? - now
Jetzt drehen Sie sich bitte nach links.	Now please turn to your left.
heute	today
Heute ist Sonntag.	It's Sunday today.
vormittags/mittags/nachmittags/abends/ nachts	every morning/every day at noon/every afternoon/ every evening/every night
Das Glockenspiel spielt um 11.00 Uhr vormittags.	The glockenspiel chimes at eleven o'clock every morning.
dann	then
Ich warte dann auf Sie.	I'll be waiting for you then.
danach	after
Was können wir danach noch machen?	What can we do afterwards?
einmal/zweimal	once/twice
Es spielt zweimal täglich.	It chimes twice a day.
manchmal	sometimes
Manchmal können Sie die Alpen sehen.	Sometimes you can see the Alps.
wieder	again
Yuki kommt schnell wieder heraus.	Yuki comes out again quickly.

Modal adverbs	
ja, gerne	please (*gerne* must be preceded by *ja* to mean please)
Kann ich Ihnen helfen? Ja, gerne.	Can I help you? Yes, please.
sehr	very
Dieses Kleid ist sehr hübsch.	This dress is very pretty.
auch	also
Hier können Sie Obst und Gemüse, aber auch Brot kaufen.	You can buy fruit and vegetables here, but also bread.
noch	still
Danach können sie noch in die Bibliothek gehen.	Afterwards you can still go to the library.
vielleicht	perhaps
Vielleicht möchten Sie hineingehen?	Perhaps you'd like to go in there.
sogar	even
Manchmal können Sie sogar die Alpen sehen.	Sometimes you can even see the Alps.

The imperative

Kommen Sie herein!	Come in!
Bitte nehmen Sie Platz!	Sit down, please!

The imperative is used for favours and requests and is always directed at a person. For this reason the imperative is only found in the 2nd person singular and plural.

singular		*plural*	
du	**Komm** herein!	ihr	**Kommt** herein!
Sie	**Kommen** Sie herein!	Sie	**Kommen** Sie herein!

2nd person singular: *du* form

The imperative is derived from the 2nd person singular in the present tense. The ending **-st** is omitted.

du komm**st**	*imperative:*	**Komm!**	Come (along)!
du nimm**st**	*imperative:*	**Nimm!**	Take (it)!
du gib**st**	*imperative:*	**Gib!**	Give (me it)!

The umlaut is omitted with irregular verbs where the vowel changes:

du läufst	*imperative:*	**Lauf!**	Run!
du fährst	*imperative:*	**Fahr!**	Drive!

The imperative form and 2nd person plural of the present tense have the same form.

ihr kommt	*imperative:*	**Kommt!**	Come (along)!
ihr nehmt	*imperative:*	**Nehmt!**	Take (it)!
ihr gebt	*imperative:*	**Gebt!**	Give (me it)!

Sie form (polite form of the singular and plural)

The imperative form and Sie polite form are the same, but the word order is reversed.

Sie kommen	*imperative:*	**Kommen Sie!**	Come (along)!
Sie nehmen	*imperative:*	**Nehmen Sie!**	Take (it)!
Sie geben	*imperative:*	**Geben Sie!**	Give (me it)!

With separable verbs the prefix comes at the end.

Example: ausfüllen

Sie	**Füllen Sie den Antrag aus!**

With reflexive verbs the reflexive pronoun comes after the verb. With the Sie-form the personal pronoun comes between the verb and the reflexive pronoun.

Example: sich bedanken

du	**Bedank dich!**	Say thank you.
ihr	**Bedankt euch!**	
Sie	**Bedanken Sie sich!**	

Der Markt

Obst	**Äpfel, Birnen, Orangen, Bananen, Pflaumen, Himbeeren, Erdbeeren, Kiwis, Aprikosen**
Gemüse	**Karotten, Erbsen, Blumenkohl, Radieschen, Rettich, Paprika, Weißkraut, Rotkohl, Sauerkraut, Kartoffeln, Zwiebeln**

Brot	Roggenbrot, Vollkornbrot, Weißbrot, Pumpernickel, Brötchen, Brezeln
Fleisch	Schweinefleisch, Kalbfleisch, Rindfleisch, Lammfleisch, Geflügel
Wurst	Leberwurst, Bierschinken, Weißwurst, Schinken
Käse	Emmentaler, Edamer, Appenzeller, Tilsiter, Frischkäse, Blauschimmelkäse
Blumen	Rosen, Tulpen, Nelken, Vergissmeinnicht, Sonnenblumen
Kräuter	Petersilie, Schnittlauch, Basilikum, Rosmarin, Salbei
Gewürze	Essig, Öl, Senf, Knoblauch, Paprika, Nelken, Muskatnuss

The market

fruit	apples, pears, oranges, bananas, plums, raspberries, strawberries, kiwi, apricots
vegetable	carrots, peas, cauliflower, radish(es), white radish, pepper, white cabbage, red cabbage, sauerkraut, potatoes, onions
bread	rye bread, wholemeal bread, white bread, pumpernickel, rolls, pretzels
meat	pork, veal, beef, lamb, poultry
cold meats	liver sausage, ham sausage, white sausage, ham
cheese	Emmentaler, Edam, Appenzeller, Tilsiter, cream cheese, blue cheese
flowers	roses, tulips, carnations, forget-me-nots, sunflowers
herbs	parsley, chives, basil, rosemary, sage
spices	vinegar, oil, mustard, garlic, paprika, cloves, nutmeg

Exercises

Exercise 1

Fill in the suitable adverbs: hinein, da, gerne, danach, auch, heute, heraus, noch, dort oben, mitten, hier, zweimal.

1 Möchten Sie .... eine Tasse Kaffee? Ja, ...

2 Das Rathaus ist .... im Stadtzentrum.

3 Die Gäste gehen in das Haus .... und nach 30 Minuten wieder ....

4 Olivia und Jean-Luc lernen .... Deutsch.

5 .... kaufen Frau Glück und Yuki ein Kleid. .... gehen sie essen.

6 .... ist die Damenabteilung.

7 Bitte unterschreiben Sie ....: einmal .... und einmal ....

Exercise 2

Using the example, make sentences using the imperative.

Platz nehmen

Sie	**Nehmen Sie Platz!**
Ihr	**Nehmt Platz!**
Du	**Nimm Platz!**

1 sich setzen ....

2 herkommen ....

3 hereinkommen ....

Exercise 3

Do you know your foods?

1 Sie machen einen Obstsalat. Welche fünf Obstsorten nehmen Sie?

....

2 Nennen Sie vier Fleischsorten. ....

3 Nennen Sie drei Brotsorten. ....

Exercise 4

Write the feminine form of the following nouns.

der Vater die Mutter

1 der Koch ....

2 der Franzose ....

3 der Lehrer ....

4 der Junge ....

5 der Herr ....

Exercise 5

Write down the opposite of the following nouns.

Guten Morgen! Guten Abend!

1 Guten Tag! ……………………………………

2 Frühling ……………………………………

3 Sommer ……………………………………

4 rechts ……………………………………

5 oben ……………………………………

6 der Morgen ……………………………………

7 hinein ……………………………………

8 Glück ……………………………………

Vocabulary

Below is a list of vocabulary encountered in this chapter.

Alpen, die (pl)	*Alps*
Appenzeller, der, -	*Appenzeller*
Aprikose, die, -n	*apricot*
auch	*also*
Auskunft, die, -¨e	*information*
Aussichtsturm, der, -¨e	*observation tower*
Banane, die, -n	*banana*
Basilikum, das	*basil*
befinden (sich)	*to be*
Bierschinken, der	*ham sausage*
Birne, die, -n	*pear*
bis nach oben	*up to the top*
Blick, der, -e	*view*
Blauschimmelkäse, der -	*blue cheese*
Blumenkohl, der	*cauliflower*
Brezel, die, -n	*pretzel*
da	*there*
Dirndl, das, -	*dirndl (traditional German dress)*
dort	*there*
dort oben	*up there*
draußen	*outside*
drehen (sich)	*to turn*
Edamer, der, -	*Edam*
einmal	*once*
Emmentaler, der, -	*Emmentaler*

Erbse, die, -n *pea*
Erdbeere, die, -n *strawberry*
fragen *to ask*
Frischkäse, der - *cream cheese*
Führung, die, -en *guided tour*
ganz *whole*
geben *to give*
Geflügel, das *poultry*
Gemüse, das *vegetables*
geradeaus *straight ahead*
Glockenspiel, das, -e *glockenspiel*
Gruppe, die, -n *group*
Haus, das, -¨er *house*
heraus *out of*
herauskommen *to come out*
hereinkommen *to come in*
herkommen *to come here*
herrlich *wonderful*
hier vorne *over there*
Himbeere, die, -n *raspberry*
hinauf *up*
hinaufkommen *to get/come up*
hinein *into*
hineingehen *to go into*
hinunter *down*
interessant *interesting*
ja, gerne *yes, please*
jetzt *now*
Jogurt, der, -s *yogurt*
Kalbfleisch, das *veal*
Karotte, die, -n *carrot*
Kiwi, die, -s *kiwi*
Knoblauch, der *garlic*
Kräuter, die *(Pl.)* *herbs*
Lammfleisch, das *lamb*
Leberwurst, die, -¨e *liver sausage*
Leute, die *(Pl.)* *people*
links *left*
manchmal *sometimes*
Markt, der, -¨e *market*
mitten *in the middle of*
Muskatnuss, die, -¨e *nutmeg*
nach links *to the left*
nach oben *to the top*
nach rechts *to the right*
nächste *nearest*
Nelke, die, -n *carnation (flower)*
Nelken, die *(pl. spice)* *cloves*
nun *now*
oben *up*
Obst, das *fruit*
Obstsalat, der, -e *fruit salad*
Orange, die, -n *orange*
Paprika, das *(spice)* *paprika*
Paprika, der, -s *pepper*
Petersilie, die, -n *parsley*
Pflaume, die, -n *plum*
Pumpernickel, der, - *pumpernickel*
Radieschen, das, - *radish*
Rathaus, das, -¨er *town hall*
rechts *right*
Rettich, der, -e *white radish*

Rindfleisch, das	*beef*
Roggenbrot, das, -e	*rye bread*
Rose, die, -n	*rose*
Rosmarin, der	*rosemary*
Rotkohl, der	*red cabbage*
Salbei, der	*sage*
Sauerkraut, das	*sauerkraut*
Schinken, der	*ham*
schnell	*quick(ly)*
Schnittlauch, der	*chives*
Schürze, die, -n	*apron*
Schweine-fleisch, das	*pork*
Senf, der, -e	*mustard*
sogar	*even*
Sonnenblume, die, -n	*sunflower*
spielen *in:* **es spielt zwei-mal täglich**	*to chime*
Stadtbesichti-gung, die, -en	*guided tour of the city*
Stadtführerin, die, -nen	*tour guide*
Straße, die, -n	*street*
Stufe, die, -n	*step*
täglich	*a day, daily*
Tilsiter, der, -	*Tilsiter (type of cheese)*
toll	*great*
Tourist, der, -en	*tourist*
Trachten-geschäft, das, -¨e	*traditional costume shop*
tragen (Kleidung)	*to wear*
Treffpunkt, der, -e	*meeting place*
Tulpe, die, -n	*tulip*
Turm, der, -¨e	*tower*
über	*over*
überqueren	*to cross*
unten	*down*
unterschreiben	*to sign*
Vergissmein-nicht, das, -e	*forget-me-not*
vielleicht	*perhaps*
viermal	*four times*
voll	*full*
Vollkornbrot, das, -e	*wholemeal/ whole wheat bread*
Wahrzeichen, das, -	*landmark*
warten	*to wait*
Weißbrot, das, -e	*white bread*
Weißkraut, das	*white cabbage*
Weißwurst, die, -¨e	*white sausage*
weitergehen	*to continue walking*
wieder	*again*
zweimal	*twice*

day:9

An evening out

Day 9 introduces the dative case. You will learn how to talk about something in the plural and learn how to use prepositions correctly. You will then get to practice all of this in the exercise section.

DRINKS...

Most Germans drink water, soft drinks, or beer with their evening meal. There are many types of beer, each with its own distinctive flavour. ***Pils*** *and* ***Export*** *are found all over Germany.* ***Pils*** *is drunk in special glasses, is light in color and slightly bitter.* ***Altbier****, a dark and bitter beer, is found mainly in Düsseldorf.* ***Kölsch*** *is drunk in the Cologne-Bonn area. It is light-colored with a low alcohol content.* ***Weißbier*** *or* ***Weizenbier*** *is drunk in Bavaria, as is* ***Starkbier****, a very strong beer that is drunk during Lent.* ***Helles*** *is also very popular.*

German conversation: Und Abends ins Konzert

Yuki und Tobias, der Sohn von Familie Gebhardt, gehen heute Abend ins Konzert.
Tobias holt Yuki von zu Hause ab.

Yuki: **Guten Abend, Tobias! Komm herein! Ich bin gleich fertig.**

Tobias: **Guten Abend, Yuki! Oh, du siehst aber schick aus!**

Yuki: **Danke für das Kompliment. Dein Anzug gefällt mir auch sehr gut. Fahren wir mit der U-Bahn oder mit dem Bus?**

Tobias: **Lieber mit der U-Bahn. Die Haltestelle ist direkt gegenüber der Philharmonie.**

Yuki: **Also gut. Gehen wir. Wem hören wir heute Abend eigentlich zu?**

Tobias: **Den Bamberger Symphonikern. Sie spielen die Wassermusik von Händel und das Erste Brandenburgische Konzert von Bach.**

Tobias und Yuki sind in der Philharmonie.

Tobias: **Wollen wir die Mäntel an der Garderobe abgeben?**

Yuki: **Ja, das ist eine gute Idee. Wo sitzen wir denn eigentlich?**

Tobias: **Wir haben gute Plätze. Wir sitzen in der zweiten Reihe in der Mitte direkt vor dem Orchester. Ich besorge noch schnell ein Programm.**

Nach dem Konzert.

Tobias: **Wie findest du die Bamberger Symphoniker?**

Yuki: **Einfach super! Ein sehr gutes Orchester mit ausgezeichneten Solisten.**

Tobias: **Das finde ich auch. Wollen wir noch etwas trinken? Ich kenne ein nettes Weinlokal in der Nähe.**

Yuki: **Ja, gerne.**

Auf dem Weg zum Lokal sehen sie einen Losverkäufer.

Tobias: **Wollen wir ein Los kaufen?**

Yuki: **Ja, vielleicht haben wir Glück. Ich wohne schließlich bei Frau Glück.**

Tobias: **Zwei Lose bitte. Yuki, du darfst wählen.**

Tobias gibt dem Losverkäufer zwei Euro. Im Weinlokal.

Tobias: **Zum Wohl, Yuki!**

Yuki: **Prost! Und vielen Dank für die Einladung zum Konzert.**

English conversation: An evening at a concert

Yuki and Tobias, Mr. and Mrs. Gebhardt's son, are going to a concert this evening. He is picking Yuki up at her place.

Yuki: **Good evening, Tobias. Come in. I'll be ready in a minute.**

Tobias: **Good evening, Yuki. Oh, you look really smart!**

Yuki: **Thank you for the compliment. I really like your suit too. Shall we go by subway or by bus?**

Tobias: **The subway is better. The station is directly opposite the Philharmonic Hall.**

Yuki: **Okay then. Let's go. Oh, by the way, who are we listening to tonight?**

Tobias: **The Bamberg Symphonic Orchestra. They are playing Händel's Water Music. And Bach's First Brandenburg concerto.**

Tobias and Yuki are at the Philharmonic Hall.

Tobias: **Shall we leave our coats in the cloakroom?**

Yuki: **Yes, that's a good idea. By the way, where are we sitting?**

Tobias: **We've got good seats. We are sitting in the middle of the second row. Right in the front of the orchestra. I'll just go and get a programme.**

After the concert.

Tobias: **How do you like the Bamberg Symphony Orchestra?**

Yuki: **They're marvellous! A very good orchestra with very good soloists.**

Tobias: **That's what I think, too. Shall we go for a drink? I know a nice little wine bar near here.**

Yuki: **Yes, let's have a drink.**

On their way to the wine bar they see a lottery ticket vendor.

Tobias: **Shall we buy a lottery ticket?**

Yuki: **Perhaps we'll be lucky. After all I live with Mrs. Glück.**

Tobias: **Two lottery tickets, please. Why don't you choose, Yuki?**

Tobias gives the lottery seller two euros. In the wine bar.

Tobias: **To your health, Yuki!**

Yuki: **Cheers. And thank you for inviting me to the concert.**

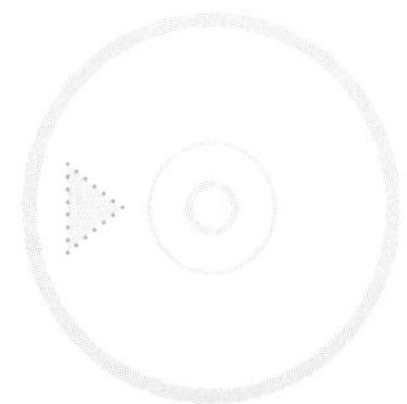

Grammar

Eigentlich

Eigentlich is a particle that is used when a new idea is introduced into a conversation.

Was hören wir uns heute Abend eigentlich an?

Oh, by the way, who are we listening to tonight?

Definite and indefinite articles

singular		
nominative	*masculine*	der/ein Mann
	neuter	das/ein Kind
	feminine	die/eine Frau
accusative	*masculine*	den/einen Mann
	neuter	das/ein Kind
	feminine	die/eine Frau
dative	*masculine*	dem/einem Mann
	neuter	dem/**ein**em Kind
	feminine	der/einer Frau

plural		
nominative	*masculine*	die/– Männer
	neuter	die/– Kinder
	feminine	die/– Frauen
accusative	*masculine*	die/– Männer
	neuter	die/– Kinder
	feminine	die/– Frauen
dative	*masculine*	den/– Männern
	neuter	den/– Kindern
	feminine	den/– Frauen

All nouns which do not end in -n take an -n in the dative plural. Exception: nouns with an -s in the plural: den Autos.

The Dative case

The dative case does not exist in English. In German, it is used after certain verbs and prepositions. These verbs sometimes have a so-called indirect object in English, as in "me" in: "Give me it", which could also be "Give it to me". However, many of the German verbs followed by the dative correspond to English verbs with a direct object, so it is best just to learn them - and the prepositions - by heart.

Verbs followed by the dative:

Tobias	*is*	*glad to help her.*	
Tobias	hilft	ihr	gerne.
subject	*verb*	*dative complement*	
Wer oder **was?**		**Wem?**	

The verb determines the case of the noun and the article. The verbs **antworten** *(answer)*, **danken** *(thank)*, **gefallen** *(like)*, **gratulieren** *(congratulate)*, **helfen** *(help)*, **passen** *(fit)*, **widersprechen** *(contradict)*, **zuhören** *(listen to)*, **zusagen** *(accept)*, **zuschauen** *(watch)* are always followed by the dative.

antworten:	Die Schüler	**antworten**	**dem Lehrer.**
danken:	Yuki	**dankt**	**dem Postbeamten.**
gefallen:	Der Anzug	**gefällt**	**dem Mann.**
gratulieren:	Die Lehrerin	**gratuliert**	**dem Schüler.**
helfen:	Der Vater	**hilft**	**der Tochter.**
passen:	Der Pullover	**passt**	**dem Kind.**
wider-sprechen:	Der Sohn	**widerspricht**	**dem Vater.**
zuhören:	Yuki	**hört**	**den Bamberger Symphonikern zu.**
zusagen:	Frau Glück	**sagt**	**der Arbeitskollegin zu.**
zuschauen:	Yuki	**schaut**	**der Bäckerin zu.**

Question words for persons: nominative, accusative and dative

nominative	
Das ist **Yuki.**	Das sind **Yuki und Frau Glück.**
Wer ist das?	**Wer** sind die zwei Frauen?
accusative	
Ich sehe **Yuki.**	Ich sehe **Yuki und Frau Glück.**
Wen sehen Sie?	**Wen** sehen Sie?
dative	
Das Kleid gefällt **Yuki.**	Das Kleid gefällt **Yuki und Frau Glück.**
Wem gefällt das Kleid?	**Wem** gefällt das Kleid?

Verbs followed by the dative and the accusative

Some verbs need two complements: one in the dative and one in the accusative (persons in the dative and objects in the accusative): These are verbs meaning "give": **anbieten** *(offer)*, **bringen** *(bring)*, **geben** *(give)*, **schenken** *(give a present)*, **schicken** *(send)*, **verkaufen** *(sell)* and verbs meaning "inform": **erzählen** *(tell)*, **empfehlen** *(recommend)*, **erklären** *(explain)*, **sagen** *(say)*, **wünschen** *(wish)*, **zeigen** *(show)*.

	Tobias	gibt	dem Losverkäufer	zwei Euro.
	subject	*verb*	*dative complement*	*accusative complement*
	Wer oder was?		Wem?	Wen or was?

anbieten:	Herr Gebhardt	bietet	den Gästen	einen Aperitif an.
bringen:	Das Mädchen	bringt	der Großmutter	einen Kuchen.
empfehlen:	Die Lehrerin	empfiehlt	dem Kursteilnehmer	ein Buch.
erklären:	Die Lehrerin	erklärt	dem Schüler	ein Wort.
erzählen:	Der Opa	erzählt	den Kindern	ein Märchen.
geben:	Die Oma	gibt	den Kindern	ein Eis.
sagen:	Herr Gebhardt	sagt	den Gästen	"Auf Wiedersehen".
schenken:	Frau Glück	schenkt	der Gastgeberin	einen Blumenstrauß.
schicken:	Yuki	schickt	der Freundin	eine Postkarte.
wünschen:	Die Lehrerin	wünscht	den Schülern	viel Glück.
zeigen:	Die Verkäuferin	zeigt	der Dame	die Hüte.

Prepositions followed by the dative

Fahren wir mit der U-Bahn oder mit dem Bus?
Shall we go by subway or by bus?
Vielen Dank für die Einladung zum Konzert.
Thank you for the invitation to the concert.

Prepositions followed by the dative only are: aus *(from, out of)*, bei *(at)*, gegenüber *(opposite)*, mit *(with)*, nach *(after)*, seit *(since)*, von *(from)*, zu *(to)*.

aus	Die Kinder kommen aus der Schule.
	The children are coming out of school.
bei	Yuki kauft Brezeln beim (= bei dem) Bäcker.
	Yuki is buying pretzels at the baker's.
gegenüber	Die Haltestelle ist gegenüber der Philharmonie.
	The station is opposite the Philharmonic Hall.
mit	Tobias spielt mit der Katze.
	Tobias is playing with the cat.
nach	Nach dem Konzert gehen Yuki und Tobias in ein Weinlokal.
	After the concert Yuki and Tobias go to a wine bar.
seit	Peter ist seit einem Monat in Deutschland.
	Peter has been in Germany for one month.
von	Yuki kommt von der Schule.
	Yuki is coming from school.
zu	Vielen Dank für die Einladung zum (= zu dem) Konzert.
	Thank you for the invitation to the concert.

bei dem = beim   von dem = vom   zu dem = zum

Prepositions that take both the accusative and the dative

Yuki fährt in die Stadt.	(Wohin?) (Akkusativ)
Yuki is going into town.	(Where to?) (accusative)
Wir sitzen in der Mitte.	(Wo?) (Dativ)
We are sitting in the middle.	(Where?) (dative)

The prepositions **an** *(on)*, **auf** *(on)*, **in** *(into)*, **neben** *(next to)*, **unter** *(under)*, **vor** *(in front of)*, **entlang** *(along)*, **hinter** *(behind)*, **über** *(over)*, **zwischen** *(between)* are prepositions that take the accusative in answer to the question *Where to?* The verb used expresses an activity. These prepositions take the dative in answer to the question *Where?* The verb used expresses a state.

Where (to)? accusative	
an	Yuki hängt das Bild an die Wand.
	Yuki is hanging the picture on the wall.
auf	Yuki legt das Buch auf den Tisch.
	Yuki is putting the book on the table.
in	Yuki fährt in die Stadt.
	Yuki is going into town.
neben	Jean-Luc setzt sich neben das Mädchen.
	Jean-Luc sits down next to the girl.
unter	Mainzel geht unter das Bett.
	Mainzel is going under the bed.
vor	Yuki setzt sich vor das Orchester.
	Yuki is sitting down in front of the orchestra.

Where? dative	
an	Das Bild hängt an der Wand.
	The picture hangs on the wall.
auf	Das Buch ist auf dem Tisch.
	The book is on the table.
in	Das Weinlokal befindet sich im Stadtzentrum.
	The wine bar is in the city center.
neben	Die U-Bahn-Haltestelle ist neben dem Haus.
	The subway station is next to the house.
unter	Mainzel ist unter dem Bett.
	Mainzel is under the bed.
vor	Yuki sitzt vor dem Orchester.
	Yuki is sitting in front of the orchestra.

Exercises

Exercise 1

Complete the following sentences by inserting the definite article in the dative.

1 Die Mutter gibt .... Baby Milch.

2 Der Vater gibt .... Kindern Schokolade.

3 Yuki gibt .... Gastgeberin einen Blumenstrauß.

4 Der Sohn widerspricht .... Vater.

5 Die Kinder widersprechen .... Eltern.

6 Tobias und Yuki hören .... Bamberger Symphonikern zu.

7 Das Kind hört .... Großvater zu.

Exercise 2

Put the articles into the dative. Remember to be careful with the endings of nouns in the plural.

1 Tobias schenkt .... einen Ring. (Freundin)

2 Die Oma kauft .... eine Brezel. (Kinder)

3 Frau Glück bringt .... eine Flasche Wein. (Gastgeber)

4 Der Postbeamte zeigt .... Sondermarken. (Touristen)

5 Herr Gebhardt sagt .... „Guten Abend". (Gäste)

6 Theresa empfiehlt .... Weißwürste. (Mann)

7 Opa erzählt .... eine Geschichte. (Kinder)

Exercise 3

Complete the sentences with a preposition that takes the dative and the correct article before the noun where necessary.

1 Yuki spricht .... (Kollege) (*pl.*)

2 Yuki wohnt .... (Frau Glück)

3 Gail kommt .... (USA)

4 Jean-Luc ist .... in Deutschland. (ein Monat)

5 .... gehen alle nach Hause. (Abendessen)

6 Die Haltestelle ist .... (Rathaus)

7 Yuki und Tobias fahren .... (U-Bahn)

8 Yuki und Tobias gehen .... etwas trinken. (Konzert)

Exercise 4

Answer the questions.

1 Wo spielen die Kinder? (das Haus/vor)

....

2 Wo zahlen wir den Hut? (die Sammelkasse/an)

....

3 Wo kaufen wir ein Kleid? (das Kaufhaus/in)

....

4 Wo ist die Haltestelle? (die Straße/neben)

....

Vocabulary

Below is a list of vocabulary encountered in this chapter.

abgeben *in:* **den Mantel abgeben**	*to leave*
abholen	*to pick up*
also gut	*okay then*
antworten	*to answer*
auf	*on*
aussehen	*to look*
besorgen	*to go and get*
Bett, das, -en	*bed*
bringen	*to bring*
Bus, der, -se	*bus*
danken	*to thank*
direkt	*directly*
Einfach super!	*Simply marvellous!*
erzählen	*to tell*
finden *in:* **wie findest du …?**	*to like* *in: How do you like…?*
Garderobe, die, -n	*cloakroom*
Gastgeber, der, -	*host*
Gastgeberin, die, -nen	*hostess*
gegenüber	*opposite*
gratulieren	*to congratulate*
in der Nähe	*near here*
Keller, der, -	*cellar*
Kompliment, das, -e	*compliment*
Konzert, das, -e	*concert*
sollen wir lieber	*is it better to*
Los, das, -e	*lottery ticket*
Losverkäufer, der, -	*lottery-ticket seller*
Märchen, das, -	*story, fairy tale*
Mitte, die	*middle*
Nähe *in:* **in der Nähe**	*near here*
neben	*next to*
Orchester, das, -	*orchestra*
Philharmonie, die, -n	*Philharmonic Hall*
Programm, das, -e	*programme*
Prost!	*Cheers!*
Reihe, die, -n	*row*
Ring, der, -e	*ring*
sagen	*to say*
schenken	*to give a present*
schließlich	*after all*
Sohn, der, -¨e	*son*
Solist, der, -en	*soloist*
spielen	*to play*
unter	*under*
von	*from*
vor	*in front of*
wählen	*to choose*
Wand, die, -¨e	*wall*
Weg, der, -e	*way*
Weinlokal, das, -e	*wine bar*
widersprechen	*to contradict*
wünschen	*to wish*
zu	*to*
zuhören	*to listen to*
zuschauen	*to watch*
zweite	*second*

day: 10

The Family

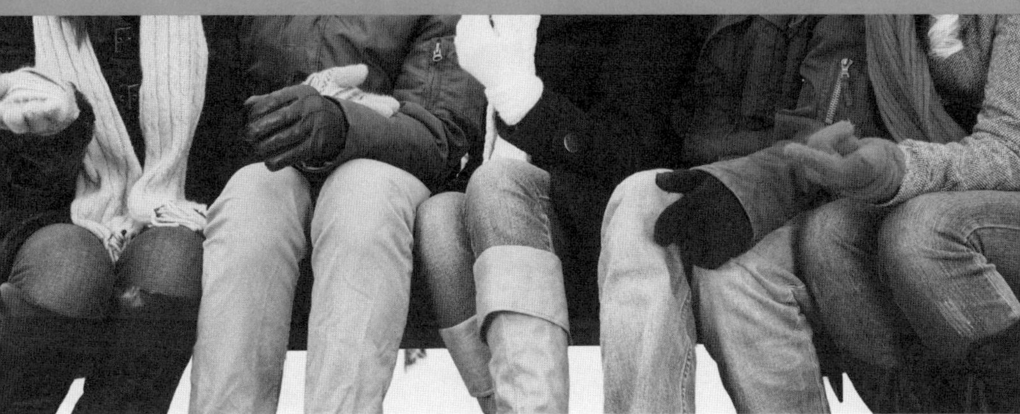

Day 10 introduces the family and possessive adjectives, as well as personal pronouns. You will build your vocabulary so you can talk about yourself and your family and you will pick up more country and culture tips about life in Germany.

FAMILY TIES…

Traditional ways of life have changed. Only one in twenty families in Germany has five members or more. The large family has more or less disappeared and, today, the average family consists of one, or at the most, two children with grandparents and relatives often living at a great distance from one another.

German conversation: Die Familie

Der Postbote bringt zwei Briefe. Ein Brief ist für Yuki, der andere für Frau Glück.

Frau Glück: **Hier ist ein Brief für Sie, Yuki.**

Yuki: **Woher kommt er?**

Frau Glück: **Ich glaube aus Amerika.**

Yuki: **Da wohnt meine Schwester Hanako. Sie ist dort verheiratet. Sie wohnt schon seit drei Jahren mit ihrer Familie in Cincinnati. Haben Sie auch Geschwister?**

Frau Glück: **Ja. Ich habe zwei Schwestern und zwei Brüder. Meine Schwester Christel wohnt in Köln und meine Schwester Elke in Hildesheim. Mein Bruder Rolf wohnt in Hamburg und mein Bruder Dieter in Dresden.**

Yuki: **Was für eine große Familie! Haben Sie noch mehr Verwandte?**

Frau Glück: **Ja. Meine Geschwister sind alle verheiratet. Ich habe also noch zwei Schwäger und zwei Schwägerinnen. Und alle haben Kinder. Deshalb habe ich Nichten und Neffen. Außerdem leben auch noch meine Eltern und ich habe viele Cousinen und Cousins. Wir sind wirklich eine sehr große Familie.**

Yuki: **Wie oft sehen Sie Ihre Familie?**

Frau Glück: **Sehr selten. Wir treffen uns nur einmal im Jahr zu meinem Geburtstag. Da kommen alle gern. Aber wir telefonieren oft miteinander. Oh, mein Brief kommt von meinem Bruder aus Dresden!**

Liebe Angelika,

endlich bekommst Du wieder einen Brief von mir. Ich habe eine Überraschung für Dich! Ich komme nächste Woche beruflich nach München und möchte dann gerne am Samstag mit Dir ins Deutsche Museum und anschließend etwas essen gehen.

Viele Grüße an Dich und Deine Mitbewohnerin aus Japan.

Dein Dieter

Frau Glück: **So eine Überraschung! Mein Bruder besucht mich. Und was schreibt Ihre Schwester?**

Yuki: **Sie möchte mich gerne besuchen, aber sie hat kein Geld. Schade!**

English conversation: The Family

The postman (mail carrier) brings two letters. One letter is for Yuki, the other is for Mrs. Glück.

Mrs. Glück: **Here's a letter for you, Yuki.**

Yuki: **Where's it from?**

Mrs. Glück: **I think it's from America.**

Yuki: **My sister Hanako lives there. She's married and has been living there with her family in Cincinnati for three years. Have you got any brothers and sisters?**

Mrs. Glück: **Oh, yes. I've got two sisters and two brothers. My sister Christel lives in Cologne and my sister Elke lives in Hildesheim. My brother Rolf lives in Hamburg and my brother Dieter in Dresden.**

Yuki: **What a big family! Have you got any more relatives?**

Mrs. Glück: **Yes, I have. My brothers and sisters are all married. So I've also got two brothers-in-law and two sisters-in-law and they've all got children. So I've got nieces and nephews. My parents are still alive as well. And I've got a lot of cousins. We're really a very big family.**

Yuki: **How often do you see your family?**

Mrs. Glück: **Very rarely. We see each other only once a year on my birthday. They all enjoy coming. But we often ring each other up. Oh, my letter is from my brother in Dresden.**

Dear Angelika,

At long last you have got a letter from me. I have a surprise for you!

I'm coming to Munich next week on business and would like to take you to the Deutsches Museum on Saturday and take you out for a meal afterwards.

Best regards to you and your guest from Japan.

Yours,

Dieter

Mrs. Glück: **What a surprise! My brother is coming to visit me. And what has your sister written in her letter?**

Yuki: **She'd like to come and visit me, but she doesn't have any money. What a pity!**

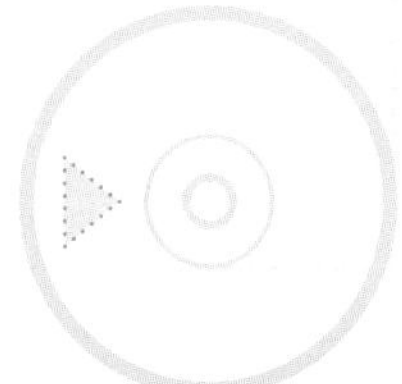

Grammar

Possessive adjectives and pronouns

Possessive adjectives usually modify a noun. They show ownership and connection.

Meine Schwester Christel wohnt in Köln.	My sister Christel lives in Köln.
Viele Grüße an **deine** Mitbewohnerin.	Best regards to your guest.

The ending of the possessive adjective agrees with the person it refers to. In the nominative, accusative and dative singular, the possessive adjectives take the same endings as the indefinite article **ein**.

singular personal pronoun	ich	du	Sie	er/es	sie
masculine/neuter	mein	dein	Ihr	sein	ihr
feminine	mein**e**	dein**e**	Ihr**e**	sein**e**	ihr**e**
plural	mein**e**	dein**e**	Ihr**e**	sein**e**	ihr**e**

plural personal pronoun	wir	ihr	Sie	sie
masculine/neuter	unser	euer	Ihr	ihr
feminine	unser**e**	eu(e)r**e**	Ihr**e**	ihr**e**
plural	unser**e**	eu(e)r**e**	Ihr**e**	ihr**e**

Personal pronouns

Hier ist ein Brief für Sie. Woher kommt **er**?	Here is a letter for you. Where's it from?
Hilfst du dem Mann? Ja, ich helfe **ihm**.	Are you helping the man? Yes, I'm helping him.

singular		
nominative	*accusative*	*dative*
ich	mich	mir
du	dich	dir
Sie	Sie	Ihnen
er	ihn	ihm
sie	sie	ihr
es	es	ihm

plural		
nominative	*accusative*	*dative*
wir	uns	uns
ihr	euch	euch
Sie	Sie	Ihnen
sie	sie	ihnen

Question words

Wer?	Wen?	Wem?
Who?	Who?	Who(m)?

Exercises

Exercise 1

Fill in the correct possessive adjectives.

1 die Mutter und .... Tochter

2 die Mutter und .... Sohn

3 die Mutter und .... Kind

4 die Cousine und .... Mann

5 der Vater und .... Sohn

6 der Vater und .... Kind

7 der Cousin und .... Frau

8 die Eltern und .... Kinder

Exercise 2

Look at the following example and answer the questions.

Was suchen Sie? (die Serviette) Ich suche meine Serviette.

1 Was suchen Sie? (der Pass) ....

2 Was sucht er? (die Fahrkarte) ....

3 Was sucht ihr? (das Klassenzimmer) ....

4 Was sucht sie? (die Brille) ....

5 Was suchst du? (der Schlüssel) ....

Exercise 3

Fill in the possessive adjectives in the nominative, accusative or dative.

1 Yuki hat eine Schwester. .... Schwester wohnt mit .... Familie in den USA.

2 Frau Glück bekommt einen Brief von .... Bruder.

3 Darf ich Ihnen .... Mann vorstellen?

4 Ist der Brief von deiner Schwester? Nein, von .... Bruder.

5 Ist der Brief von deinem Bruder? Nein, von .... Schwester.

Exercise 4

Fill in the personal pronoun in the dative.

1 Kannst du .... bitte einen Kaffee bringen? (ich)

2 Wie geht es ....? Danke, ... geht es gut. (du) (ich)

3 Möchtest du mit .... ausgehen? (er)

4 Komm doch mit.. (wir)

5 Könnt ihr .... helfen? Wir helfen .... gerne. (wir) (ihr)

Vocabulary

Below is a list of vocabulary encountered in this chapter.

also	*so, therefore*
andere	*other*
anschließend	*afterwards*
außerdem	*as well*
bald	*soon*
beruflich	*on business*
besuchen	*to visit*
Brille, die, -n (sing.)	*glasses*
Bruder, der, -¨	*brother*
Cousin, der, -s	*cousin (male)*
Cousine, die, -n	*cousin (female)*
dein	*your (in letters - yours)*
deshalb	*therefore*
dich *(Acc.)*	*you*
dir *(Dat.)*	*to you*
Eltern, die *(pl.)*	*parents*
endlich	*at long last*
erzählen	*to talk about*
es *(Acc.)*	*it*

euch	*you (pl.)*
euer	*your (pl.)*
Geburtstag, der, -e	*birthday*
Geschwister, die *(pl.)*	*brothers and sisters*
Großeltern, die *(pl.)*	*grandparents*
Großmutter, die, -¨	*grandmother*
Großvater, der, -¨	*grandfather*
Gruß, der, -¨e	*regards*
herzliche Grüße	*best regards*
hören	*to hear*
ihm *(Dat.)*	*(to) him*
ihn *(Acc.)*	*him*
ihnen	*(to) them*
ihr	*(to) her*
Jahr, das, -e	*year*
Klassen-zimmer, das, -	*classroom*
mehr	*more*
mein	*my*
mich *(Acc.)*	*me*
mir *(Dat.)*	*(to) me*
Mitbewohne-rin, die, -nen	*guest*
miteinander	*with each other*
nächste Woche	*next week*
Neffe, der, -n	*nephew*
Nichte, die, -n	*niece*
Onkel, der, -	*uncle*
Pass, der, -¨e	*passport*
Postbote, der, -n	*postman/mail carrier*
schade	*what a pity*
Schlüssel, der, -	*key*
schreiben	*to write*
Schwager, der, -¨	*brother-in-law*
Schwägerin, die, -nen	*sister-in-law*
Schwester, die, -n	*sister*
sein	*his, its*
seit *in:* **seit drei Jahren**	*for three years*
selten	*seldom, rarely*
sie *(Acc. sing.)*	*her*
sie *(Acc. pl.)*	*(to) them*
So eine Überraschung!	*What a surprise!*
Spaß, der, -¨e	*fun*
Tante, die, -n	*aunt*
Tochter, die, -¨	*daughter*
treffen (sich)	*to see each other*
Überraschung, die, -en	*surprise*
uns *(Acc.)*	*us*
uns *(Dat.)*	*(to) us*
unser	*our*
verheiratet sein	*to be married*
Verwandte, die *(Pl.)*	*relatives*
Was gibt es Neues?	*What's new?*
wem*? (Dat.)*	*(to) who(m)?*
wen*? (Acc.)*	*who?*
Wie oft?	*How often?*
wirklich	*really*
Woche, die, -n	*week*

day: 11

Finding work

Day 11 discusses finding work and professions and you will learn how to talk about how long you have been doing something. You will also learn how to spell out words phonetically, as well as further expanding your vocabulary.

LOOKING FOR A JOB…

If you are looking for a job in Germany, check the weekend edition of a national newspaper like the ***Frankfurter Rundschau*** *or the* ***Süddeutsche Zeitung*** *or put your own advertisement in a newspaper. Also, check various internet sites under* ***Stellenangebote, Stellenanzeigen*** *or* ***Jobs****.*

Another way to find a job is to look at the jobs offered by the ***Arbeitsagentur*** *(Job Center).*

German conversation: Jobsuche

Yuki: Ich glaube, ich muss Geld verdienen. Meine Schwester möchte mich so gerne besuchen. Sie kann die Reise nach Deutschland aber nicht bezahlen. Ich möchte ihr den Flug finanzieren.

Frau Glück: Vielleicht lesen Sie mal die Stellenangebote in der Zeitung. Ich glaube, ich habe noch die Zeitung vom Samstag. Ja, da ist sie. Also wollen wir mal sehen, welche Stellen es gibt. Schauen Sie, hier ist ein interessantes Angebot:

Reisebüro sucht freundliche junge Dame für leichte Büroarbeit. Englischkenntnisse erwünscht. Kenntnisse in Japanisch von Vorteil. Arbeit am PC erforderlich. Arbeitszeit: 18–21 Uhr. Gute Bezahlung. Informationen unter Tel. 346178

Rufen Sie doch mal an!

Yuki: Meinen Sie wirklich?

Frau Glück: Natürlich!

Yuki ruft im Reisebüro an.

Frau Dietl: Reisebüro Sonnenschein. Guten Tag! Frau Dietl am Apparat. Was kann ich für Sie tun?

Yuki: Hier spricht Yuki Naito. Ich möchte mich gerne um die Stelle bewerben. Sie suchen jemand mit Kenntnissen in Englisch und Japanisch.

Frau Dietl: Können Sie auch am Computer arbeiten?

Yuki: Ja, das kann ich auch.

Frau Dietl: Wie gut sind Ihre Japanisch- und Englischkenntnisse?

Yuki: Japanisch ist meine Muttersprache. Englisch lerne ich schon seit zehn Jahren.

Frau Dietl: Seit wann sind Sie denn schon in Deutschland?

Yuki: Seit drei Monaten.

Frau Dietl: Ihr Deutsch ist wirklich ausgezeichnet! Ich mache Ihnen einen Vorschlag: Kommen Sie doch einfach bei uns vorbei und stellen Sie sich vor. Unser Reisebüro ist in der Königinstraße 4. Wissen Sie, wie Sie zu uns kommen?

Yuki: Ich denke ja. Wann kann ich zu Ihnen kommen?

Frau Dietl: Geht es morgen Nachmittag, sagen wir um 17 Uhr?

Yuki: Ja, das geht.

Frau Dietl: Also, dann bis morgen, Frau… Wie ist Ihr Name?

Yuki: Naito. Ich buchstabiere: N wie Nordpol, A wie Anton, I wie Ida, T wie Theodor und O wie Otto. Mein Vorname ist Yuki, Y wie Ypsilon, U wie Ulrich, K wie Kaufmann und I wie Ida. Naito Yuki. Also dann bis morgen, Frau Dietl. Auf Wiederhören!

English conversation: Looking for a job

Yuki: **I think I'll have to earn some money. My sister would like to visit me. But she can't afford to pay for the trip to Germany. I'd like to pay for the flight for her.**

Mrs. Glück: **Perhaps you should take a look at the job offers in the newspaper. I think I still have Saturday's paper. Oh, yes, there it is. Let's have a look and see what jobs there are. Look, here's an interesting job offer:**

Travel agency seeks friendly young lady for light office work. Knowledge of English desirable. Knowledge of Japanese an advantage. Required to work on PC. Working hours: 6 – 9 p.m. Good pay. For further information call 34 61 78

Why don't you give them a call?

Yuki: **Do you think I should?**

Mrs. Glück: **Of course.**

Yuki telephones the travel agency.

Mrs. Dietl: **Sonnenschein Travel Agency. Good afternoon, Mrs. Dietl speaking. What can I do for you?**

Yuki: **This is Yuki Naito speaking. I would like to apply for the vacancy. You are looking for someone with knowledge of English and Japanese.**

Mrs. Dietl: **Can you use a computer?**

Yuki: **Yes, I can.**

Mrs. Dietl: **How good is your knowledge of Japanese and English?**

Yuki: **Japanese is my native language and I've been learning English for ten years.**

Mrs. Dietl: **How long have you been in Germany?**

Yuki: **For three months.**

Mrs. Dietl: **Your German is really excellent. Let me make a suggestion: why don't you just come and see us and introduce yourself. Our travel agency is at number four Königinstraße. Do you know how to get to us?**

Yuki: **I think I do. When can I come and see you?**

Mrs. Dietl: **Is tomorrow afternoon okay? Let's say about 5 p.m.**

Yuki: **Yes, that's okay.**

Mrs. Dietl: **I'll see you tomorrow then, Ms. … What was your name?**

Yuki: **Naito. I'll spell it for you: N A I T O. My first name is Yuki, Y U K I. Naito Yuki. I'll see you tomorrow then, Mrs. Dietl. Goodbye.**

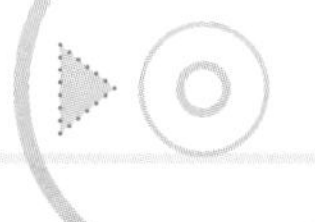

Grammar

Phonetic alphabet

A	wie Anton	J	wie Julius	S	wie Samuel
Ä	wie Ärger	K	wie Kaufmann	Sch	wie Schule
B	wie Berta	L	wie Ludwig	T	wie Theodor
C	wie Cäsar	M	wie Martha	U	wie Ulrich
Ch	wie Charlotte	N	wie Nordpol	Ü	wie Übermut
D	wie Dora	O	wie Otto	V	wie Viktor
E	wie Emil	Ö	wie Ökonom	W	wie Wilhelm
F	wie Friedrich	P	wie Paula	X	wie Xanthippe
G	wie Gustav	Q	wie Quelle	Y	wie Ypsilon
H	wie Heinrich	R	wie Richard	Z	wie Zacharias
I	wie Ida				

Professions

male	female	
der Architekt	die Architektin	architect
der Arzt	die Ärztin	doctor
der Bauer	die Bäuerin	farmer
der Friseur	die Friseurin	hairdresser
der Ingenieur	die Ingenieurin	engineer
der Kellner	die Kellnerin	waiter/waitress
der Krankenpfleger	die Krankenschwester	male nurse/nurse
der Lehrer	die Lehrerin	teacher
der Mechaniker	die Mechanikerin	mechanic
der Polizist	die Polizistin	policeman/policewoman
der Schreiner	die Schreinerin	carpenter
der Sekretär	die Sekretärin	secretary

Seit…

Seit is a preposition which is always followed by the dative and is used before dates and times. Although it is used in the present tense, it refers to the past.

Paul arbeitet seit einer Stunde am Computer.	Paul has been working on the computer for an hour.
Yuki ist seit drei Monaten in Deutschland.	Yuki has been in Germany for three months.

Wann?

Wann kommen Sie? Um 11 Uhr.	When are you coming? At 11 a.m.
Seit wann ist Yuki in Deutschland? Seit drei Monaten.	How long has Yuki been in Germany? For three months.

Exercises

Exercise 1

Answer the questions.

1 Seit wann kennt Yuki Tobias?

(drei/Woche) ....

2 Seit wann sind Sie schon in Deutschland?

(fünf/Monat) ....

3 Seit wann arbeitest du am Computer?

(drei/Stunde) ....

4 Seit wann spielen die Kinder Fußball?

(dreißig/Minute) ....

5 Seit wann liest du das Buch?

(fünf/Tag) ....

Exercise 2

Fill in the following words: buchstabieren, die Stellenangebote, Englischkenntnisse, sich bewerben, sich vorstellen, Computer, verdienen.

Change the form of the verbs where necessary.

1 Yuki möchte Geld ....

2 Yuki .... um eine Stelle.

3 Frau Glück liest .... in der Zeitung.

4 Yuki hat ....

5 Yuki .... ihren Namen.

6 Yuki kann auch am .... arbeiten.

7 Yuki .... im Reisebüro ....

Exercise 3

Match the following sentences.

1 Deutsche Lufthansa. Guten Tag!	**a** Ja, ich lerne seit vier Jahren Französisch.
2 Haben Sie Computerkenntnisse?	**b** Geht es morgen Vormittag?
3 Also dann bis übermorgen!	**c** Mein Name ist Janzen. Was kann ich für Sie tun?
4 Sprechen Sie auch Französisch?	**d** Ja. Auf Wiederhören!
5 Wann kann ich zu Ihnen kommen?	**e** Ja, natürlich!

Exercise 4

Match the German jobs below to the corresponding English word:

Lehrerin/Mechaniker/Sekretärin/Bauer/Ärztin/Schreiner

1 Doctor	**2** Secretary ....
3 Carpenter..	**4** Mechanic ....
5 Teacher...	**6** Farmer ....

Vocabulary

Below is a list of vocabulary encountered in this chapter.

Abendstunde	*evening*
in: **in den Abendstunden**	*in the evening(s)*
Also dann bis morgen.	*I'll see you tomorrow then.*
am PC	*on the PC*
Angebot, das, -e	*offer*
Anruf, der, -e	*call*
Arbeit, die, -en	*work*
arbeiten	*to work*
Arbeitszeit, die, -en	*working hours*
Architekt, der, -en	*architect*
Architektin, die, -nen	*architect (fem.)*
Arzt, der, -¨e	*doctor*
Ärztin, die, -nen	*doctor (fem.)*
auf Wiederhören *(am Telefon)*	*goodbye (on the phone)*
Bäcker, der, -	*baker*
Bäckerin, die, -nen	*baker (fem.)*
Bauer, der, -n	*farmer*
Bäuerin, die, -nen	*farmer (fem.)*
Beruf, der, -e	*profession*
bewerben (sich) um	*to apply for*
Bezahlung, die, -en	*pay, payment*
buchstabieren	*to spell*
Büroarbeit, die, -en	*office work*
Busfahrer, der	*bus driver*
Busfahrerin, die, -nen	*bus driver (fem.)*
Computer, der, -	*computer*
Dame, die, -n	*lady*
denken	*to think*
Englischkenntnisse, die *(p.)*	*knowledge of English*
erforderlich	*required*
erwünscht	*desirable*
finanzieren	*to pay for*
Flug, der, -¨e	*flight*
Frau Dietl am Apparat	*Mrs. Dietl speaking*
Friseur, der, -e	*hairdresser*
Friseurin, die, -nen	*hairdresser (fem.)*
Information, die, -en	*information*
Ingenieur, der, -e	*engineer (male)*
Ingenieurin, die, -nen	*engineer (fem.)*
jemand	*someone*
Jobsuche, die	*looking for a job*
jung	*young*
Kaufmann, der, *(pl.)* **Kaufleute**	*salesperson*

Kellner, der, -	*waiter*
Kellnerin, die, -nen	*waitress*
Kenntnis, die, -se	*knowledge*
Kranken-pfleger, der, -	*male nurse*
Kranken-schwester, die, -n	*nurse (fem.)*
leicht	*light, easy*
mal *in:* **lesen Sie mal**	*you should read*
Mechaniker, der, -	*mechanic*
Mechanikerin, die, -nen	*mechanic (fem.)*
meinen	*to think*
Muttersprache, die, -n	*native language*
Nordpol, der	*North Pole*
Personalbüro, das, -s	*personnel department*
Polizist, der, -en	*policeman*
Polizistin, die, -nen	*policewoman*
Reise, die, -n	*trip*
Reisebüro, das, -s	*travel agency*
schauen	*to look*
Schreiner, der, -	*carpenter*
Schreinerin, die, -nen	*carpenter (fem.)*
Seit wann?	*How long?*
Sekretär, der, -e	*secretary*
Sekretärin, die, -nen	*secretary (fem.)*
Sonnenschein, der	*sunshine*
Stelle, die, -n	*job*
Stellenange-bot, das, -e	*job ad*
tun	*to do*
verdienen	*to earn*
Verkäufer, der, -	*shop assistant*
Verkäuferin, die, -nen	*shop assistant (fem.)*
vorbeikommen	*to come by*
in: **einfach vor-beikommen**	*just come and see*
Vorschlag *in:* **einen Vorschlag machen**	*to suggest*
Vorstellungs-gespräch, das, -e	*job interview*
Vorteil, der, -e	*advantage*
Wie ist Ihr Name?	*What's your name?*
wie*?*	*how?*
wissen	*to know*
Ypsilon	*y (as in the letter y)*

day: 12

The Interview

Day 12 gives you an introduction to a typical interview situation with some basic questions and answers. You will also learn more job-related vocabulary and discover more about the culture and lifestyle in Germany.

SOCIAL INSURANCE…

*Anyone in employment is a member of a number of employment schemes/plans. She/he must pay compulsory contributions to the national insurance system. There are **Kranken-**, **Arbeitslosen-**, **Pflege-** and **Rentenversicherung** (health, unemployment, nursing-care and pension insurance plans). Parts of the contributions are paid by the employer. This entitles the insured person to receive benefits when sick, unemployed or in need of care in old age.*

German conversation: Der Vorstellungstermin

Yuki stellt sich im Reisebüro Sonnenschein vor.

Yuki: **Guten Tag! Meine Name ist Yuki Naito. Ich habe um 17 Uhr einen Vorstellungstermin bei Frau Dietl.**

Frau Dietl: **Guten Tag, Frau Naito! Ich bin Frau Dietl. Bitte nehmen Sie Platz! Möchten Sie etwas zu trinken?**

Yuki: **Ein Mineralwasser, bitte.**

Frau Dietl schenkt Yuki ein Glas Mineralwasser ein.

Yuki: **Vielen Dank!**

Frau Dietl: **Also, Sie sind Japanerin. Wir suchen dringend jemand, der Japanisch kann.**

Yuki: **Das freut mich.**

Frau Dietl: **Wie gut sprechen Sie Englisch?**

Yuki: **Ich lerne seit zehn Jahren Englisch.**

Frau Dietl: **Gut. Wie sieht es mit Ihren Computerkenntnissen aus? Welche Programme können Sie anwenden?**

Yuki: **Ich kann ein Textverarbeitungsprogramm, nämlich Word sowie ein Buchhaltungsprogramm.**

Frau Dietl: **Sehr gut.**

Yuki: **Darf ich Sie etwas fragen?**

Frau Dietl: **Ja, natürlich!**

Yuki: **Für wie viele Abende suchen Sie jemand?**

Frau Dietl: **Eigentlich für vier Abende. Ich habe noch einen anderen Bewerber. Er möchte gerne drei Abende übernehmen. Können Sie den vierten Abend übernehmen?**

Yuki: **Ja, gerne. Und was verdiene ich?**

Frau Dietl: **Wir zahlen zwölf Euro die Stunde. Sind Sie krankenversichert?**

Yuki: **Ja. Wann soll ich denn mit der Arbeit beginnen?**

Frau Dietl: **Am nächsten Mittwoch. Können Sie immer am Mittwochabend arbeiten?**

Yuki: **Ja, das geht sehr gut.**

Frau Dietl: **An Ihrem ersten Arbeitstag beginnen Sie um 18.00 Uhr. Also dann bis nächsten Mittwoch.**

Yuki: **Bis Mittwoch. Auf Wiedersehen!**

English conversation: The job interview

Yuki arrives at the Sonnenschein Travel Agency for her interview.

Yuki: **Good afternoon. My name is Yuki Naito. I have an interview with Mrs. Dietl at 5 p.m.**

Mrs. Dietl: **Good afternoon, Ms. Naito. I'm Mrs. Dietl. Please take a seat. Would you like something to drink?**

Yuki: **A glass of mineral water, please.**

Mrs. Dietl pours Yuki a glass of mineral water.

Yuki: **Thank you very much.**

Mrs. Dietl: **So you are Japanese. We urgently need someone who can speak Japanese.**

Yuki: **I'm glad to hear that.**

Mrs. Dietl: **How good is your English?**

Yuki: **I've been learning English for ten years.**

Mrs. Dietl: **Good. What about your computer skills? Which programs do you use?**

Yuki: **I work with one word processing programme, Word, and one bookkeeping programme.**

Mrs. Dietl: **Very good.**

Yuki: **May I ask you something?**

Mrs. Dietl: **Yes, of course.**

Yuki: **How many evenings are you looking for someone?**

Mrs. Dietl: **For four evenings, actually. There is another candidate. He'd like to take on three evenings. Could you do the fourth evening?**

Yuki: **Yes, I could. And how much will I earn?**

Mrs. Dietl: **We pay twelve euros an hour. Do you have health insurance?**

Yuki: **Yes, I have. When do I start work?**

Mrs. Dietl: **Next Wednesday. Can you always work on a Wednesday evening?**

Yuki: **Yes, that's no problem.**

Mrs. Dietl: **You start at 6 p.m. on your first evening. I'll see you next Wednesday, then.**

Yuki: **Yes, see you on Wednesday. Goodbye.**

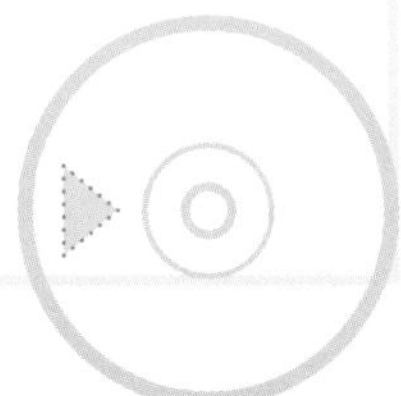

Grammar

The adverb *nämlich*

Ich kann ein Textverarbeitungsprogramm, nämlich Word.

To express a statement more exactly, the adverb nämlich (namely, you see) is used. Nämlich is never put at the beginning of a sentence.

Exercises

Exercise 1

Insert nämlich in the right position.

1 Ich muss mich beeilen, ich möchte bald zu Hause sein.

....

2 Wie geht es dir? Mir geht es nicht gut.

....

3 Wann kommen Sie? Wir wollen weggehen.

....

4 Ich habe heute Abend leider keine Zeit. Ich gehe ins Konzert.

....

Exercise 2

Answer the questions.

Herr Natsumura sucht eine Arbeit am Abend. Er lernt seit sechs Jahren Englisch. Heute stellt er sich bei dem Personalchef von Wiedemann & Co, Herrn Würtz, vor.

1 Was sagt Herr Natsumura zuerst?

....

2 Was antwortet Herr Würtz?

....

3 Dann fragt Herr Würtz nach den Sprachkenntnissen. Was sagt er?

....

4 Herr Würtz fragt, welche Computerprogramme Herr Natsumura anwenden kann.

....

5 Herr Natsumura kann zwei Computerprogramme.

....

6 Herr Natsumura fragt, wie viele Stunden er am Abend arbeiten muss.

....

7 Herr Natsumura fragt, wie viel er an einem Abend verdient.

....

8 Herr Würtz sagt, 10 Euro die Stunde.

....

Exercise 3

Tick the correct answer.

1 In welchem Beruf verdient man am besten?

a Mechaniker **b** Krankenschwester **c** Architekt

2 In welchem Beruf muss man kreativ sein?

a Steuerberater **b** Lehrer **c** Architekt

3 In welchem Beruf braucht man Fremd-sprachenkenntnisse?

a Sekretärin **b** Bäcker **c** Mechaniker

Vocabulary

Below is a list of vocabulary encountered in this chapter.

Arbeitstag, der, -e	*working day*
aussehen mit	*to be about*
in: **Wie sieht es mit Ihren Computerkenntnissen aus?**	*What about your computer skills?*
bar auf die Hand	*all in cash*
beeilen (sich)	*to hurry*
benutzen	*to work*
Bewerber, der, -	*applicant*
Buchhaltungsprogramm, das, -e	*bookkeeping programme*
dringend	*urgently*
einschenken	*to pour out*
Fremdsprachenkenntnis, die, -se	*knowledge of a foreign language*
krankenversichert sein	*to have health insurance*
Krankenversicherung, die, -en	*health insurance*
kreativ	*creative*
Mineralwasser, das	*mineral water*
nachfragen	*to enquire*
Sozialversicherung, die, -en	*social insurance*
Steuer, die, -n	*tax*
Steuerberater, der, -	*tax adviser*
Textverarbeitungsprogramm, das, -e	*word processing programme*
übernehmen	*to do, to take over*
Vorstellungstermin, der, -e	*interview*

Test 2

Work your way around the board. Each correct answer will take you to the next question until you have completed the exercise. Enjoy!

1
Choose one of the solutions. Then go to the square showing the number of the solution you think is correct.

2
Yuki kauft einen … Mantel.
hellen ▶ 8
helle ▶ 15

3
Wrong!
Go back to number 5.

8
Correct.
Next one: Dein Mantel gefällt …
mich ▶ 6
mir ▶ 25

9
Wrong!
Go back to number 25.

10
Wrong!
Go back to number 14.

11
Wrong!
Go back to number 29.

16
Good. Continue:
Gehen Sie … weiter.
geradeaus ▶ 22
mitten ▶ 18

17
Wrong!
Go back to number 22.

18
Wrong!
Go back to number 16.

19
Correct!
End of exercise.

24
Wrong!
Go back to number 12.

25
Very good. Continue:
Yuki legt das Buch auf … Tisch.
den ▶ 14
dem ▶ 9

26
Wrong!
Go back to number 30.

27
Good. Continue:
Ich suche … Schlüssel.
mein ▶ 23
meinen ▶ 12

4

Good. Continue:
Ich rufe morgen …
an ▶ 20
auf ▶ 7

5

Correct.
Continue: Bitte
bedienen Sie …
euch ▶ 3
sich ▶ 13

6

Wrong!

Go back to number 8.

7

Wrong!

Go back to number 4.

12

Very good.
Go on: Der Vater hilft
… Sohn.
dem ▶ 16
der ▶ 24

13

Correct! Continue: Ich
spreche mit… Kollegen.
der ▶ 21
dem ▶ 29

14

Very good. Next one:
Die Haltestelle ist …
dem Bahnhof.
zu ▶ 10
gegenüber ▶ 30

15

Wrong!

Go back to number 2.

20

Well done.
Go on: … Sie
den Antrag aus!
Füllen ▶ 5
Füllt ▶ 28

21

Wrong!

Go back to number 13.

22

Correct!
Yuki schickt der
Freundin … Postkarte.
ein ▶ 17
eine ▶ 19

23

Sorry!

Go back to number
27.

28

Wrong!

Go back to number 20.

29

Well done. Continue:
Kannst du … bitte
einen Kaffee bringen!
mich ▶ 11
mir ▶ 27

30

Correct. Continue:
Deutsche Lufthansa.
Guten Tag! Was kann ich
für … tun?
dich ▶ 26 Sie ▶ 4

day: 13

The Lottery!

Day 13 teaches you how to talk in the past (perfect) tense using both *haben* and *sein*. You will then have the chance to practice what you have learnt, and learn more about everyday conversation.

LOTTO…

Lotto, *the national lottery, is very popular in Germany. Every week millions of people hope to win a fortune when they hand in their lottery ticket at their local lottery counter. They mark with crosses 6 numbers from 1–49 on a lottery ticket. Every Saturday evening in a special television programme called* ***Ziehung der Lottozahlen*** *the winning numbers are drawn and announced. In addition to the Saturday lottery, there is also one on Wednesday. You must have at least three correct numbers to win.*

German conversation: Hurra, ich habe gewonnen!

Yuki kommt nach Hause. Frau Glück gibt ihr einen Brief.

Frau Glück: **Dieser Brief ist heute für Sie gekommen.**

Yuki: **Von wem ist denn der Brief?**

Frau Glück: **Der Absender ist die Staatliche Lotterieverwaltung.**

Yuki öffnet den Brief.

Sehr geehrte Frau Naito,

Ihr Los mit der Nummer 98052687 hat € 5 000 gewonnen. Wir gratulieren Ihnen herzlich und freuen uns, Ihnen einen Scheck über € 5000 senden zu können.

Mit freundlichen Grüßen

Staatliche Lotterieverwaltung

Yuki: **Ich kann es nicht glauben! Ich habe gewonnen! 5000 Euro! Das ist ja fantastisch!**

Frau Glück: **Ich gratuliere Ihnen. Wo haben Sie denn das Los gekauft?**

Yuki: **Neulich sind Tobias und ich ins Konzert gegangen. Anschließend haben wir noch ein Glas Wein getrunken. Auf dem Weg zum Weinlokal haben wir einen Losverkäufer gesehen und wir haben zwei Lose gekauft. Jedes Los hat einen Euro gekostet. Und jetzt habe ich 5000 Euro gewonnen.**

Frau Glück: **Vielleicht wollen Sie es Tobias erzählen? Rufen Sie ihn doch an!**

Yuki: **Ja, das ist eine gute Idee. Hoffentlich ist er zu Hause.**

Yuki ruft an.

Frau Gebhardt: **Gebhardt, guten Tag!**

Yuki: **Hier spricht Yuki. Kann ich bitte Tobias sprechen?**

Frau Gebhardt: **Tobias ist leider nicht zu Hause. Er ist heute Morgen nach Frankfurt geflogen. Er kommt erst heute Abend zurück. Kann ich etwas ausrichten?**

Yuki: **Nein, danke. Ich versuche es morgen noch einmal. Vielen Dank und viele Grüße an Tobias.**

English conversation: Hurrah, I've won!

Yuki comes home. Mrs. Glück gives her a letter.

Mrs. Glück:	**This letter arrived for you today.**
Yuki:	**Who is the letter from?**
Mrs. Glück:	**It's from the Lottery Commission.**

Yuki opens the letter.

Dear Mrs. Naito,

Your lottery ticket number 98 052 687 has won you € 5000.

We offer you our warmest congratulations and are delighted to send you a cheque for € 5000.

Yours sincerely,

Lottery Commission

Yuki:	**I can't believe it! I've won! 5000 euros! That's just wonderful!**
Mrs. Glück:	**Congratulations. Where did you buy the lottery ticket?**
Yuki:	**Tobias and I went to a concert the other day. Afterwards we went to have a glass of wine. On the way to the wine bar we saw a lottery ticket seller and bought two lottery tickets. Each lottery ticket cost one euro. And now I've won 5000 euros.**
Mrs. Glück:	**Perhaps you want to tell Tobias about it. Why don't you phone him?**
Yuki:	**Yes, that's a good idea. I hope he's at home.**

Yuki phones.

Mrs. Gebhardt:	**Hello, Mrs. Gebhardt speaking.**
Yuki:	**This is Yuki speaking. Can I speak to Tobias, please?**
Mrs. Gebhardt:	**I'm afraid Tobias is not at home. He flew to Frankfurt this morning. He won't be back until this evening. Can I give him a message?**
Yuki:	**No, thank you. I'll try again tomorrow. Thank you very much and give my regards to Tobias, please.**

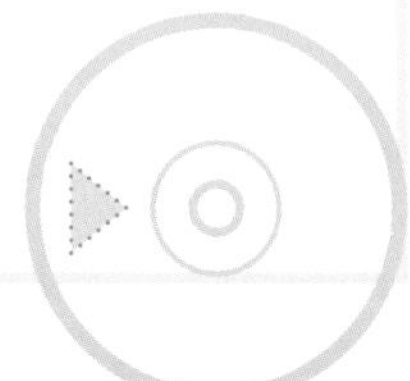

Grammar

The particle *doch*

Rufen Sie ihn **doch** an!	Why don't you telephone him?

Doch is used to reinforce suggestions and advice.

The perfect tense

Wir **haben** Wein **getrunken**.	We drank some wine.
Tobias **ist** nach Frankfurt **geflogen**.	Tobias has flown to Frankfurt.

The perfect tense and the preterite tense are used to talk about the past. The perfect tense is mainly used in spoken language. It is formed by using the present tense of the auxiliary verbs **haben** or **sein** + past participle.

The perfect tense with *haben*

Most verbs, including reflexive verbs, form the perfect tense with **haben**.

Yuki **hat** Kartoffelsalat **gegessen**.	Yuki ate potato salad.

(**essen**: past participle **gegessen**)

haben			
	present		*past participle*
ich	**habe**	Wein	**getrunken**
du	**hast**	Wein	**getrunken**
Sie	**haben**	Wein	**getrunken**
er/sie/es	**hat**	Wein	**getrunken**
wir	**haben**	Wein	**getrunken**
ihr	**habt**	Wein	**getrunken**
Sie	**haben**	Wein	**getrunken**
sie	**haben**	Wein	**getrunken**

The perfect tense with *sein*

Verbs of movement, verbs expressing change of state as well as the verbs **sein** and **bleiben** form the perfect tense with **sein**.

Tobias **ist** nach Frankfurt **geflogen**.	Tobias has flown to Frankfurt.

(**fliegen**: past participle **geflogen**)

Ich **bin** um 8 Uhr **aufgewacht**.	I woke up at 8 a.m.

(**aufwachen**: past participle **aufgewacht**)

Yuki und Tobias **sind** am Sonntag im Konzert **gewesen**.	Yuki and Tobias were at the concert on Sunday.

(**sein**: past participle **gewesen**)

Wir sind zehn Tage in Amerika geblieben.	We stayed in America for ten days.
(bleiben: past participle geblieben)	

sein	to be		
	present		*past participle*
ich	bin	heute	gekommen
du	bist	heute	gekommen
Sie	sind	heute	gekommen
er/sie/es	ist	heute	gekommen
wir	sind	heute	gekommen
ihr	seid	heute	gekommen
Sie	sind	heute	gekommen
sie	sind	heute	gekommen

The past participle of regular verbs

Regular verbs form the past participle with the prefix ge- and with the ending -t. With separable verbs, ge- is in the middle, between the verb and the prefix.

infinitive		*past participle*
fragen	to ask	gefragt
kaufen	to buy	gekauft
machen	to make	gemacht
sagen	to say	gesagt
zahlen	to pay	gezahlt
anfragen	to ask	angefragt
einkaufen	to go shopping	eingekauft
zusagen	to accept	zugesagt

The regular inseparable verbs with the prefix be-, emp-, ent-, er-, ge-, miss-, ver- and zer- form the past participle without ge- and always take the ending -t.

besuchen	to visit	besucht
besichtigen	to tour	besichtigt

The past participle of irregular verbs

Irregular verbs usually form the perfect tense with the prefix ge- and the ending -en. The vowels in the verb stem often change. With separable verbs -ge- is in the middle. These are best learnt by heart.

infinitive		*past participle*
bleiben	to stay	geblieben
essen	to eat	gegessen
finden	to find	gefunden
fliegen	to fly	geflogen
geben	to give	gegeben
kommen	to come	gekommen

nehmen	to take	genommen
treffen	to meet	getroffen
ankommen	to arrive	angekommen
hinfahren	to drive (to)	hingefahren
mitkommen	to come with	mitgekommen
zurückrufen	to call back	zurückgerufen

Exceptions:

infinitive		*past participle*
bringen	to bring	gebracht
denken	to think	gedacht
wissen	to know	gewusst

Inseparable irregular verbs with the prefixes **be-**, **emp-**, **ent-**, **er-**, **ge-**, **miss-**, **ver-** and **zer-** as well as most verbs ending in **-ieren** form the past participle without **ge-**. The past participle of verbs ending in **-ieren** always takes the ending **-t**.

infinitive		*past participle*
beginnen	to begin	begonnen
empfehlen	to recommend	empfohlen
entscheiden	to decide	entschieden
erfinden	to invent	erfunden
gewinnen	to win	gewonnen
misslingen	to fail	misslungen
vergessen	to forget	vergessen
versuchen	to try	versucht
zerbrechen	to break	zerbrochen
probieren	to try	probiert
studieren	to study	studiert

Note the position of the auxiliary and the participle in the below examples:

Yuki **hat** einen Brief **erhalten**.	Yuki has received a letter.
Tobias **hat** die Zeitung **gelesen**.	Tobias has read the newspaper.
Ich **bin** in Berlin **angekommen**.	I have arrived in Berlin.
Du **bist** nach Hause **gefahren**.	You have gone home.
Bist du nach Hause **gefahren**?	Have you gone home?
Ist Tobias nach Frankfurt **geflogen**?	Has Tobias flown to Frankfurt?

Exercises

Exercise 1

Complete the sentences using sein or haben.

1 Ich .... in die Schule gegangen.

2 Was .... du gestern Abend gemacht?

3 Wo .... ihr am Nachmittag gewesen?

4 Wir .... euch gesucht.

5 Was .... Sie für das Auto gezahlt?

6 Warum .... du nicht mitgekommen?

7 Ich .... den Antrag unterschrieben.

8 Was .... ihr zum Frühstück gegessen?

Exercise 2

Talk about what you did yesterday and put the expression of time at the beginning of the sentence.

Um 8.00 Uhr frühstücken

Um 8.00 Uhr habe ich gefrühstückt.

1 Um 8.30 Uhr in die Stadt fahren

....

2 Danach den Sprachunterricht besuchen

....

3 Um 12.00 Uhr Mittagspause machen

....

4 Um 13.00 Uhr zurück zur Schule kommen

....

5 Ab 15.00 Uhr in der Bibliothek Zeitung lesen

....

6 Danach meine Freundinnen abholen

....

7 Anschließend wir Kuchen essen und Kaffee trinken

....

8 Um 18.00 Uhr mich meine Freundinnen nach Hause bringen

....

9. Am Abend Deutsch lernen

....

10 Nachts gut schlafen

....

Exercise 3

Ask questions in the Sie form.

Freunde einladen

Haben Sie Freunde eingeladen?

1 Geld umtauschen

....

2 nach Frankfurt fliegen

....

3 U-Bahn fahren

....

4 ins Konzert gehen

....

5 Wiener Schnitzel essen

....

Exercise 4

Form the past participle of the following verbs and place in the correct column: absagen, anprobieren, bedienen, besuchen, bringen, einkaufen, erledigen, eröffnen, fahren, fliegen, geben, gehen, hinfahren, kaufen, kommen, laufen, lesen, machen, suchen, versuchen, wissen, zahlen

1.ge..en 2.ge ....t 3. ....t

ge..en ge..................................t ....t

ge..en ge..................................t ....t

ge..en ge..................................t ....t

ge..en ge..................................t ....t

ge..en ge..................................t ....t

ge..en ge..................................t ....t

ge..en ge..................................t ....t

Exercise 5

Answer the questions using the perfect tense.

Wann hat das Konzert begonnen? (19.30 Uhr)

Das Konzert hat um 19.30 Uhr begonnen.

1 Wann hast du die Gebhardts besucht? (gestern)

....

2 Wann bist du nach Hamburg geflogen? (vor 2 Tagen)

....

3 Wann hast du gefrühstückt? (7.00 Uhr)

....

4 Wann hast du Tobias angerufen? (heute Morgen)

....

5 Wann hast du Geld umgetauscht? (am Montag)

....

Vocabulary

Below is a list of vocabulary encountered in this chapter.

abfahren	*to leave*
Absender, der, -	*sender*
anfragen	*to ask*
aufwachen	*to wake up*
ausrichten	*to give a message*
Bank, die, -en	*bank*
bayerisch	*Bavarian*
besichtigen	*to visit*
bleiben	*to stay*
erfinden	*to invent*
erhalten	*to receive*
eröffnen	*to open*
erst	*not until*
fantastisch (*also:* **phantastisch**)	*just wonderful*
fliegen	*to fly*
Frühstück, das, -e	*breakfast*
gewinnen	*to win*
hinfahren	*to drive (to)*
hoffentlich	*I hope, hopefully*
hurra	*hurrah*
kalt	*cold*
kochen	*to cook*
Leberkäse, der, -	*Bavarian meat speciality*
leider	*I'm afraid*
misslingen	*to fail*
mitkommen	*to come along*
neulich	*the other day*
noch einmal	*once again*
Nummer, die, -n	*number*
öffnen	*to open*
Postsparbuch, das, -¨er	*post office savings account book*
probieren	*to try*
pünktlich	*punctual*
schmecken	*to taste*
senden	*to send*
studieren	*to study*
Taxifahrer, der, -	*taxi driver*
Telefonnummer, die, -n	*telephone number*
treffen	*to meet*
vergessen	*to forget*
wissen	*to know*
zurückrufen	*to call back*

day: 14

Café culture

Day 14 talks about the all-important café culture in Germany. You will also learn how adverbs can change the word order in sentences and will further build your vocabulary. The exercises will help to reinforce what you have learnt in the previous chapters.

CAFE CULTURE…

Coffee houses are extremely popular in Germany. You might order ***eine Tasse Kaffee*** *(a cup of coffee) or* ***ein Kännchen Kaffee*** *(a small pot of coffee), which is about two cups of coffee, and a slice of cake. To attract the waiter's attention you call out* ***Entschuldigung !*** *and once you have their attention you can say* ***Bezahlen bitte!*** *(The bill, please!). It is not unusual for them to ask you what you ordered.*

German conversation: Im Café

Yuki trifft sich mit zwei Freundinnen im Café.

Yuki: **Ich möchte euch einladen.**
Maria: **Hast du Geburtstag?**
Yuki: **Nein, aber feiern möchte ich trotzdem. Ich habe nämlich gewonnen.**
Beatrice: **Was hast du denn gewonnen?**
Yuki: **Ich habe ein Los gekauft und Geld gewonnen. Deshalb möchte ich euch einladen. Bitte sucht euch etwas aus.**
Beatrice: **Windbeutel, gefüllt mit Sahne, Schwarzwälder Kirschtorte, Wiener Apfelstrudel. Ich weiß gar nicht, was ich bestellen soll.**
Maria: **Linzer Torte, Schwäbischer Käsekuchen, Sachertorte. Ich glaube, ich muss die Bedienung fragen.**
Yuki: **Hier kommt sie gerade.**
Bedienung: **Guten Tag, meine Damen! Haben Sie schon gewählt?**
Yuki: **Wir sind gerade dabei, aber vielleicht können Sie uns helfen?**
Bedienung: **Gerne!**
Beatrice: **Was ist Schwarzwälder Kirschtorte?**
Bedienung: **Das ist eine Torte aus schwarzem und weißem Biskuit mit Schwarzwälder Kirschwasser, Sahne, Schokoladenstreusel und Kirschen. Ich kann diese Torte sehr empfehlen.**
Beatrice: **Gut, dann nehme ich ein Stück.**
Maria: **Und was ist Sachertorte?**
Bedienung: **Das ist eine Schokoladentorte mit Aprikosenkonfitüre und Schokoladenglasur.**
Maria: **Ich glaube, ich nehme ein Stück.**
Bedienung: **Mit oder ohne Sahne?**
Maria: **Mit Sahne, bitte.**
Bedienung: **Und was möchten Sie?**
Yuki: **Eine Käsesahnetorte, bitte.**
Bedienung: **Und was möchten Sie trinken?**
Beatrice: **Ein Kännchen Kaffee, bitte.**
Maria: **Einen Becher heiße Schokolade, bitte.**
Yuki: **Eine Tasse Kaffee, aber bitte koffeinfrei.**

Die Bedienung kommt wieder.

Yuki: **Das sieht ja lecker aus!**
Maria: **Die Sachertorte schmeckt himmlisch!**
Beatrice: **Ich weiß gar nicht, was ich zuerst probieren soll: die Kirschen, die Schokoladenstreusel oder die Sahne.**
Yuki: **Meine Käsesahne ist auch köstlich.**

Die Bedienung kommt wieder.

Bedienung:	**Hat es Ihnen geschmeckt?**
Beatrice:	**Wirklich vorzüglich.**
Yuki:	**Ich möchte bitte bezahlen.**
Bedienung:	**Alles zusammen?**
Yuki:	**Ja, bitte.**
Bedienung:	**Was haben Sie gehabt?**
Yuki:	**Einmal Schwarzwälder Kirschtorte, einmal Sachertorte mit Sahne und einmal Käsesahne. Außerdem ein Kännchen Kaffee, eine Tasse koffeinfreien Kaffee und eine heiße Schokolade.**
Bedienung:	**Das macht zusammen 13,80 Euro.**

Yuki legt einen 20-Euro-Schein auf den Tisch.

Yuki:	**15 Euro, bitte.**
Bedienung:	**Vielen Dank!**

English conversation: In a café

Yuki meets two friends in a cafe.

Yuki:	**I want to treat you.**
Maria:	**Is it your birthday?**
Yuki:	**No, but I want to celebrate something nevertheless. The reason is I've won something.**
Beatrice:	**What have you won?**
Yuki:	**I bought a lottery ticket and have won some money. That's why I want to treat you. Please choose something.**
Beatrice:	**Cream puff, Black Forest Gateau, Viennese apple strudel. I don't know what I should order.**
Maria:	**Linzer Torte, Swabian cheesecake, Sachertorte. I think I'll have to ask the waitress.**
Yuki:	**She's just coming.**
Waitress:	**Good afternoon, ladies. Have you decided what you want?**
Yuki:	**We're just thinking about it. But perhaps you could help us.**
Waitress:	**Sure.**
Beatrice:	**What is Black Forest Gateau?**
Waitress:	**It's a cake made of chocolate and vanilla sponge cake soaked in Black Forest liqueur with whipped cream, flaked chocolate and cherries. I can highly recommend this cake.**
Beatrice:	**Good, then I'll have a piece.**

Maria: **And what is Sachertorte?**
Waitress: **It's a chocolate cake filled with apricot jam and chocolate icing.**
Maria: **I think I'll have a piece.**
Waitress: **With or without whipped cream?**
Maria: **With whipped cream, please.**
Yuki: **A piece of cream cheese cake, please.**
Waitress: **And what would you like to drink?**
Beatrice: **A small pot of coffee, please.**
Maria: **A mug of hot chocolate, please.**
Yuki: **A cup of coffee, but decaffeinated.**
The waitresss comes back again.
Yuki: **That looks delicious.**
Maria: **The Sachertorte tastes absolutely wonderful.**
Beatrice: **I don't know what to try first: the cherries, the flaked chocolate or the cream.**
Yuki: **My cream cheese cake is also very tasty.**
The waitress comes back again.
Waitress: **Did you enjoy it?**
Beatrice: **Really excellent.**
Yuki: **The bill, please.**
Waitress: **Just one bill?**
Yuki: **Yes, please.**
Waitress: **What did you have?**
Yuki: **One Black Forest cake, one Sachertorte with whipped cream, and one cream cheese cake, and one pot of coffee, one cup of decaffeinated coffee and one hot chocolate.**
Waitress: **That's 13 euros and 80 cents.**
Yuki puts €20 on the table.
Yuki: **15 euros, please.**
Waitress: **Thank you very much.**

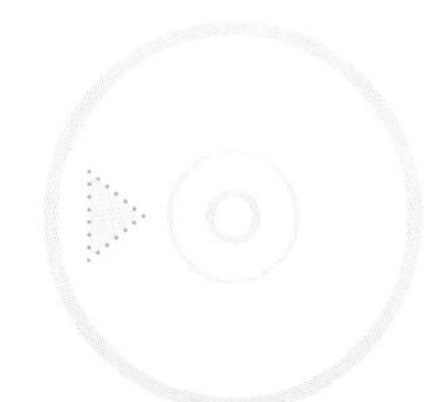

Grammar

Change of word order with adverbs

Hier kommt sie gerade.	She is just coming.
Deshalb möchte ich euch einladen.	That's why I want to treat you (to coffee and cake).

If the adverb is at the beginning of a sentence, the word order changes.

Er ist hoffentlich zu Hause.
Hoffentlich ist er zu Hause.

Exercises

Exercise 1

Put the adverbs at the beginning of the sentence.

1 Die Freundinnen gehen sonntags spazieren.

....

2 Tobias ist leider nicht zu Hause.

....

3 Yuki lädt heute Maria und Beatrice ins Café ein.

....

4 Wir haben gestern Kuchen gegessen.

....

5 Wir nehmen gerne eure Einladung an.

....

Exercise 2

Form the past participle of the following verbs and place in the correct column: gewinnen, haben, essen, trinken, schmecken, kaufen, wählen, probieren, frühstücken, studieren.

1.ge..............................en	2.ge ....t	3. ....t
ge..............................en	ge..............................t	..............................t
ge..............................en	ge..............................t	..............................t

ge..en ge.................................. t ....t

ge..en ge.................................. t ....t

Exercise 3

Complete the sentences using the past participle of the following verbs: finden, trinken, sein, schmecken, essen, bestellen.

1 Wir haben Kuchen .... und Kaffee ....

2 Welchen Kuchen hast du ....?

3 Bedienung: "Hat es Ihnen ....?"

4 Habt ihr das Café ....?

5 Maria und Beatrice sind am Nachmittag im Café ....

Exercise 4

What do you say and what does the waitress say in the following situations?

1 Sie sind mit Freunden im Café.

Sie wollen bestellen.

....

2 Die Bedienung kommt.

....

3 Sie haben gegessen und getrunken und wollen bezahlen.

....

4 Was fragt die Bedienung dann?

....

Vocabulary

Below is a list of vocabulary encountered in this chapter.

alles zusammen	*just one bill*
Aprikosen-konfitüre, die, -n	*apricot jam*
aussuchen	*to choose*
Becher, der, -	*mug*
bestellen	*to order*
Biskuit, der, -s	*sponge cake*
dabei sein *in:* **wir sind gerade dabei**	*we're just thinking about it*
einladen	*to treat, to invite*
feiern	*to celebrate*
füllen	*to fill*
gar nicht *in:* **ich weiß gar nicht**	*not at all* *I don't know*
gerade	*just*
gestern	*yesterday*
himmlisch	*absolutely wonderful*
Kännchen, das, -	*(small) pot*
Käsesahne-torte, die, -n	*cream cheese cake*
Kirsche, die, -n	*cherry*
Kirschwasser, das	*kirsch*
koffeinfrei	*decaffeinated*
köstlich	*tasty*
lecker	*delicious*
leider	*unfortunately*
Linzer Torte, die, -n	*Linzer Torte*
normalerweise	*normally*
probieren	*to taste/to try*
Sachertorte, die, -n	*Sachertorte*
Sahne, die	*cream*
Schokoladen-glasur, die, -n	*chocolate icing*
Schokoladen-streusel, die *(pl.)*	*flaked chocolate*
Schwäbischer Käsekuchen, der, -	*Swabian cheesecake*
Schwarzwälder Kirschtorte, die, -n	*Black Forest cake*
spazieren gehen	*to go for a walk*
Stück, das, -e	*piece*
Torte, die, -n	*cake, gateau*
trotzdem	*nevertheless*
Vanilleeis, das	*vanilla ice cream*
vorzüglich	*excellent*
wieder-kommen	*to come back*
Wiener Apfelstrudel, der, -	*Viennese apple strudel*
Windbeutel, der, -	*cream puff*
Zwanzig-Euro-Schein, der, -e	*twenty-euro note/bill*

day:15

Celebrations

Day 15 is an introduction to celebrations in Germany. You will also learn all about adjectives and how to compare things, as well as how to use *dass* (that). You will also have the opportunity to put all of your new grammar into practice, and further increase your vocabulary.

HOLIDAYS...

*Germans love a party and the country's old traditions live on in a range of colorful festivals held throughout the year - from the parades of **Carnival** and the **Munich Oktoberfest**, to town and village celebrations. Many street festivals take a theme such as the wine harvest, the May blossom, summer flowers or the fruit harvest. Others may have religious significance or commemorate historical events. Classical and opera music festivals are also popular throughout the country.*

German conversation: Geburtstagsfeier mit Freunden

Heute ist der 1. Mai und Yuki hat Geburtstag. Sie hat Freunde eingeladen.

Maria: **Herzlichen Glückwunsch zum Geburtstag, Yuki!**

Yuki: **Vielen Dank! Ich freue mich, dass du gekommen bist.**

Maria gibt Yuki ein kleines Geschenk.

Yuki: **Vielen Dank!**

Beatrice: **Auch von mir alles Gute zum Geburtstag! Hier ist eine kleine Überraschung für dich.**

Yuki: **Das ist aber nett von dir. Danke!**

Beatrice gibt Yuki ein großes Päckchen.

Yuki: **Ein Gast fehlt noch.**

Maria: **Wen erwartest du noch?**

Yuki: **Ich habe auch Tobias eingeladen. Ihr kennt ihn noch nicht.**

Frau Glück: **Männer sind doch meistens pünktlich!**

Es klingelt.

Tobias: **Entschuldigung, Yuki, ich habe die Straßenbahn verpasst. Darf ich dir alles Gute zum Geburtstag wünschen? Dieser Blumenstrauß ist für dich.**

Yuki: **Vielen Dank! So ein herrlicher Frühlingsstrauß! Oh, da ist ja auch noch ein Päckchen und eine Karte. Vielen herzlichen Dank, Tobias!**

Yuki legt das Päckchen auf den Tisch.

Frau Glück: **Jetzt müssen Sie aber Ihre Geschenke auspacken.**

Yuki: **Welches soll ich zuerst auspacken?**

Maria: **Mach doch das kleinste Geschenk zuerst auf!**

Yuki: **Also, gut.**

Yuki packt zuerst das kleinste Geschenk aus: Es ist eine CD der Bamberger Symphoniker. Danach öffnet sie das größere Päckchen: Es ist ein deutsch-japanisches Wörterbuch. Zuletzt öffnet sie das größte Päckchen: Es ist ein Schokoladen-Maikäfer.

Yuki: **So viele Geschenke! Eines ist schöner als das andere. Damit habt ihr mir eine große Freude bereitet.**

Es ist Abend. Die Gäste sind gegangen.

Frau Glück: **Wie hat Ihnen denn Ihr Geburtstag gefallen, Yuki?**

Yuki: **Wirklich sehr gut. Ich weiß gar nicht, was mir am besten gefallen hat: die Geschenke oder das Essen.**

English conversation: Celebrating a birthday with friends

Today is May 1st and it's Yuki's birthday. She has invited friends.

Maria:	**Happy birthday, Yuki.**
Yuki:	**Thank you very much. I'm glad that you could come.**

Maria gives Yuki a small present.

Yuki:	**Thank you very much.**
Beatrice:	**Happy birthday from me, too. Here's a little surprise for you.**
Yuki:	**That's very nice of you, thank you.**

Beatrice gives Yuki a big parcel.

Yuki:	**One guest is still to come.**
Maria:	**Who are you expecting?**
Yuki:	**I've invited Tobias, too. You don't know him yet.**
Mrs. Glück:	**I thought men were usually punctual.**

The bell rings.

Tobias:	**Sorry, Yuki, I missed the tram. I'd like to wish you a very happy birthday. This bunch of flowers is for you.**
Yuki:	**Thank you very much. What a lovely bunch of spring flowers. Oh, and there's a present and card, too. Thank you ever so much, Tobias.**

Yuki puts the box on the table.

Mrs. Glück:	**Now you must open your presents.**
Yuki:	**Which one should I open first?**
Maria:	**Why don't you open the smallest present first?**
Yuki:	**Okay, then.**

Yuki opens the smallest present first; it's a CD of the Bamberg Symphony Orchestra. Then she opens the larger present: it is a German-Japanese dictionary. Finally she opens the largest present: it is a chocolate bug.

Yuki:	**I've got so many presents. I don't know which is the nicest. You've really made my day.**

It's evening. The guests have left.

Mrs. Glück:	**How did you enjoy your birthday?**
Yuki:	**It was really very nice. I don't know what I liked best, the presents or the meal.**

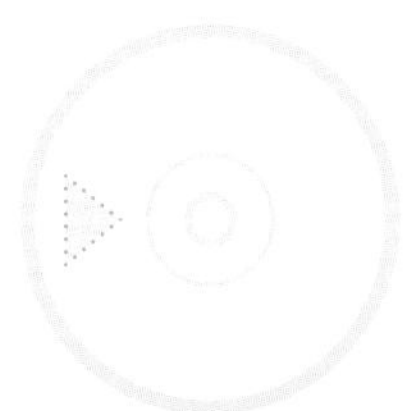

Grammar

The comparison of adjectives

The degrees of comparison are:

positive	*comparative*	*superlative*
groß	größer	am größten
large	larger	(the) largest

Predicative adjectives

Predicative adjectives follow a verb such as "to be" and do not have any additional endings.

Dieses Päckchen ist **schwer**.	This parcel is heavy.
Das andere Päckchen ist **schwerer**.	The other parcel is heavier.
Das Päckchen von Beatrice ist am **schwersten**.	Beatrice's parcel is the heaviest.

The comparative is formed by adding the ending **-er** and the superlative by placing **am** before the adjective and adding the ending **-sten** to the adjective.

positive	*comparative*	*superlative*
klein	klein**er**	am klein**sten**
small	smaller	(the) smallest

Specials forms:

a, o, u → ä, ö, ü

warm	w**ä**rm**er**	am w**ä**rm**sten**
warm	warmer	(the) warmest
groß	gr**ö**ß**er**	am gr**ö**ß**ten**
large	larger	(the) largest
jung	j**ü**ng**er**	am j**ü**ng**sten**
young	younger	(the) youngest

-est in the superlative after **-t**, **-ß** and **-sch**

breit	brei**t**er	am breit**est**en
wide	wider	(the) widest
heiß	hei**ß**er	am heiß**est**enst
hot	hotter	(the) hottest
hübsch	hüb**sch**er	am hübsch**est**en
pretty	prettier	(the) prettiest

Irregular forms:

gut	besser	am besten
good	better	(the) best
viel	mehr	am meisten
much	more	(the) most
gern	lieber	am liebsten
a lot	more	(the) most
hoch	höher	am höchsten
high	higher	(the) highest
nah	näher	am nächsten
near	nearer	(the) nearest
teuer	teurer	am teuersten
expensive	more expensive	(the) most expensive
dunkel	dunkler	am dunkelsten
dark	darker	(the) darkest

Attributive adjectives

Attributive adjectives are used before a noun and have endings to agree with the noun.

Yuki öffnet das **größere** Päckchen nach dem **kleinsten** Geschenk.
Yuki opens the larger parcel after the smallest present.

The comparative attributive adjective takes the ending **-er** plus the adjectival ending. The superlative attributive adjective takes the ending **-st** plus the adjectival ending.

Comparison using *als*

Yuki ist 150 cm groß.	Tobias ist 184 cm groß.
Yuki is 150 cm *(tall)*.	Tobias is 184 cm *(tall)*.
Yuki ist **kleiner als** Tobias.	Tobias ist **größer als** Yuki.
Yuki is smaller than Tobias.	Tobias is taller than Yuki.
Yuki ist 20 Jahre alt.	Tobias ist 24 Jahre alt.
Yuki is 20 years old.	Tobias is 24 years old.
Yuki ist **jünger als** Tobias.	Tobias ist **älter als** Yuki.
Yuki is younger than Tobias.	Tobias is older than Yuki.

In comparison, the comparative + **als** is used when comparing items or persons with each other.

Subordinate clauses with *dass*

Ich freue mich, **dass** du gekommen bist.	I am glad that you have come.

Dass is a conjunction which links the main clause **Ich freue mich** and the subordinate clause **du gekommen bist**.

Dass is often used after words which express an opinion and verbs which express a wish or feeling. Examples of such verbs include:
sagen (say), **meinen** (think), **glauben** (believe), **wissen** (know), **hoffen** (hope), **mögen** (like), **wünschen** (wish), **sich freuen** (be glad), **vorschlagen** (suggest)

As you will see in the table below, the main and subordinate clauses are separated by a comma. The verb is always found at the end of the subordinate clause.

subject	*verb*	*conjunction*	*subject*	*verb*
Yuki	freut sich,	**dass**	du	gekommen bist.
Yuki is glad that you have come.				
Ich	hoffe,	**dass**	er	kommt.
I hope that he'll come.				
Ich	schlage vor,	**dass**	wir	uns im Café treffen.
I suggest that we meet in the café.				
Du	weißt doch,	**dass**	er	nicht pünktlich ist.
You know very well that he is not punctual.				
Die Mutter	möchte,	**dass**	das Kind	in die Schule geht.
The mother wants her child to go to school.				
Der Lehrer	wünscht,	**dass**	die Schüler	fleißig lernen.
The teacher wants his pupils to study hard.				
Ich	glaube,	**dass**	der Zug	pünktlich ankommt.
I believe the train will arrive on time.				
Wir	gehen davon aus,	**dass**	du	den Job bekommst.
We assume that you'll get the job.				

Exercises

Exercise 1

Make sentences using the adjectives below in the positive, comparative and superlative.

e.g. Stuttgart/München/Berlin

Stuttgart ist groß, München ist größer und Berlin ist am größten.

1. Hans/Tobias/Franz **fleißig**

....

....

2 Rathaus/Olympiaturm/Alpen **hoch**

....

....

3 Fahrrad/U-Bahn/Flugzeug **schnell**

....

....

Exercise 2

Fill in the comparative and the superlative.

1 viel

comparative .... superlative ....

2 klein

comparative .... superlative ....

3 groß

comparative .... superlative ....

4 gut

comparative .... superlative ....

5 teuer

comparative .... superlative ....

Exercise 3

Yuki goes shopping. Make comparative sentences with als.

Weißwein: vier Euro,

Rotwein: fünf Euro (teuer)

Der Rotwein ist teurer als der Weißwein.

1 Äpfel, Kirschen (groß)

....

2 Roggenbrot, Weißbrot (dunkel)

....

3 Kleid rot, Kleid weiß (schön)

....

4 Schuhe schwarz, Schuhe grüne (schick)

....

Exercise 4

Form sentences using dass.

1 Wir freuen uns/du lädst uns zum Geburtstag ein

....

2 Ich hoffe/wir sehen am Wochenende die Alpen

....

3 Frau Glück meint/Yuki ist eine ruhige Mitbewohnerin

....

4 Frau Gebhardt hofft/ihr Mann hat Wein gekauft

....

5 Tobias geht davon aus/er bekommt einen neuen Job

....

Vocabulary

Below is a list of vocabulary encountered in this chapter.

Alles Gute zum Geburtstag!	*Happy birthday!*
am liebsten	*(the) most*
am meisten	*(the) most*
auspacken	*to open*
bereiten *in:*	*to give*
Freude bereiten	*to give pleasure*
berühmt	*famous*
breit	*wide*
CD, die, -s	*CD*
damit	*with that*
Darf ich dir alles Gute zum Geburtstag wünschen?	*I'd like to wish you a very happy birthday.*
dass	*that*
davon ausgehen	*to assume*
dunkel	*dark*
erwarten	*to expect*
fehlen	*to be missing*
Feiertag, der, -e	*holiday*
fleißig	*hard*
Freude bereiten	*to give pleasure*
Frühlingsstrauß, der, -¨e	*bunch of spring flowers*
gar nicht	*not at all*
Geburtstagsfeier, die, -n	*birthday party*
Geschenk, das, -e	*present*
Herzlichen Glückwunsch zum Geburtstag!	*Happy birthday!*
hoch	*high*
Job, der, -s	*job*
Karte, die, -n	*card*
legen	*to put*
meistens	*usually*
nah	*near*
Päckchen, das, -	*small parcel*
schön	*nice*
Schokoladenmaikäfer, der, -	*chocolate bug*
Straßenbahn, die, -en	*tram*
Tomate, die, -n	*tomato*
verpassen	*to miss*
vorschlagen	*to suggest*
Werktag, der, -e	*working week*
Wörterbuch, das, -¨er	*dictionary*
zuletzt	*finally, last of all*

day: 16

At the doctor's

Day 16 sees you pay a visit to the doctor. You will learn how to express the negative in a variety of ways (including how to say no!), pick up all the essential vocabulary you need to explain to a doctor or pharmacist how you are feeling. You will be able to practice all that you have learned in the exercises.

THE HEALTH SERVICE…

Healthcare is very good in Germany. The country has a national health system whereby doctors and hosiptal fees are covered by insurance and only a token fee has to be paid for medication. Treatment and medication is also free of charge for EU members (on presentation of a European Health Insurance Card). All other foreign nationals should ensure they have adequate health insurance.

German conversation: Beim Arzt

Heute ist der 2.Mai. Yuki hat schlecht geschlafen.

Frau Glück: **Guten Morgen, Yuki! Geht es Ihnen nicht gut? Sie sehen so blass aus.**

Yuki: **Ich weiß nicht, was mit mir los ist. Mir ist übel und ich habe kaum geschlafen. Ich glaube, ich bin krank.**

Frau Glück: **Jetzt trinken Sie erst einmal einen schwarzen Tee. Vielleicht geht es Ihnen dann besser.**

Yuki: **Nein danke, ich möchte nichts trinken.**

Frau Glück: **Sie sollten zum Arzt gehen. Ich sehe gleich mal nach, wann mein Hausarzt Sprechstunde hat.**

Frau Glück sucht im Telefonbuch die Nummer von Dr. Köhler, ihrem Hausarzt, und findet auch die Sprechzeiten.

Frau Glück: **Montag bis Freitag von 9–12 Uhr und von 14–18 Uhr außer Mittwochnachmittag. Ohne vorherige Anmeldung. Alle Kassen.**

Yuki: **Was bedeutet "Alle Kassen"?**

Frau Glück: **Das heißt, er behandelt nicht nur Privatpatienten, sondern auch Kassenpatienten. Bei welcher Krankenkasse sind Sie denn versichert?**

Yuki: **Bei der AOK.**

Frau Glück: **Dann haben Sie ein Versicherungskärtchen. Das müssen Sie mitnehmen und der Sprechstundenhilfe geben. Wollen Sie gleich zum Arzt gehen?**

Yuki: **Ja. Ich glaube, ich nehme ein Taxi.**

Yuki ist bei Dr. Köhler.

Dr. Köhler: **Was fehlt Ihnen denn?**

Yuki: **Mir ist so übel.**

Dr. Köhler: **Sie sehen nicht gut aus. Seit wann ist Ihnen denn übel?**

Yuki: **Seit heute Morgen.**

Dr. Köhler: **Haben Sie Fieber?**

Yuki: **Nein, ich glaube nicht.**

Dr. Köhler: **Was haben Sie gestern gegessen und getrunken?**

Yuki: **Ich habe zwei Stück Käsesahnetorte gegessen und Kaffee getrunken, anschließend Käse und Brot gegessen und dann noch zwei Gläser Weißwein getrunken. Ich habe gestern nämlich meinen Geburtstag gefeiert.**

Dr. Köhler: **Herzlichen Glückwunsch nachträglich. Ihrem japanischen Magen ist das deutsche Essen aber nicht bekommen. Kaffee und Weißwein übersäuern den Magen, und dann noch Käsesahnetorte. Da ist es kein Wunder, dass Ihr Magen rebelliert.**

Yuki: **Was soll ich jetzt machen?**

Dr. Köhler: **Heute jedenfalls nichts mehr essen. Trinken Sie Kamillentee und nehmen Sie von diesen Tropfen dreimal täglich zwanzig. Ich verschreibe sie Ihnen. Hier, Ihr Rezept. Und legen Sie sich heute am besten ins Bett. Morgen wird es Ihnen wieder besser gehen.**

Yuki: **Ja, das mache ich.**

Dr. Köhler: **Gute Besserung!**

English conversation: At the doctor's

It's May 2nd today. Yuki hasn't slept very well.

Mrs. Glück: **Good morning, Yuki! Don't you feel very well? You look very pale.**

Yuki: **I don't know what's wrong with me. I feel sick and I've hardly slept at all. I think I'm ill.**

Mrs. Glück: **Well, first of all have some tea. Perhaps you'll feel better then.**

Yuki: **No thanks. I don't want anything to drink.**

Mrs. Glück: **You ought to go to the doctor's. I'll have a look and see when my general practitioner has his surgery/office hours.**

Mrs. Glück looks in the phone book for Dr. Köhler's number and also finds his hours.

Mrs. Glück: **Monday to Friday from 9–12 a.m. and from 2–6 p.m. except Wednesday afternoons. No appointment necessary. All insurance schemes.**

Yuki: **What does "All insurance schemes" mean?**

Mrs. Glück: **That means he doesn't only treat private patients but also non-private patients. What insurance do you have?**

Yuki: **The AOK.**

Mrs. Glück: **Then you've got a medical insurance card. You'll have to take it with you and give it to the receptionist. Do you want to go to the doctor's immediately?**

Yuki: **Yes, I do. I think I'll take a taxi.**

Yuki is at Doctor Köhler's.

Dr. Köhler: **What's wrong with you?**

Yuki: **I feel sick.**

Dr. Köhler: **You certainly don't look very well. How long have you been feeling sick?**

Yuki: **Since this morning.**

Dr. Köhler: **Have you got a temperature?**

Yuki: **No, I don't think so.**

Dr. Köhler: **What did you have to eat and drink yesterday?**

Yuki: **I had two pieces of cream cheese cake and some coffee, afterwards some bread and cheese and then I drank two glasses of white wine. I was celebrating my birthday yesterday, you see.**

Dr. Köhler: **Well, a belated happy birthday. But our German food didn't agree with your Japanese stomach. Coffee and white wine give you an acid stomach and then the cream cheese cake on top of that. It's not surprising that your stomach is rebelling.**

Yuki: **What should I do now?**

Dr. Köhler: **Well, you certainly shouldn't eat anything more today. Drink chamomile tea and take twenty of these drops three times a day. I'll give you a prescription for them. Here you are. And the best thing is to stay in bed today. You'll feel much better tomorrow.**

Yuki: **Yes. I'll do that.**

Dr. Köhler: **I hope you feel better soon.**

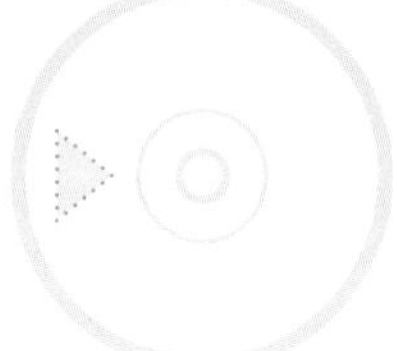

Grammar

Negation with *nicht* or *kein*

Haben Sie das Fieberthermometer?	Ich habe es **nicht**.
Do you have the thermometer?	I don't have it.
Haben Sie ein Versicherungskärtchen?	Ich habe **keine** Karte.
Do you have an insurance card?	I don't have a card.
Haben Sie Fieber?	Ich habe **kein** Fieber.
Do you have a temperature?	I don't have a temperature.

When the noun has a definite article, the negative particle **nicht** is used. When the noun has an indefinite article or no article, the negative particle **kein** is used.

nicht or *nichts*

Yuki hat den indischen Tee getrunken.	Yuki has drunk the Indian tea.
Negative:	Yuki hat den indischen Tee **nicht** getrunken.
	Yuki hasn't drunk the Indian tea.
	Yuki möchte etwas trinken.
	Yuki would like something to drink.
	Yuki möchte schwarzen Tee trinken.
	Yuki would like to drink black tea.
Negative:	Yuki möchte **nichts** trinken.
	Yuki doesn't want to drink anything.

Nicht –not (anything)– makes a sentence negative. **Nichts** –nothing, not anything– stands for a nominative or accusative complement.

Additional words of negation

nie/niemals	
Er ruft **nie** an.	He never phones.
Er ruft **niemals** an.	He never ever phones.
niemand	
Niemand ist im Haus.	Nobody is at home.
nirgends/nirgendwo	
Ich kann das Buch **nirgends** finden.	I can't find the book anywhere.
Ich kann das Buch **nirgendwo** finden.	I can't find the book anywhere at all.
nie und nimmer	
Ich will Sie **nie und nimmer** sehen.	I never ever want to see you again.

nicht nur … sondern auch

Er behandelt **nicht nur** Privatpatienten, **sondern auch** Kassenpatienten.
He doesn't treat only private patients, but also non-private patients.
Yuki spricht **nicht nur** Deutsch, **sondern auch** Englisch.
Yuki doesn't speak only German, but also English.

The coordinating conjunctions **nicht nur … sondern auch** (not only … but also) join words or groups of words. They indicate that something will be added to what has already been said.

Exercises

Exercise 1

Complete the sentences with nicht or kein.

1 Wo ist die Wärmflasche? Ich finde sie ....

2 Haben Sie einen Termin? Nein, ich habe .... Termin.

3 Haben Sie Husten? Nein, ich habe .... Husten.

4 Ich habe die Apotheke .... gleich gefunden.

5 Frau Glück hat .... Zahnschmerzen.

Exercise 2

What is the positive equivalent?

1 nie	a jemand	1 ....
2 niemand	b irgendwo	2 ....
3 nirgendwo	c etwas	3 ....
4 keiner	d immer	4 ....
5 nichts	e einer	5 ....

Exercise 3

Combine the statements below using nicht nur ..., sondern auch.

1 Tobias Deutsch sprechen – Englisch

....

2 Frau Glück kaufen Obst – Gemüse

....

3 Der Bäcker backen Brot – Brötchen

....

4 Wir Kuchen essen – Kaffee trinken

....

5 Du lesen Bücher – hören Konzerte

....

Exercise 4

Form sentences using nicht nur ... sondern auch.

Complete the text using the following words:

nicht (4x), nichts (3x), keine (3x), kein, nicht nur ..., sondern auch, nie, nie und nimmer.

Eine phantastische Geschichte

Eine Maus geht in der Stadt spazieren. Sie heißt Mona. Sie hat seit Tagen gegessen und nur Wasser getrunken. Sie ist hungrig und traurig. Sie sieht gut aus. Da trifft sie eine Katze. Sie heißt Lisa. Sie hat gegessen. Sie ist satt und glücklich.

Die Katze sagt zur Maus: "Was ist los mit dir, Mona? Du siehst .... gut aus." Die Maus antwortet: "Ich habe seit Tagen .... gegessen und .... getrunken. Ich habe .... Wohnung, ... Kleider, ... Freunde und .... Geld. Ich bin unglücklich."

Lisa sagt zu Mona: "Komm doch mit zu mir. Ich lade dich ein."

Die Maus kann das .... glauben. Sie fragt vorsichtig: "Darf ich wirklich zu dir kommen?" "Warum glaubst du mir .... ?", fragt die Katze. "Noch .... ist eine Katze so freundlich zu mir gewesen", antwortet die Maus. "Katzen und Mäuse können............................ Freundinnen werden." "Wir probieren es einfach", antwortet die Katze. Dann hat sie die Maus mit nach Hause genommen. Sie hat ihr zu essen und zu trinken gegeben, sie hat ihre Freundinnen kennengelernt und sie hat bei ihr gewohnt.

Nach einigen Wochen sagt die Maus zur Katze: "Du hast mir .... zu essen und zu trinken gegeben, ... mir .... Kleider und deine Wohnung gegeben. Was kann ich für dich tun? Ich möchte dir etwas schenken."

"Schenk mir einfach dein Herz", antwortete die Katze. Seitdem heißen sie Mona-Lisa.

Vocabulary

Below is a list of vocabulary encountered in this chapter.

Anmeldung, die, -en *in:* **ohne vorherige Anmeldung**	*appointment*
außer	*except*
behandeln	*to treat*
Besserung *in:* **gute Besserung!**	*I hope you'll feel better soon*
blass	*pale*
erst einmal	*first of all*
fehlen *in:* **Was fehlt Ihnen denn**?	*What's wrong with you?*
Fieber, das	*temperature*
Fieberthermometer, das, -	*thermometer*
gehen *in:* **es geht mir besser**	*I feel better*
Geschichte, die, -n	*story*
Hausarzt, der, -¨e	*general practitioner*
Herz, das, -en	*heart*
Husten, der	*cough*
jedenfalls	*certainly*
Kamillentee, der, -s	*chamomile tea*
Kasse, die, -n in: Krankenkasse	*health insurance (provider)*
Kassenpatient, der, -en	*non-private patient*
kaum	*hardly*
Kleider, die *(pl.)*	*clothes*
krank	*ill*
Krankenhaus, das -¨er	*hospital*
Krankenkasse, die, -en	*health insurance*
los sein *in:* **etwas ist mit mir los**	*something is wrong with me*
Magen, der, -¨	*stomach*
Maus, die, -¨e	*mouse*
messen	*to measure*
mitnehmen	*to take with you*
nachsehen	*to have a look*
nachträglich	*belated*
nicht nur ..., sondern auch	*not only ... but also*
nie	*never*
nie und nimmer	*never ever*
niemals	*never (ever)*
niemand	*nobody*
nirgends	*nowhere*
nirgendwo	*nowhere at all*
phantastisch *(also:* **fantastisch***)*	*fantastic*
Privatpatient, der, -en	*private patient*
rebellieren	*to rebel*
Rezept, das, -e	*prescription*
satt *in:* **satt sein**	*full*

schlecht	*bad*
seitdem	*since*
Sprechstunde, die, -n	*doctor's surgery/ doctor's office hours*
Sprechstundenhilfe, die, -n	*receptionist*
Sprechzeit, die, -en	*surgery / office hours*
Telefonbuch, das, -¨er	*phone book*
Termin, der, -e	*appointment*
traurig	*sad*
Tropfen, der, -	*drop*
übel	*sick*
übersäuerter Magen	*acidity of the stomach*
verschreiben	*to prescribe*
Versicherungskärtchen, das, -	*medical insurance card*
vorherig	*previous*
Wärmflasche, die, -n	*hot water bottle*
Weißwein, der, -e	*white wine*
Wunder, das,	*miracle*
in: **kein Wunder**	*not surprising*
Zahnschmerzen, die *(pl.)*	*toothache*

day: 17

The pharmacy

Day 17 continues on to the pharmacy, where you will learn how to make comparisons using *so... wie*. You will learn more vocabulary covering the essential items you might require in this setting, as well as picking up some more information about life in Germany and the German healthcare system.

112...

All hospitals have an emergency outpatients' department, which is open day and night. The general emergency number is 112, which also includes the fire services. For the police, dial 110. For less urgent cases, the local pharmacy will provide the addresses and telephone numbers of doctors who are on call. Pharmacies have normal shop opening times. When closed, the address of the nearest pharmacy offering a 24-hour service will be posted on the door.

German conversation: In der Apotheke

Auf dem Weg nach Hause kommt Yuki an einer Apotheke vorbei.

Apothekerin: **Bitte schön?**

Yuki: **Ich habe ein Rezept.**

Apothekerin: **Einen Moment, bitte.**

Die Apothekerin holt das Medikament für Yuki.

Apothekerin: **Hier sind Ihre Tropfen. Sie müssen dreimal täglich zwanzig Tropfen nehmen. Am besten vor dem Essen. Brauchen Sie sonst noch etwas?**

Yuki: **Ja, Kopfschmerztabletten.**

Apothekerin: **Möchten Sie eine bestimmte Sorte?**

Yuki: **Können Sie mir eine bestimmte Sorte empfehlen?**

Apothekerin: **Ich empfehle Ihnen Aspirin plus C®. Wollen Sie die große oder die kleine Packung?**

Yuki: **Wie viele Tabletten sind in der großen Packung?**

Apothekerin: **Die große Packung enthält 40 Tabletten und kostet €6,20, und die kleine mit 20 Stück kostet €3,50.**

Yuki: **Ich nehme die große Packung.**

Apothekerin: **Möchten Sie sonst noch etwas?**

Yuki: **Haben Sie auch Sonnenmilch?**

Apothekerin: **Ja, ich zeige Ihnen unsere Auswahl.**

Yuki: **Gerne.**

Apothekerin: **Also, hier ist eine Flasche mit 200 ml zu €9,50. Diese Flasche enthält 150 ml und kostet €7,10. Und diese hier ist im Angebot und kostet nur €6,95. Sie enthält 200 ml.**

Yuki: **Das heißt, diese Flasche enthält so viel wie diese?**

Apothekerin: **Ja, die Flasche im Angebot ist aber billiger als diese.**

Yuki: **Dann nehme ich die günstigere Sonnenmilch.**

Apothekerin: **Ist das alles?**

Yuki: **Ja, das ist alles. Was macht das?**

Apothekerin: **Also, die Tropfen ... für die kleinste Packung müssen Sie €4,50 zuzahlen, die Kopfschmerztabletten kosten €6,20 und die Sonnenmilch €6,95. Macht zusammen €17,65.**

Yuki bezahlt und bekommt ein Tütchen mit ihren Medikamenten und der Sonnenmilch und eine kleine Packung Taschentücher.

Yuki: **Vielen Dank.**

Apothekerin: **Auf Wiedersehen und gute Besserung!**

English conversation: At the chemist's

On her way home Yuki passes a chemist's.

Chemist:	**Can I help you?**
Yuki:	**I've got a prescription.**
Chemist:	**Just a moment, please.**

The chemist gets the medicine for Yuki.

Chemist:	**Here are your drops. You must take twenty drops three times a day, preferably before a meal. Do you need anything else?**
Yuki:	**Yes, please. Headache tablets.**
Chemist:	**Do you want any particular kind?**
Yuki:	**Can you recommend any?**
Chemist:	**I'd recommend Aspirin plus C®. Do you want the large or the small packet?**
Yuki:	**How many tablets are there in the large packet?**
Chemist:	**The large packet contains 40 tablets and costs 6 euros 20 cents and the small one with 20 tablets costs 3 euros 50 cents.**
Yuki:	**I'll take the large packet.**
Chemist:	**Do you want anything else?**
Yuki:	**Have you got any suntan lotion?**
Chemist:	**Yes, we have. I'll show you our selection.**
Yuki:	**Thank you.**
Chemist:	**Well, here's a 200 ml bottle for 9 euros 50 cents. This bottle contains 150 ml and costs 7 euros 10 cents. And this one here is a special offer and costs only 6 euros 95 cents. It contains 200 ml.**
Yuki:	**That means this bottle contains as much as that one?**
Chemist:	**Yes, but the special offer is cheaper than that one.**
Yuki:	**I'll take the cheaper one, then.**
Chemist:	**Is that all?**
Yuki:	**Yes, that's all. How much is that?**
Chemist:	**Let me see, the drops … for the smallest packet you have to pay a contribution of 4 euros 50 cents, the aspirin costs 6 euros 20 cents and the suntan lotion costs 6 euros 95 cents. That makes 17 euros and 65 cents altogether.**

Yuki pays and is given a small plastic bag with her medicine, the suntan lotion and a small packet of tissues.

Yuki:	**Thank you very much.**
Chemist:	**Goodbye and I hope you feel better soon.**

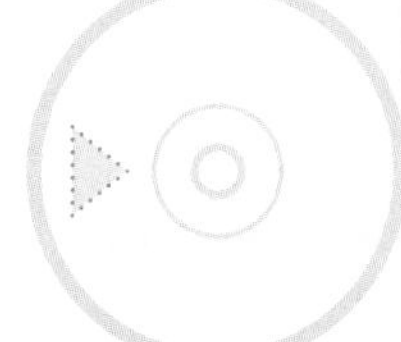

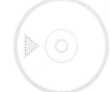

Grammar

Comparisons with *so ... wie*

Diese Flasche enthält so viel wie diese.	This bottle contains as much as that one.
Franz ist so groß wie Hans.	Franz is as tall as Hans.

In comparative sentences so ... wie is used when the subjects are equal.

Exercises

Exercise 1

Make sentences with so ... wie.

1 Hose/Jacke/teuer

....

2 Frau Gebhardt/Frau Glück/alt

....

3 Nelken/Rosen/schön

....

4 Vollkornbrot/Pumpernickel/gesund

....

Exercise 2

Match the two columns to form full sentences.

1 Das Empire State Building ist höher	**a** als der Lastwagen.	1 ....
2 David ist so groß	**b** als der Film.	2 ....
3 Der Porsche fährt schneller	**c** wie Hans.	3 ....
4 Das Buch ist spannender	**d** als der Eiffelturm.	4 ....

Exercise 3

Tick the correct answers.

1. Was kann man in einer Apotheke kaufen?

a ☐ Sonnenmilch

b ☐ Pflaster

c ☐ Salben

d ☐ Zäpfchen

e ☐ Tabletten

f ☐ Rezepte

2 Wer arbeitet im Krankenhaus?

a ☐ Krankenschwester

b ☐ Apothekerin

c ☐ Anästhesist

d ☐ Patient

e ☐ Sprech-stundenhilfe

f ☐ Ärztin

Exercise 4

Form compounds from the following nouns. Note that some nouns are comprised of three words and certain words are linked with an s**. The last noun of the compound determines its gender.** die Versicherung **(2x)**, der Kopf, die Hilfe, der Tag, das Geschenk, die Brause, das Haus **(2x)**, das Kärtchen, die Sprechstunde, die Kranken *(pl.)*, die Tabletten *(pl.)*, die Ärztin, die Schmerzen *(pl.)*, die Geburt

1 ....

2 ....

3 ....

4 ....

5 ....

6 ....

7 ....

8 ....

Vocabulary

Below is a list of vocabulary encountered in this chapter.

Anästhesist, der, -en	*anaesthetist*
Apotheke, die, -n	*chemist's / pharmacy*
Apotheker, der, -	*chemist / pharmacist*
Apothekerin, die, -nen	*chemist/pharmacist (f)*
billig	*cheap*
Brausetabletten, die *(pl.)*	*soluble tablets*
Eiffelturm, der	*the Eiffel Tower*
enthalten	*to contain*
Film, der, -e	*film*
Kopfschmerztabletten, die (pl.)	*headache tablet (aspirin)*
Lastwagen, der, -	*lorry / truck*
Medikament, das, -e	*medicine*
Packung, die, -en	*packet*
Patient, der, -en	*patient*
Pflaster, das, -	*plaster /Band Aid*
Salbe, die, -n	*ointment*
Schrank, der, -¨e	*cupboard*
so … wie	*as … as*
spannend	*exciting*
Papiertaschentücher, die *(pl.)*	*tissues*
Tütchen, das, -	*plastic bag*
Zäpfchen, das, -	*suppository*
zuzahlen *in:* **Sie müssen dazuzahlen**	*you have to pay a contribution*
Sonnenmilch, die	*suntan lotion*
Diät, die, -en	*diet*
Notdienst, der, -e	*emergency service*
Verband, der, -¨e	*bandage*
verschreibungspflichtig	*available by prescription only*
wirken	*to take effect*

day: 18

At the station

Day 18 introduces you to rail travel in Germany. You will continue to build your comprehension and conversation skills as well as learn about conditional clauses and how to use the particle *und zwar*. Finally, you will further build your vocabulary.

DEUTSCHE BAHN...

Traveling in Germany by train is a pleasant experience. The ***InterCityExpress (ICE)*** *is a quite luxurious mode of transport and is equipped with comfortable seats with ample leg room, dedicated phone and catering carriages and WiFi. The* ***InterCity*** *and* ***EuroCity*** *are fast trains with catering cars. There is also the* ***RegionalExpress (RE)*** *and* ***Regionalbahn (RB)*** *that link regional towns with cities, both offering a good commuter service. The* ***S-Bahn*** *runs every few minutes and serves the larger cities and their surroundings.*

German conversation: Am Bahnhof

Yuki ist wieder gesund. Sie möchte am Wochenende nach Bamberg fahren.

Angestellter: **Ja, bitte.**
Yuki: **Ich möchte eine Fahrkarte 2.Klasse nach Bamberg.**
Angestellter: **Wissen Sie schon mit welchem Zug?**
Yuki: **Nein. Ich möchte am Samstag fahren, und zwar vormittags.**

Der Angestellte schaut in den Computer.

Angestellter: **Also, es gibt einen ICE um 7.52 Uhr bis Nürnberg und dann weiter mit dem Regional-Express. Sie sind dann um 10.30 Uhr in Bamberg. Sie können auch mit dem IC direkt nach Bamberg fahren. Wenn Sie den Zug um 8.49 Uhr nehmen, sind Sie um 11.12 Uhr in Bamberg.**
Yuki: **Ich fahre lieber mit dem ICE.**
Angestellter: **Möchten Sie einen Sitzplatz reservieren?**
Yuki: **Ja, bitte.**
Angestellter: **Einfache Fahrt oder Rückfahrkarte?**
Yuki: **Eine Rückfahrkarte, bitte.**
Angestellter: **Wollen Sie für die Rückfahrt auch reservieren?**
Yuki: **Ja, am Sonntagabend gegen 19 Uhr.**
Angestellter: **Wenn Sie den IC um 18.49 Uhr nehmen, sind Sie um 21.12 Uhr in München.**
Yuki: **Ja, das passt mir.**
Angestellter: **Raucher oder Nichtraucher?**
Yuki: **Nichtraucher.**
Angestellter: **Großraumwagen oder Abteil?**
Yuki: **Was ist da der Unterschied?**
Angestellter: **Im Großraumwagen sitzen viele Reisende in einem Wagen, im Abteil nur sechs. Außerdem können Sie im Großraumwagen einen Platz mit Tisch reservieren.**
Yuki: **Dann reservieren Sie bitte im Großraumwagen.**
Angestellter: **Also, Nichtraucher und Großraumwagen. Haben Sie eine BahnCard?**
Yuki: **Nein, was ist das?**
Angestellter: **Eine Ermäßigungskarte. Wenn Sie eine BahnCard kaufen, erhalten Sie 25 Prozent Ermäßigung auf alle Rabatte.**
Yuki: **Was kostet denn die BahnCard?**
Angestellter: **Die BahnCard kostet €60. Sie können dann ein Jahr lang mit 25 Prozent Ermäßigung auf alle Normalpreise und Sparpreise fahren.**
Yuki: **Aber ich bleibe nur für sechs Monate in Deutschland. Ich glaube, die Karte rentiert sich nicht für mich.**
Angestellter: **Das kommt darauf an. Wenn Sie in den sechs Monaten viel reisen, dann rentiert sich die BahnCard auch für Sie.**

Yuki: **Aber ich reise nicht so viel. Was kostet die Rückfahrkarte ohne BahnCard?**
Angestellter: **€52, der IC-Zuschlag €7 und die Platzreservierung €2,60. Macht zusammen €61,60.**
Yuki: **Kann ich mit Kreditkarte bezahlen?**
Angestellter: **Natürlich. Hier sind Ihre Reiseunterlagen. Ich wünsche Ihnen eine gute Reise und einen schönen Aufenthalt in Bamberg.**
Yuki: **Danke schön.**

English conversation: At the train station

Yuki is better now. She wants to go to Bamberg for the weekend by train.
Booking clerk: **Can I help you?**
Yuki: **I'd like a second class ticket to Bamberg.**
Booking clerk: **Do you know which train you're taking?**
Yuki: **No, I don't. I want to travel on Saturday, Saturday morning.**
The booking clerk looks at the computer.
Booking clerk: **Well, there's an ICE at 7:52 a.m. to Nuremberg and then you continue your journey on a regional express train. You arrive in Bamberg at 10:30 a.m. You can also travel direct to Bamberg on the IC. If you take the 8:49 a.m., you arrive in Bamberg at 11:12 a.m.**
Yuki: **I'd prefer the ICE.**
Booking clerk: **Do you want to reserve a seat?**
Yuki: **Yes, please.**
Booking clerk: **Single or return/one way or round trip?**
Yuki: **Return/round trip, please.**
Booking clerk: **Do you want to reserve a seat for the return journey?**
Yuki: **Yes, for Sunday evening, around 7 p.m.**
Booking clerk: **If you take the IC at 6:49 p.m., you arrive in Munich at 9:21 p.m.**
Yuki: **That would suit me.**
Booking clerk: **Smoking or non-smoking?**
Yuki: **Non-smoking.**
Booking clerk: **Open-plan carriage or compartment?**
Yuki: **What's the difference?**
Booking clerk: **In the open-plan carriage there are a lot of passengers in one large carriage and in a compartment there are only six passengers. In addition, in an open-plan carriage you can reserve a seat with a table.**

Yuki:	**Reserve a seat in the open-plan carriage then, please.**
Booking clerk:	**Right, non-smoking and open-plan carriage. Have you got a BahnCard?**
Yuki:	**No, what's that?**
Booking clerk:	**A card which entitles you to a reduction. If you buy a BahnCard, you get a 25% reduction on all discounts.**
Yuki:	**What does a BahnCard cost?**
Booking clerk:	**The BahnCard costs 60 euros. You can then travel at a 25% reduction on all regular and discount prices for one year.**
Yuki:	**But I'm only staying in Germany for six months, so it wouldn't really be worth it.**
Booking clerk:	**It depends. If you travel a lot in the six months, it would be worth having a BahnCard.**
Yuki:	**But I won't be travelling a lot. What does a return ticket cost without a BahnCard?**
Booking clerk:	**52 euros, the IC surcharge 7 euros, and the seat reservation 2 euros 60 cents. That makes 61 euros 60 cents altogether.**
Yuki:	**Can I pay by credit card?**
Booking clerk:	**Yes, of course. Here are the travel documents. Have a good trip and a nice stay in Bamberg.**
Yuki:	**Thank you very much.**

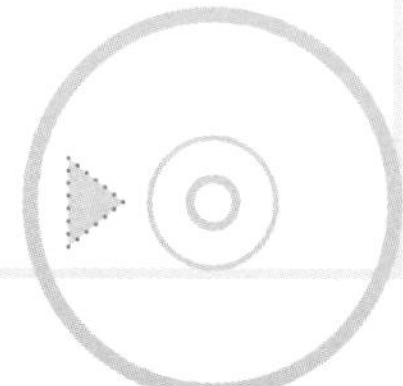

Grammar

Conditional clauses

subordinate clause	*main clause*
Wenn Sie eine BahnCard haben,	erhalten Sie 25% Rabatt.
If you have a BahnCard	you get a 25% reduction.

The subordinate clause can also follow the main clause. The meaning of the sentence remains unchanged.

main clause	*subordinate clause*
Sie erhalten 25% Rabatt,	wenn Sie eine BahnCard haben.
You get a 25% reduction	if you have a BahnCard.

Conditional clauses with **wenn** give a condition that must be fulfilled before the action of the main clause can be true, possible or done. In the subordinate clause the verb is always found at the end of the sentence.

Und zwar

The particle **und zwar** is used to focus on the detail that follows. A comma always goes before **und zwar**. There is no direct equivalent in English.

Ich möchte am Samstag fahren, und zwar vormittags.

I want to travel on Saturday, (namely) Saturday morning.

Exercises

Exercise 1

Match up the following sentences using wenn.

1	Wenn die Sonne scheint,	**a**	erhält sie 25 Prozent Ermäßigung auf alle Rabatte.
2	Wenn ich Deutsch gelernt habe,	**b**	kann man eine Tablette nehmen.
3	Wenn Yuki einkauft,	**c**	gehen wir in die Berge.
4	Wenn Frau Gebhardt Gäste hat,	**d**	kommen wir schneller ins Konzert.
5	Wenn Yuki eine BahnCard hat,	**e**	kaufe ich mir eine Wohnung.
6	Wenn ich im Lotto gewinne,	**f**	zahlt sie mit der Kreditkarte.
7	Wenn man Kopfschmerzen hat,	**g**	finde ich einen besseren Job.
8	Wenn wir die U-Bahn nehmen,	**h**	kocht sie besonders gut.

1 .... **2** .... **3** .... **4** .... **5** .... **6** .... **7** .... **8** ....

Exercise 2

Form sentences using wenn.

die Sonne nicht scheint   Deutsch lernen

Wenn die Sonne nicht scheint, lerne ich Deutsch.

1 ich habe die U-Bahn   Bus nehmen   verpasst

....

2 der Bäcker kein Brot   Brötchen kaufen   mehr hat

....

3 mein Magen übersäuert   nichts essen, sondern nur Tee   ist   trinken

....

4 ich kein Geld mehr habe   am Automaten Geld holen

....

5 mein Hausarzt keine   einen anderen Arzt suchen   Sprechstunde hat

....

Exercise 3

Form sentences with und zwar.

1 Yuki fährt mit dem Zug; mit dem ICE

....

2 Sie geht gern einkaufen; am Abend

....

3 Tobias isst gern Käse; Emmentaler

....

4 Frau Glück hört gern Musik; Mozart

....

Vocabulary

Below is a list of vocabulary encountered in this chapter.

Abteil, das, -e	*compartment*
Angestellte, die, -n *(am Schalter)*	*booking clerk*
Anschluss, der, -¨e	*connection*
Bahnhof, der, -¨e	*station*
Bahnsteig, der, -e	*platform*
Berg, der, -e	*mountain*
das kommt darauf an	*that depends*
Ermäßigung, die, -en	*reduction*
Ermäßigungskarte, die, -n	*a card which entitles you to a reduction*
Fahrkarte *in:* **einfache Fahrkarte**	*single / one-way ticket*
gesund	*healthy*
Gleis, das, -e	*track*
IC (InterCity), der, -s	*InterCity train*
IC-Zuschlag, der, -¨e	*IC surcharge*
ICE (InterCityExpress), der, -s	*InterCity express train*
Nichtraucherabteil, das -e	*non-smoking compartment*
Normalpreis, der, -e	*normal/regular price*
passen *in:* **das passt mir**	*to suit (that suits me)*
einen platz	*a space/place*
Platzreservierung, die, -en	*seat reservation*
Preis, der, -e	*price*
Prozent, das, -e	*percent*
Rabatt, der, -e	*discount*
Raucherabteil, das, -e	*smoking compartment*
Regional Express (RE), der, -e	*regional express train*
Reiseunterlagen, die *(pl.)*	*travel documents*
rentieren (sich)	*to be worthwhile*
Rückfahrkarte, die, -n	*return/ round-trip ticket*
Schaffner, der, -	*conductor*
Sitzplatz, der, -¨e	*seat*
Schlafwagen, der, -	*sleeping car*
Schließfach, das, -¨er	*locker*

Sparpreis, der, -e	*discount price*
Speisewagen, der, -	*restaurant car*
und zwar	*namely (but usually transalted*
Unterschied, der, -e	*difference*
Wochenende, das, -n	*weekend*
Verspätung, die, -en	*delay*
Zuschlag, der, -¨e	*surcharge*

day: 19

A trip to Bamberg

Day 19 sees you take a trip to Bamberg. Along the way, you will learn all about the subordinate clause with *um … zu* + infinitive, and how to use *der, die, das* as demonstrative pronouns. You will learn more about train travel and continue to build your vocabulary. Finally, you can try out the fun game on page 180 to see how well you are progressing.

RESERVATIONS…

*Before buying a train ticket, you should enquire about special fares and cheap rates offered by **Deutsche Bahn**. There is also a special **Wochenendticket**, which allows groups to travel on regional trains at a reduced fare, and special rates apply if you start your journey after 7:00 p.m at weekends. For longer trips, advance reservations are advisable. However, tickets for shorter journeys can be obtained from machines at the station.*

German conversation: In Bamberg

Yuki ist in Bamberg angekommen. Jetzt will sie die Stadt erkunden.
Sie geht zuerst ins Fremdenverkehrsamt.

Yuki: **Guten Tag! Ich möchte gerne einen Stadtplan.**

Herr Fösel: **Bitte schön. Sie möchten unser romantisches Bamberg anschauen?**

Yuki: **Ja. Können Sie mir empfehlen, welche Sehenswürdigkeiten ich hier anschauen soll?**

Herr Fösel: **Natürlich! Sind Sie zu Fuß?**

Yuki: **Ja.**

Herr Fösel: **Gut, denn um die Stadt kennenzulernen, geht man am besten zu Fuß. Also, Sie sind jetzt am Bahnhof, gehen Sie einfach die Luitpoldstraße entlang bis zur Oberen Königstraße, dann rechts und nach ungefähr 200 Metern biegen Sie links in die Königstraße und Sie kommen zur Kettenbrücke. Sie führt über die Regnitz.**

Yuki: **Und wie komme ich in die Innenstadt?**

Herr Fösel: **Um in die Innenstadt zu kommen, gehen Sie einfach über die Brücke und schon sind Sie mitten im Zentrum.**

Yuki: **Und was kann ich dort alles besichtigen?**

Herr Fösel: **Viel. Zuerst den Maxplatz mit seinen bunten Marktständen, dann die St. Martinskirche, die Universität mit ihren herrlichen renovierten Gebäuden und natürlich das Alte Rathaus. Es steht auf einer Brücke mitten im Fluss.**

Yuki: **Und es gibt auch die Bamberger Symphoniker.**

Herr Fösel: **Oh, die kennen Sie?**

Yuki: **Ja. Ich habe sie schon in München in der Philharmonie gehört. Wann geben sie denn ihr nächstes Konzert?**

Herr Fösel: **Das kann ich Ihnen ganz genau sagen: heute Abend. Ich habe nämlich eine Karte und kann leider nicht hingehen. Möchten Sie die Karte haben?**

Yuki: **Was kostet denn die Karte?**

Herr Fösel: **Gar nichts. Die schenke ich Ihnen.**

Yuki: **Das ist sehr nett von Ihnen! Und was kann ich sonst noch alles in Bamberg sehen?**

Herr Fösel: **Natürlich müssen Sie in den Dom gehen und den Bamberger Reiter anschauen. Dann laufen Sie an der Alten Hofhaltung vorbei weiter zur Michaelskirche. Von dort oben haben Sie einen herrlichen Blick über die ganze Stadt. Und wenn Sie zurück über die Rathausbrücke gehen, werfen Sie einen Blick auf Klein-Venedig.**

Yuki: **Ich glaube, der Tag wird ganz schön anstrengend.**

Herr Fösel:	**Anstrengend, aber auch schön. Und hier Ihre Karte für die Bamberger Symphoniker. Ich wünsche Ihnen einen schönen Aufenthalt in unserer Stadt.**
Yuki:	**Vielen Dank. Es lohnt sich wirklich, ins Land der Franken zu fahren!**

English conversation: In Bamberg

Yuki has arrived in Bamberg. She wants to explore the town. She starts by going to the Tourist Information Office.

Yuki:	**Good morning! I'd like a map of the town.**
Mr. Fösel:	**Here you are. Do you want to have a look around our romantic town of Bamberg?**
Yuki:	**Yes, I do. Can you recommend which sights I should have a look at?**
Mr. Fösel:	**Of course. Are you on foot?**
Yuki:	**Yes, I am.**
Mr. Fösel:	**Good, it's best to go on foot to get to know the town. OK. You're now at the station, just walk down Luitpoldstraße as far as Obere Königstraße, then turn right, and after about 200 meters turn left into Königstraße and then you come to the Kettenbrücke. It crosses the Regnitz.**
Yuki:	**And how do I get to the town centre?**
Mr. Fösel:	**To get to the town centre you simply cross the bridge and then you're right in the middle of the town.**
Yuki:	**And what is there to see there?**
Mr. Fösel:	**There's a lot to see. First of all, Maxplatz with all the colourful market stalls, St Martin's Church, the university with its beautifully renovated buildings and Old Town Hall, of course. It is situated on a bridge in the middle of the river.**
Yuki:	**And there's the Bamberg Symphony Orchestra, too.**
Mr. Fösel:	**Oh, you've heard of them?**
Yuki:	**Yes, I heard them play in Munich at Philharmonic Hall. When are they giving their next concert?**
Mr. Fösel:	**I can tell you exactly when: this evening. I've got a ticket, you see, but unfortunately I can't go. Would you like to have the ticket?**
Yuki:	**How much is it?**
Mr. Fösel:	**It won't cost you anything. It's a present.**
Yuki:	**That's very kind of you! And what else can I see in Bamberg?**
Mr. Fösel:	**You must go to the cathedral, of course, and have a look at the Bamberger Reiter, the rider. Then you walk past the Alte**

	Hofhaltung, the old court, as far as the church, St Michael's. From the top, you have a wonderful view of the whole town. And when you walk back to the Rathausbrücke, the Town Hall bridge, take a look at KleinVenedig, little Venice.
Yuki:	**I think it is going to be a very tiring day.**
Mr. Fösel:	**Tiring, yes, but also very interesting. And here's your ticket for the Bamberg Symphony Orchestra. I hope you have a very pleasant day in Bamberg.**
Yuki:	**Thank you very much. It's really worth coming to Franconia.**

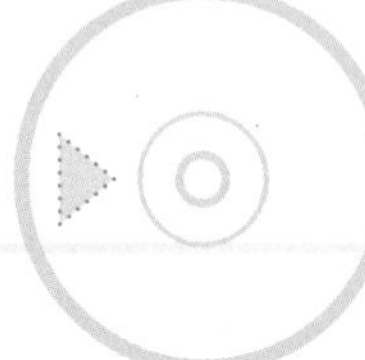

Grammar

Subordinate clause with um … zu + infinitive

Um die Stadt kennen**zu**lernen,	gehen Sie am besten zu Fuß.
To get to know the town	it's best to go on foot.
subordinate clause	*main clause*
Gehen Sie am besten zu Fuß,	**um** die Stadt kennen**zu**lernen.
It's best to go on foot	to get to know the town.
main clause	*subordinate clause*

The conjunction **um … zu + infinitive** refers to a destination or an intention. **Um … zu + infinitive** can only be used when the persons in the main clause and the subordinate clause are the same.

Der, die, das as demonstrative pronouns

In spoken German **der**, **die**, **das** can be used as demonstrative pronouns instead of personal pronouns. The demonstrative pronouns refer to the person or subject matter mentioned in the previous sentence. They have the same form as the definite article with the exception of the dative plural form, which is **denen**.

singular	*masculine*	*neuter*	*feminine*
nominative	**der**	**das**	**die**
accusative	**den**	**das**	**die**
dative	**dem**	**dem**	**der**

plural	masculine	neuter	feminine
nominative	die	die	die
accusative	die	die	die
dative	denen	denen	denen

For example:

Die Bamberger Symphoniker. Oh, die kennen Sie schon?

The Bamberg Symphony Orchestra. Oh, you've heard of them already?

Wie geht es deinen Eltern? Denen geht es gut.

How are your parents? They are very well.

Exercises

Exercise 1

Link the sentences with um … zu + infinitive.

Yuki geht nach Deutschland. Sie möchte Deutsch lernen.

Yuki geht nach Deutschland, um Deutsch zu lernen.

1 Yuki arbeitet abends. Sie (muss) Geld verdienen.

....

2 Sie geht abends ins Konzert. Sie (möchte) die Bamberger Symphoniker hören.

....

3 Sie fährt mit dem ICE. Sie (möchte) schneller in Bamberg sein.

....

4 Sie geht zu Fuß. Sie (möchte) die Stadt kennenlernen.

....

Exercise 2

Complete the sentences by adding the demonstrative pronouns der, die, das or denen.

1 Was hast du von den Gebhardts gehört? Von .... habe ich schon lange nichts gehört.

2 Siehst du das rote Kleid auf dem Tisch? .... ziehe ich heute Abend an.

3 Wo hält der Bus in der Innenstadt? .... hält an der Königstraße.

4 Wie geht es deinen Geschwistern? .... geht es gut.

Exercise 3

Match the sentences.

1 Wohin fährt dieser Bus?
2 Kennst du die Bamberger Symphoniker?
3 Du kennst den Autor Goethe nicht?
4 Möchten Sie diesen Anzug?
5 Was kosten die Brezeln?
6 Fährt diese U-Bahn zum Marienplatz?
7 Kann ich die Zeitung haben?
8 Wie findest du meinen neuen Haarschnitt?

a Den finde ich gut.
b Ja, die fährt zum Marienplatz.
c Ja, den nehme ich.
d Der fährt in die Innenstadt.
e Von denen habe ich eine CD.
f Nein, von dem habe ich noch nichts gelesen.
g Die kosten 50 Cent das Stück.
h Ja, die brauche ich nicht mehr.

1 .... **2** .... **3** .... **4** .... **5** .... **6** .... **7** .... **8** ....

Vocabulary

Below is a list of vocabulary encountered in this chapter.

anschauen	*to have a look at*
anstrengend	*tiring*
Aufenthalt, der, -e	*stay*
Autor, der, -en	*author*
besichtigen	*to look at*
biegen	*to turn*
Brücke, die, -n	*bridge*
Dom, der, -e	*cathedral*
entlang	*along*
erkunden	*to explore*
Fluss, der, -¨e	*river*
Fremden-verkehrsamt, das, -¨er	*Tourist Information Office*
führen *in:* **die Brücke führt über die Regnitz**	*the bridge crosses the Regnitz*
Fuß *in:* **zu Fuß sein**	*on foot*
Gebäude, das, -	*building*
genau	*exact*
Haarschnitt, der, -e	*haircut*
Innenstadt, die, -¨e	*town/city centre*
Karte, die, -n *in:* **Konzert-karte**	*ticket*
Kirche, die, -n	*church*
Land der Franken	*Franconia*
Land, das, -¨er	*country*
lohnen (sich)	*to be worthwhile*
Marktstand, der, -¨e	*market stall*
Reiter, der, -	*rider*
renovieren	*to renovate*
romantisch	*romantic*
Stadtplan, der, -¨e	*map of the town/city*
um … zu	*in order to*
ungefähr	*about*
Universität, die, -en	*university*
vorbeilaufen	*to walk past*
weiter zur	*as far as*
werfen *in:* **einen Blick werfen auf**	*to have a look at*

Test 3

Work your way around the board. Each correct answer will take you to the next question until you have completed the exercise. Enjoy!

1
Choose one of the two possible solutions. Then go to the square showing the number of the solution you think is correct.

2
Ich bin gestern nach Frankfurt …
geflogen ▶8
gefliegt ▶15

3
Wrong!
Go back to number 5.

8
Correct.
Go on:
Ich bin ins Café …
gegingen ▶6
gegangen ▶25

9
Wrong!
Go back to number 25.

10
Wrong!
Go back to number 14.

11
Wrong!
Go back to number 29.

16
Good. Continue:
Ich kann den Pass … finden.
nirgends ▶22
niemand ▶18

17
Wrong!
Go back to number 22.

18
Wrong!
Go back to number 16.

19
Correct!
End of exercise.

24
Wrong!
Go back to number 12.

25
Very good. Next one:
In der Apotheke kann man … kaufen.
Pflaster ▶14
Rezepte ▶9

26
Wrong!
Go back to number 30.

27
Good. Next one:
… Sie eine BahnCard haben, erhalten Sie 25% Ermäßigung.
Wen ▶23 Wenn ▶12

4

Good. Go on:
Wir … eine Woche in Berlin geblieben.
sind ▶20
haben ▶7

5

Correct, continue:
Ich habe Geld …
umtauscht ▶3
umgetauscht ▶13

6

Wrong!

Go back to number 8.

7

Wrong!

Go back to number 4.

12

Very good. Go on:
München ist groß, aber Berlin ist …
größer ▶ 16
größten ▶ 24

13

Correct! Continue:
Dieses Brot schmeckt mir am …
besser ▶21
besten ▶29

14

Very good.
Next one:
Ich habe … Termin.
nicht ▶10
keinen ▶30

15

Wrong!

Go back to number 2.

20

Well done! Continue:
Yuki spricht nicht nur Deutsch, … Englisch.
sondern auch ▶5
dass ▶28

21

Wrong!

Go back to number 13.

22

Correct!
Diese Flasche enthält so viel … diese.
als ▶17
wie ▶19

23

Wrong!

Go back to number 27.

28

Wrong!

Go back to number 20.

29

Well done. Continue:
Ich hoffe, … er pünktlich ist.
wenn ▶11
dass ▶27

30

Correct! Continue:
Ich habe guten Wein …
trinken ▶26
getrunken ▶4

day: 20

Eco-conscious

Day 20 covers the verbs *legen, liegen, stellen, stehen, hängen, sich setzen* and *sitzen* in the accusative and dative. You will also learn indefinite pronouns *ein- / kein-/welche* to express the notion of one, some or none. You will also further build your vocabulary. Finally, you will learn more about German culture and the German people's regard for the environment.

RECYCLE...

Germans are by and large environmentally aware and tend to purchase environmentally-friendly products as a preference. Conservation of resources and recycling are concepts that are taken very seriously and are observed in the home. Moreover, waste avoidance is a primary objective of German environmental policy.

German conversation: Mülltrennung

Yuki trifft Frau Glück in der Küche. Vor ihr liegt ein großer Haufen mit Dosen, Flaschen, Zeitungen und Plastiktüten.

Yuki:	**Was machen Sie denn da?**
Frau Glück:	**Ich sortiere Flaschen, Dosen, Alufolie, Plastik und Papier und lege alles getrennt auf einen Haufen.**
Yuki:	**Was machen Sie dann damit?**
Frau Glück:	**Ich bringe alles in die entsprechenden Container. Die Flaschen kommen in Glascontainer. Es gibt einen für Weißglas, Braunglas und Grünglas. Die Zeitungen und Kartons kommen in den Behälter für Papier. Alle Plastikdosen kommen in den Container für Plastik. Und die Blechdosen und Alufolien kommen in den für Blech.**
Yuki:	**Warum machen Sie das?**
Frau Glück:	**Ja, wir müssen den Müll trennen. Das ist eine neue Vorschrift.**
Yuki:	**Das ist neu für mich.**
Frau Glück:	**Wir sammeln erst den Abfall und dann sortieren wir ihn. Wissen Sie, andere Länder sammeln Olympiamedaillen und Fußballsiege, und wir sammeln eben Müll.**
Yuki:	**Wenn ich etwas in Deutschland gelernt habe, dann ist es das Sprichwort: Wenn schon, denn schon.**
Frau Glück:	**Sie haben doch schon einmal eine Tafel Schokolade gekauft oder einen Joghurt?**
Yuki:	**Ja, natürlich.**
Frau Glück:	**Eine Tafel Schokolade ist zuerst in Alufolie eingepackt und noch einmal in Papier. Wenn Sie die Schokolade gegessen haben, werfen Sie die Alufolie in diese Tüte hier und das Papier in den Papierkorb. Beim Joghurt trennen Sie das Plastik von der Alufolie. Das Plastik kommt in diese Tüte, und die Alufolie kommt in die Tüte mit Blechdosen.**
Yuki:	**Das ist aber ziemlich kompliziert und umständlich.**
Frau Glück:	**Das ist aber noch nicht alles. Auf dem Balkon steht mein Komposteimer. In den werfe ich alle organischen Abfälle, wie zum Beispiel Filtertüten, Gemüsereste, Obstschalen, Eierschalen und Papierservietten.**
Yuki:	**Wie kann ich das alles behalten?**
Frau Glück:	**Man gewöhnt sich daran!**

English conversation: Separating waste

Yuki meets Mrs. Glück in the kitchen. In front of her is a huge pile of cans, bottles, newspapers and plastic bags.

Yuki: **What are you doing?**

Mrs. Glück: **I'm sorting out the bottles, cans, aluminium/aluminum foil, plastic and paper and putting them in different piles.**

Yuki: **What are you going to do with them, then?**

Mrs. Glück: **I'm going to take them to special containers. The bottles go in the bottle bank (container for glass). There's one for clear glass, brown glass and green glass. The newspapers and the cardboard go in the scrap paper container. All the plastic goes in the container for plastic waste, and the cans and aluminium/ aluminum go in the one for metal.**

Yuki: **Why are you doing that?**

Mrs. Glück: **Because we are supposed to separate waste. It's a new regulation.**

Yuki: **That's new to me.**

Mrs. Glück: **Well, first of all we collect the rubbish/garbage and then we sort it. Other countries collect Olympic medals and football trophies, and we collect waste!**

Yuki: **If there's one thing I've learnt in Germany, it's that if a job's worth doing, it's worth doing well.**

Mrs. Glück: **Have you ever bought a bar of chocolate or a yoghurt?**

Yuki: **Yes, of course.**

Mrs. Glück: **A bar of chocolate is first packed in aluminium/aluminum foil and then in paper. When you've eaten the chocolate, you throw the foil in this bag here and the paper in the wastepaper basket. With a yoghurt you take the foil off the plastic. The plastic goes in this bag and the foil in the bag with the cans.**

Yuki: **But that's all rather complicated and a lot of trouble.**

Mrs. Glück: **That's not all. There's a compost bin on the balcony. I throw all my organic waste into it – for example paper filters, vegetable peelings, fruit peel, eggshells and paper napkins.**

Yuki: **How am I supposed remember all that?**

Mrs. Glück: **You'll get used to it!**

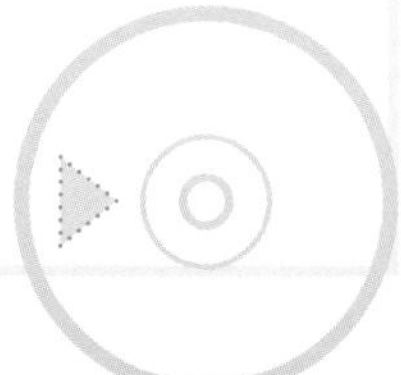

Grammar

Verbs

The verbs **legen**, **stellen**, **sich setzen** and **hängen** are regular verbs that describe an activity. The prepositions which indicate place are followed by the accusative. You can ask **Wohin**?
The verbs **liegen**, **stehen**, **sitzen** and **hängen** are irregular verbs that focus on the result of the activity. The prepositions which indicate place are followed by the dative. You can ask **Wo**?

legen **to put**	**liegen** **to lie**
Frau Glück **legt** alles getrennt auf einen Haufen.	Die Zeitungen **liegen** auf einem Haufen.
Mrs. Glück puts everything in different piles.	The newspapers are lying in a pile.
infinitive: **legen**	*infinitive:* **liegen**
present perfect: **hat gelegt**	*present perfect:* **hat gelegen**

stellen **to put**	**stehen** **to be**
Frau Glück **stellt** den Komposteimer auf den Balkon.	Der Komposteimer **steht** auf dem Balkon.
Mrs. Glück puts the compost bin on the balcony.	The compost bin is on the balcony.
infinitive: **stellen**	*infinitive:* **stehen**
present perfect: **hat gestellt**	*present perfect:* **hat gestanden**

hängen **to hang**	**hängen** **to hang**
Frau Glück **hängt** den Mantel an die Garderobe.	Der Mantel **hängt** an der Garderobe.
Mrs. Glück hangs the coat on the hook.	The coat is hanging on the hook.
infinitive: **hängen**	*infinitive:* **hängen**
present perfect: **hat gehängt**	*present perfect:* **hat gehangen**

sich setzen **to sit down**	**sitzen** **to sit**
Yuki **setzt sich** auf die Bank.	Yuki **sitzt** auf der Bank.
Yuki sits down on the bench.	Yuki is sitting on the bench.
infinitive: **sich setzen**	*infinitive:* **sitzen**
present perfect: **hat gesetzt**	*present perfect:* **hat gesessen**

Indefinite pronouns ein-/kein-/welche

The indefinite pronouns **einer**, **ein(e)s**, **eine** (one) stand for one person or for one object from a number of persons or objects. The plural in the nominative and the accusative is always **welche** (some), and in the dative **welchen**.
The negative form is **kein** and it is declined like **ein**.

Ich habe vier Orangen gekauft.	I've bought four oranges.
Eine habe ich schon gegessen.	I've eaten one of them already.
Fünf Kollegen sind zur Arbeit gefahren. Alle fünf sind mit dem Auto gefahren.	Five colleagues went to work. All five went by car.
Keiner hat die U-Bahn genommen.	None of them went by underground/ subway.
Hast du Kirschen gekauft?	Have you bought some cherries?
Ja, ich habe **welche** gekauft.	Yes, I bought some.

singular	*masculine*	*neuter*	*feminine*
nominative	**einer/keiner**	**ein(e)s/kein(e)s**	**eine/keine**
accusative	**einen/keinen**	**ein(e)s/kein(e)s**	**eine/keine**
dative	**einem/keinem**	**einem/keinem**	**einer/keiner**

plural	*masculine*	*neuter*	*feminine*
nominative	**welche/keine**	**welche/keine**	**welche/keine**
accusative	**welche/keine**	**welche/keine**	**welche/keine**
dative	**welchen/keinen**	**welchen/keinen**	**welchen/keinen**

Exercises

Exercise 1

Complete the sentences using the following verbs: legen, liegen, hängen, setzen, stehen or stellen.

1 Die Container .... in der Nähe.

2 Frau Glück .... die Mülltüten auf den Balkon.

3 Das Familienfoto .... an der Wand.

4 Frau Glück hat den Prospekt zwischen die Zeitungen ....

5 Die Zeitungen .... auf einem Haufen.

6 Die Mutter .... ihre Tochter auf den Stuhl.

Exercise 2

Complete the sentences using the appopriate prepositions.

1 Ich habe .... der Bushaltestelle auf dich gewartet.

2 Bist du .... der Küche?

3 Kannst du den Blumenstrauß .... das Fensterbrett stellen?

4 Die Kinder gehen .... den Kindergarten.

5 Tobias setzt sich ....Yuki und Frau Glück.

Exercise 3

Complete the sentences with the indefinite pronoun.

1 Hast du zwei Briefmarken für mich?

Ja, auf meinem Schreibtisch, oben rechts, liegen ....

2 Hast du einen Mann mit einem grünen Hemd gesehen?

Ja, da vorne steht ....

3 Ein Buch liegt auf dem Fensterbrett. Auf dem Tisch liegen auch noch ....

4 Ich hole mir einen Hamburger. Möchtest du auch ....

Vocabulary

Below is a list of vocabulary encountered in this chapter.

Abfall, der, -̈e	*waste*
Alufolie, die, -n	*aluminium/aluminum foil*
Balkon, der, -e	*balcony*
Bank, die, -̈e	*bench*
in: **sich auf eine Bank setzen**	
behalten	*to remember*
Behälter, der, -	*container*
Blech, das, -e	*tin*
Braunglas, das	*brown glass*
Bushaltestelle, die, -n	*bus stop*
Container, der, -	*container*
Dose, die, -n	*can*
Eierschale, die, -n	*eggshell*
einpacken	*to wrap up*

entsprechend *proper*
erst *in:* **wir sammeln erst** *first of all*
Familienfoto, das, -s *family picture*
Fenster, das, - *window*
Fensterbrett, das, -er *window sill*
Filtertüte, die, -n *paper filter*
Fußballpokal, der, -e *football trophy*
Garderobe, die, -en *hook, cloakroom*
Gemüserest, der, -e *vegetable peelings*
gewöhnen (sich) *to get used to*
Glascontainer, der, - *bottle bank/ glass container*
Grünglas, das *green glass*
Haufen, der, - *pile*
Karton, der, -s *cardboard*
Kindergarten, der, -¨ *kindergarten*
Kino, das, -s *cinema /movie theater*
Kollege, der, -n *colleague*
kompliziert *complicated*
Komposteimer, der, - *compost bin*
liegen *to lie*
Mülltonne, die, -n *dustbin/ garbage can*
Obstschale, die, -n *fruit peel*
Olympiamedaille, die, -n *Olympic medal*
organisch *organic*
Papier, das, -e *paper*
Papierkorb, der, -¨e *wastepaper basket*
Papierserviette, die, -n *serviette/ paper napkin*
Plastik, das *plastic*
Prospekt, der, -e *brochure*
sammeln *to collect*
Sammlung, die, -en *collection*
sortieren *to sort*
stehen *to stand*
stellen *to put*
Tafel, die, -n *in:* **Tafel Schokolade** *bar of chocolate*
trennen *to separate*
Trennung, die, -en *separation*
Tüte, die, -n *bag*
umständlich *complicated*
Veranstaltung, die, -en *event*
vermeiden *to avoid*
Vorschrift, die, -en *regulation*
Weißglas, das *clear glass*
zum Beispiel *for example*
zwischen *between*

day: 21

At the gym

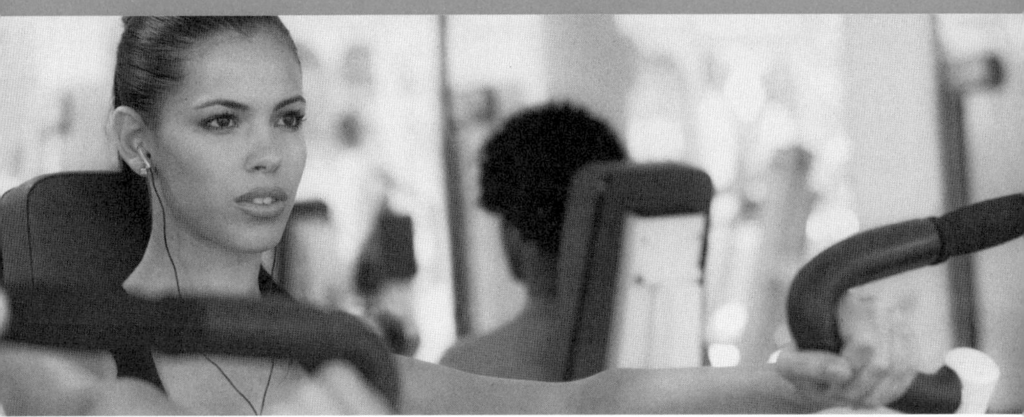

Day 21 delves into word formation and creating nouns from verbs and adjectives, as well as an introduction to the subjunctive using *würde*. You will discover more cultural information about Germany and you will further expand your vocabulary.

MEMBERS ONLY…

There is no shortage of clubs in Germany. Every sport has its own club, from alpine clubs to soccer and fishing clubs and some professions also have their own societies such as choirs or music societies.

***Trachten- und Kulturvereine** (societies to preserve national costumes and foster local traditions) also play an important role; the **Trachtenzug** (the parade of traditional costumes) on the first Sunday of the **Oktoberfest** relies heavily on the assistance of thousands of society members, as does the Rhine Carnival for its **Trachtengarden** (guards in traditional costume).*

German conversation: Sport ist gesund

Yuki und ihre Freundinnen möchten Sport treiben. Sie überlegen, für welche Sportart sie sich entscheiden sollen.

Yuki: **Ich würde am liebsten Fitness-Gymnastik machen. Da kann ich mich richtig bewegen und ich kann andere Leute kennenlernen.**

Maria: **Ich würde lieber schwimmen und anschließend in die Sauna gehen. Ist das keine gute Idee?**

Beatrice: **Ich mache lieber Sport an der frischen Luft. Lasst uns doch bergsteigen.**

Yuki: **Beim Bergsteigen sind wir an der frischen Luft und treiben gleichzeitig Sport. Und nach dem Bergsteigen können wir noch in ein Schwimmbad oder in eine Sauna gehen.**

Maria: **Und was machen wir, wenn es regnet?**

Beatrice: **Wir haben doch alle Regenmäntel! Also ich mache euch einen Vorschlag. Wir probieren das Bergsteigen einfach mal aus. Wenn wir Spaß am Bergsteigen haben, machen wir weiter. Wenn nicht, suchen wir uns eine andere Sportart aus.**

Maria: **Ja, das ist ein guter Vorschlag.**

Yuki: **Wann treffen wir uns?**

Beatrice: **Gleich übermorgen – am Sonntag um 6.00 Uhr am Bahnhof. Der Zug nach Mittenwald fährt um 6.10 Uhr. Ich habe mich erkundigt.**

Maria: **Ist das nicht ein bisschen früh?**

Beatrice: **Überhaupt nicht. Morgenstund hat Gold im Mund. Vergesst die Regenmäntel nicht!**

English conversation: Sport is healthy

Yuki and her friends would like to do some sport. They are wondering which sport they should decide on.

Yuki: **I'd really like to work out at the gym. I can get plenty of exercise that way and I can get to know other people.**

Maria: **I'd rather go swimming and then afterwards go to the sauna. Isn't that a good idea?**

Beatrice: **I'd rather do sport in the open air. Let's go climbing in the mountains.**

Yuki: **When we go climbing, we're in the fresh air and are doing some sport at the same time. And afterwards we can still go to a swimming pool or a sauna.**

Maria:	And what will we do if it rains?
Beatrice:	We've all got raincoats. Let me make a suggestion. We can have a go at climbing in the mountains. If we enjoy it, then we can carry on doing it. If we don't, we'll choose another kind of sport.
Maria:	Yes, that's a good idea.
Yuki:	When shall we meet?
Beatrice:	The day after tomorrow, on Sunday, at 6 a.m. at the railway station. The train to Mittenwald leaves at 6:10. I've already made enquiries.
Maria:	Isn't that a bit early?
Beatrice:	Not at all. The early bird catches the worm. Don't forget your raincoats!

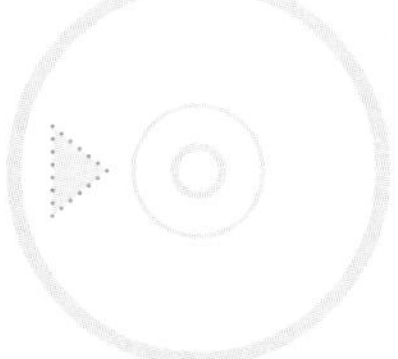

Grammar

Nouns from verbs

schwimmen	das Schwimmen

A noun can be formed from a verb by putting the article das before the verb and writing the noun with a capital letter.

Nouns from adjectives

Alles Gute zum Geburtstag!	Best wishes on your birthday!
Das Neue am ICE ist das	What's new about the ICE is
Abteil für Mutter und Kind.	the compartment for mothers and children.

Nouns can also be formed from adjectives by capitalizing them and adding the ending -e.

groß	das Große	rot	das Rot
big	the big thing	red	the red one

Nouns from verb + noun

schwimmen	das Bad	das Schwimmbad	swimming pool
schlafen	das Zimmer	das Schlafzimmer	bedroom

New nouns can also be formed from verbs by dropping the ending -en and adding a noun.

Nouns from adjective + noun

Another way to form nouns is by combining a noun with an adjective.

groß	die Stadt	die Großstadt	city
klein	die Stadt	die Kleinstadt	small town

Subjunctive with *würde* + infinitive

The subjunctive is a grammatical "mood", usually used to express wishes, emotions, possibilities and the like, and is fairly common in German. One way of expressing the subjunctive in German is with würde. Subjunctive with würde + infinitive.

Ich würde **am liebsten Gymnastik** machen.	I'd really like to do gymnastics.
Würdest du **mich zum Bahnhof** bringen?	Would you take me to the station?

Exercises

Exercise 1

Form nouns by joining the following words and add the article.

Brot, Zimmer, Stunde, Glas, schlafen, sprechen,schwarz, grün

1 ....

2 ....

3 ....

4 ....

Exercise 2

Form nouns from the verbs below and complete the sentences using the appropriate noun.

wandern, joggen, wohnen, zahlen

1 Das .... im Wald ist gesund.

2 Das .... mit der Kreditkarte geht ganz einfach.

3 Beim .... kann man nette Leute kennenlernen.

4 Das .... in einer Großstadt ist oft teuer.

Exercise 3

Using the subjunctive with würde + infinitive is a polite way of asking favours and expressing wishes. Write down what you would really like to do.

Ich würde am liebsten ein Buch lesen.

1 in die Disko gehen

....

2 einen Kuchen backen

....

3 die Zeitung lesen

....

4 ins Schwimmbad gehen

....

Exercise 4

Complete the sentences using the following reflexive verbs and reflexive pronouns.

sich auskennen, sich treffen, sich entscheiden, sich gewöhnen, sich erkundigen

1 Hast du .... schon .... , wohin du fahren möchtest?

2 Sie .... , wann der Zug fährt.

3 Die Deutschen haben .... daran ...., Müll zu sortieren.

4 Wir .... um 6.00 Uhr am Bahnhof.

5 .... Sie .... in der Altstadt aus?

Vocabulary

Below is a list of vocabulary encountered in this chapter.

auskennen (sich)	*to know one's way around*
aussuchen	*to pick out*
bergsteigen	*to go mountain climbing*
bewegen (sich)	*to get some exercise*
bisschen	*a little*
doch	*instead*
erkundigen (sich)	*to make enquiries*
Fitness-Gymnastik, die	*to do workouts*
frisch	*fresh*
gleichzeitig	*at the same time*
glücklich	*happy*
Großstadt, die, -¨e	*city*
joggen	*to go jogging*
Kleinstadt, die, -¨e	*small town*
lassen	*to let*
lohnen (sich)	*to be worthwhile*
Luft, die, -¨e	*air*
Morgenstund hat Gold im Mund *(Sprichwort)*	*the early bird catches the worm (proverb)*
Regenmantel, der, -¨	*raincoat*
Sauna, die, -s	*sauna*
Schwimmbad, das, -¨er	*swimming pool*
schwimmen	*to swim*
Sport treiben	*to do sports*
Sportart, die, -en	*sport*
tanzen	*to dance*
überhaupt nicht	*not at all*
überlegen	*to think about*
übermorgen	*the day after tomorrow*
wandern	*hike*
weitermachen	*to carry on*

day: 22

On the phone

Day 22 will help you with making phone calls, and covers all the vocabulary you will need to do this. You will also learn how to use *entweder/oder* (either/or) to discuss different possibilities and you will learn some more separable verbs. Finally, there are more practice exercises to help reinforce what you have learnt so far.

TALK TIME...

If you wish to phone Germany from abroad, you dial the international code first, then the country/national code 49, then the area code without the zero, then the telephone number. (The country code for Austria is 43, and 41 for Switzerland.)

German conversation: Ein Telefonanruf

Es ist Mittwochabend. Yuki ist im Reisebüro Sonnenschein. Das Telefon klingelt.

Yuki: **Reisebüro Sonnenschein. Guten Tag! Frau Naito am Apparat. Was kann ich für Sie tun?**

Herr Zacher: **Grüß Gott. Mein Name ist Zacher. Ich möchte die Reiseunterlagen für meine Amerikareise abholen.**

Yuki: **Wann fliegen Sie denn nach Amerika, Herr Zacher?**

Herr Zacher: **Am 12. Juli. Ich bleibe bis zum 27. Juli. Zuerst fliege ich nach Cincinnati und dann nach Portland.**

Yuki: **Einen Moment, bitte.**

Yuki holt die Reiseunterlagen.

Yuki: **Hören Sie? Ihre Reiseunterlagen sind fertig. Sie können sie abholen. Sie haben bereits €1000 angezahlt. Die Reise kostet €2145. Sie können den Restbetrag bei Abholung der Unterlagen mit EC-Karte oder Kreditkarte bezahlen.**

Herr Zacher: **In Ordnung. Wie lange haben Sie abends geöffnet?**

Yuki: **Wir haben bis 20.00 Uhr offen. Sie treffen entweder meinen Kollegen Herrn Wagner oder mich an.**

Herr Zacher: **Gut, dann komme ich in den nächsten Tagen vorbei. Auf Wiederhören!**

Yuki: **Auf Wiederhören!**

Eine Woche später.

Yuki: **Sie wünschen, bitte?**

Herr Zacher: **Mein Name ist Zacher.**

Yuki: **Ach ja, wir haben letzte Woche miteinander telefoniert. Ich hole Ihre Reiseunterlagen. Einen Moment. Bitte nehmen Sie doch Platz.**

Herr Zacher: **Vielen Dank.**

Yuki kommt mit den Reiseunterlagen für Herrn Zacher zurück.

Yuki: **Hier sind Ihre Reiseunterlagen. Zahlen Sie mit EC-Karte?**

Herr Zacher: **Ich würde lieber mit Kreditkarte zahlen.**

Yuki: **Kein Problem.**

English conversation: A telephone call

It is Wednesday evening and Yuki is at Sonnenschein Travel Agency.
The telephone rings.

Yuki:	**Sonnenschein Travel Agency. Good evening! Ms. Naito speaking. Can I help you?**
Mr. Zacher:	**Good evening. My name is Zacher. I'd like to pick up my travel documents for my trip to the States.**
Yuki:	**When are you flying to the States, Mr. Zacher?**
Mr. Zacher:	**On July 12th. I'm staying until July 27th. First of all, I'm flying to Cincinnati and then to Portland.**
Yuki:	**Just a moment, please.**

Yuki fetches the travel documents.

Yuki:	**Hello? Your travel documents are ready. You can pick them up. You have already paid a deposit of 1000 euros. The trip costs 2145 euros. You can pay the outstanding sum by EC card or credit card when you collect the travel documents.**
Mr. Zacher:	**OK. How long are you open in the evening?**
Yuki:	**We're open until 8 p.m. You'll find either my colleague Mr. Wagner or myself here.**
Mr. Zacher:	**Good, then I'll come by sometime during the next few days. Goodbye.**
Yuki:	**Goodbye.**

A week later.

Yuki:	**Can I help you?**
Mr. Zacher:	**My name's Zacher.**
Yuki:	**Oh, yes, we spoke on the telephone last week. I'll go and get your travel documents. Just a minute. Please take a seat.**
Mr. Zacher:	**Thank you very much.**

Yuki comes back with Mr. Zacher's travel documents.

Yuki:	**Here are your travel documents. Are you paying by EC card?**
Mr. Zacher:	**I'd prefer to use my credit card.**
Yuki:	**No problem.**

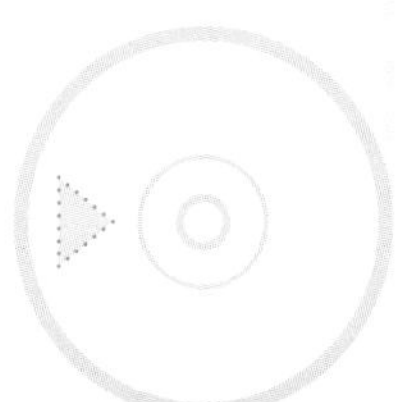

Grammar

Conjunction *entweder ... oder*

Wir gehen entweder ins Kino oder in die Disko.	We'll either go to the movies or we'll go to the disco.

The conjunction entweder ... oder is used when there are two possibilities.

Separable verbs

You have already seen some separable verbs with the prepositions ab-, an-, auf-, aus-, ein-, mit-, zurück-, zu- as prefixes.
Other separable prefixes are: her-, hinaus-, nach-, vor-, weg-, weiter- and zusammen-.
See the table below to see how these are used:

her-	herkommen	Wissen Sie, wie Sie herkommen können?
	to get here	Do you know how to get here?
hinaus-	hinausgehen	Lasst uns an die frische Luft hinausgehen.
	to go out	Let's go out and get some fresh air.
nach-	nachschauen	Ich schaue in den Reiseunterlagen nach.
	to have a look	I'll have a look at the travel documents.
weg-	wegkommen	Mit der großen Packung kommen Sie günstiger weg.
	to be better off	You're better off with the large packet.
weiter-	weitergehen	Geht schon weiter; ich komme nach.
	to go ahead	Go ahead; I'll follow.
zusammen-	zusammenkommen	Wann kommen wir drei wieder zusammen?
	to meet	When will the three of us meet again?

Note: a separable verb can also be formed by combining an adjective + verb:

Adjective + verb		
fern-	fernsehen	Am Abend sieht Frau Glück fern.
	to watch television	Mrs Glück watches television in the evening.

There are some fixed expressions which split in the same way as the separable verbs do:

Verb + verb	
liegen lassen	Lassen Sie Ihre Kreditkarte nicht liegen.
to leave behind	Don't leave your credit card behind.
spazieren gehen	Wir gehen abends gerne spazieren.
to go for a walk	We like going for a walk in the evenings.
kennenlernen	Beim Bergsteigen lernt man neue Leute kennen.
to get to know	When you go mountain climbing, you get to know new people.

Noun + verb	
Rad fahren	to go cycling.
Am Wochenende **fahren** wir **Rad**	At weekends/On the weekend we go cycling.
Probe fahren	to test-drive
Er **fährt** das neue Auto am Samstag **Probe**.	He is test-driving the new car on Saturday.

Essential phrases for making phone calls

eine Telefonnummer wählen	to dial a telephone number
die Auskunft anrufen	to phone directory enquiries
einen Anruf erhalten	to receive a call
den Anruf weiterleiten	to forward a call
zurückrufen	to call back
um Rückruf bitten	to ask someone to call back
eine Nachricht hinterlassen	to leave a message
eine Telefonnummer hinterlassen	to leave a telephone number
den Anrufbeantworter einschalten	to switch on the answering machine
den Anrufbeantworter abhören	to listen to the answering machine
eine E-Mail verschicken	to send an email
eine E-Mail erhalten	to receive an email

Exercises

Exercise 1

Complete the sentences using the following words (put the verbs in the correct tense and form): schicken, Anrufbeantworter, hinterlassen, anrufen, Nummer, ankommen, erhalten, um Rückruf.

Frau Dietl kommt ins Büro.

Frau Dietl	Hat jemand für mich .... ?
Herr Wagner	Ja. Herr Schmölder bittet ....
Frau Dietl	Hat er seine Nummer .... ?
Herr Wagner	Nein.
Frau Dietl	Ich glaube, ich habe seine ....
Herr Wagner	Sie haben auch ein Fax .... Ich habe es auf Ihren Schreibtisch gelegt.
Frau Dietl	Haben Sie die E-Mail nach Amerika .... ?
Herr Wagner	Ja. Sie ist schon ....
Frau Dietl	Bitte schalten Sie den .... ein, bevor Sie gehen.

Exercise 2

Make alternative suggestions to a friend. Make sentences with entweder ... oder.

1 Tennis spielen; Disko gehen

....

2 ins Theater; ins Kino gehen

....

3 nach München; nach Berlin fahren

....

4 Restaurant gehen; zu Hause kochen

....

Exercise 3

Complete the sentences using the prefixes ab-, an-, auf-, aus-, ein-, herein-, nach-, um-, weiter-.

1 Das Kind packt das große Geschenk als erstes ....

2 Yuki tauscht auf der Post Geld ....

3 Yuki gibt den Brief an ihre Schwester auf der Hauptpost ....

4 Ich gebe den Mantel an der Garderobe ....

5 Frau Dietl nimmt das Telefonat .... und leitet es ....

6 Yuki schaut .... , ob die Reiseunterlagen fertig sind.

7 Herr Wagner schaltet den Anrufbeantworter ....

8 Der Lieferant kommt durch die Hintertür ....

Vocabulary

Below is a list of vocabulary encountered in this chapter.

abholen	*to collect*
abhören	*to listen to*
Amerikareise, die, -n	*trip to the States*
Anrufbeantworter, der, -	*answering machine*
antreffen	*to find*
anzahlen	*to make a down payment*
(Telefon-) Apparat, der, -e	*telephone*
bereits	*already*
bitten *in:* **um Rückruf bitten**	*to ask somone to call back*
E-Mail, die, -s	*email*
einschalten	*to switch on*
entweder ... oder	*either ... or*
Fax, das, -e	*fax*
Grüß Gott *(esp. in Southern Germany)*	*good morning, good afternoon or good evening*
Hauptpost, die	*main post office*
herkommen	*to get here*
hinausgehen	*to go out*
hinterlassen	*to leave*
holen	*to go and get*
Lieferant, der, -en	*supplier*
liegen lassen	*to leave behind*

Nachricht, die, -en	*message*
nachschauen	*to have a look*
Name, der, -n	*name*
offen	*open*
in Ordnung	*OK*
Platz nehmen	*to take a seat*
Probe fahren	*to test-drive*
Rad fahren	*to go cycling*
Reiseunterlagen, die *(pl.)*	*travel documents*
Restaurant, das, -s	*restaurant*
Restbetrag, der, -¨e	*outstanding sum*
Rückruf, der, -e	*return call*
Sie wünschen, bitte?	*Can I help you?*
später	*later*
Supermarkt, der, -¨e	*supermarket*
Telefonhörer, der, -	*receiver*
Tennis spielen	*to play tennis*
Theater, das, -	*theater*
übrig	*left*
verschicken	*to send*
vorbeikommen	*to come by*
wählen	*to dial*
Was kann ich für Sie tun?	*What can I do for you?*
wegkommen *in:* **günstiger wegkommen**	*to be better off*
weitergehen	*to go ahead*
weiterleiten	*to forward*
zusammenkommen	*to meet*

day:23

The wedding

Day 23 sees you receive an invitation to a wedding. You will learn about definite articles and possessive pronouns using the genitive (to describe possession or the relationships between people/things), how to talk about the family in more detail, and further build your conversation skills and vocabulary.

DRINK DRIVING...

Germans do enjoy a drink, especially at festive occasions. However, be warned, the police carry out regular alcohol checks on drivers. Even those who are not driving in a conspicuous manner can be stopped and breathalysed. If the 0.2 legal limit is exceeded, the driver has to undergo a blood test in a hospital. If the result is positive, they may be fined or lose their driving licence.

German conversation: Eine Hochzeitsfeier

Frau Glück und Yuki sind zur Hochzeit von Frau Glücks Nichte Hanna eingeladen.
Die Hochzeitsgäste warten am Standesamt auf das Brautpaar.

Yuki: **Wer ist die ältere Dame mit dem Kostüm und dem großen Hut?**
Frau Glück: **Das ist die Mutter des Bräutigams, Frau Käfer. Neben ihr steht ihr Mann.**
Yuki: **Aha. Und wo sind die Schwiegereltern des Bräutigams?**
Frau Glück: **Die steigen gerade aus dem blauen Auto. Die Frau in dem schwarzen Kleid ist Hannas Mutter. Hannas Vater sitzt noch am Steuer. Ach, da kommen ja auch die Geschwister der Braut, meine Nichte Lena und mein Neffe Martin. Da sehe ich auch noch Tante Elfriede. Sie ist die Cousine meiner Mutter. Neben ihr steht Tante Ena, eine Cousine meines Vaters. Grüß dich, Tante Elfriede. Wie schön, dass du da bist! Darf ich dir Yuki, meine japanische Mitbewohnerin vorstellen? Sie ist zum ersten Mal auf einer Hochzeit in Deutschland.**
Elfriede: **Das ist aber schön, dass Sie auch gekommen sind.**
Yuki: **Ich habe mich über die Einladung sehr gefreut. Ich bin schon ganz gespannt.**
Elfriede: **Da kommt das geschmückte Auto mit dem Brautpaar. Ist die Braut nicht entzückend!**

Das Brautpaar und die Hochzeitsgesellschaft gehen in das Standesamt. Nach der Trauung gratulieren die Hochzeitsgäste dem Brautpaar. Anschließend werfen ein paar Gäste Reis über das Brautpaar.

Yuki: **Oh, das machen wir in Japan auch. Das bringt Glück. Welchen Namen trägt das Ehepaar denn jetzt?**
Frau Glück: **Beide haben ihre Namen behalten. Hanna heißt weiterhin Hanna Glück und Michael weiterhin Michael Käfer.**
Yuki: **Und wenn Hanna und Michael einmal Kinder bekommen, wie heißen denn die?**
Frau Glück: **Entweder Glück oder Käfer. Glückskinder sind es auf jeden Fall.**

English conversation: A wedding reception

Mrs. Glück and Yuki have been invited to the wedding of Hanna, Mrs. Glück's niece. The wedding guests are waiting at the registry office for the bride and groom.

Yuki:	**Who is the older lady in the suit and the big hat?**
Mrs. Glück:	**That's Mrs. Käfer. She's the groom's mother. Her husband is standing next to her.**
Yuki:	**I see! And where are the groom's parents-in-law?**
Mrs. Glück:	**They are just getting out of that blue car. The woman in the black dress is Hanna's mother. Hanna's father is still sitting behind the steering wheel. Oh, look! There are the bride's brother and sister, my niece Lena and my nephew Martin. I can also see Aunt Elfriede over there. She's my mother's cousin. Aunt Ena, a cousin of my father's, is standing next to her. Hello, Auntie Elfriede. Nice to see you here. I'd like to introduce my Japanese flat mate/roommate Yuki to you. This is the first time she has been to a German wedding.**
Elfriede:	**It's nice you could come, too.**
Yuki:	**I was very pleased to get the invitation. I'm very excited.**
Elfriede:	**Look, there's the bride and groom in the car decorated with flowers. Isn't the bride lovely!**

The bride and groom and the wedding party go into the registry office. After the wedding ceremony the guests congratulate the couple. Afterwards some guests throw rice over the bride and groom.

Yuki:	**Oh, we do that in Japan, too. That brings the newly-weds good luck. What will the married couple's name be?**
Mrs. Glück:	**They've both kept their own names. Hanna will continue to be called Hanna Glück and Michael, Michael Käfer.**
Yuki:	**And when Hanna and Michael have children, what will they be called?**
Mrs. Glück:	**Either Glück or Käfer. At any rate they'll be born under a lucky star.**

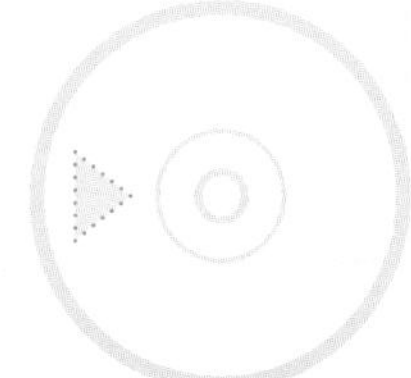

Grammar

Definite article: genitive

Das ist die Mutter des Bräutigams, Frau Käfer.	That's Mrs. Käfer, the groom's mother.
Da kommen die Geschwister der Braut.	Look, there are the bride's brother and sister.

singular	*masculine*	*neuter*	*feminine*
nominative	der Mann	das Kind	die Frau
accusative	den Mann	das Kind	die Frau
dative	dem Mann	dem Kind	der Frau
genitive	des Mann(e)s	des Kind(e)s	der Frau

plural	*masculine*	*neuter*	*feminine*
nominative	die Männer	die Kinder	die Frauen
accusative	die Männer	die Kinder	die Frauen
dative	den Männern	den Kindern	den Frauen
genitive	der Männer	der Kinder	der Frauen

The genitive is used to express possession or relationship: **die Mutter des Bräutigams**.

Masculine and neuter nouns and nouns ending in **-ss/ß**, **-z** and **-tz** take the ending **-es** in the genitive singular.

der Freund	des Freund**es**	friend
der Fluss	des Fluss**es**	river
der Schmerz	des Schmerz**es**	pain
der Arzt	des Arzt**es**	doctor

Nouns ending in **-nis** double the **-s** in the genitive.

das Erlebnis	des Erlebni**sses**	experience

With names an **-s** is added:

Frau Glück**s** Nichte Hanna	Mrs. Glück's niece Hanna
Hanna**s** Schwiegereltern	Hanna's parents-in-law

In spoken German instead of using the genitive ending, it is more common to say:

die Nichte von Frau Glück	Mrs. Glück's niece

Wessen Geschenke stehen auf dem Tisch?	Die Geschenke der Hochzeitsgäste.
Whose presents are on the table?	The wedding guests' presents.

Wessen is used to ask about possession when referring to persons.

Possessive pronouns: genitive

Neben Tante Elfriede steht Tante Ena, eine Cousine meines Vaters.	Aunt Ena, a cousin of my father's, is standing next to Aunt Elfriede.
Ich liebe den Garten vor dem Haus meiner Eltern.	I love the garden in front of my parents' house.

singular	*masculine*	*neuter*	*feminine*
nominative	mein Freund	mein Kind	meine Frau
accusative	meinen Freund	mein Kind	meine Frau
dative	meinem Freund	meinem Kind	meiner Frau
genitive	meines Freund(e)s	meines Kind(e)s	meiner Frau

plural	*masculine*	*neuter*	*feminine*
nominative	meine Freunde	meine Kinder	meine Frauen
accusative	meine Freunde	meine Kinder	meine Frauen
dative	meinen Freunden	meinen Kindern	meinen Frauen
genitive	meiner Freunde	meiner Kinder	meiner Frauen

The genitive ending for possessive pronouns is -es in the masculine and neuter singular, and -er in the feminine singular and in all plural forms.

Exercises

Exercise 1

Complete the sentences using the genitive.

1 Die Tante .... ist auch gekommen. (der Bräutigam)

2 Das Kleid .... ist am schönsten. (die Braut)

3 Die Geschenke . ... sind fantastisch. (die Hochzeitsgäste)

4 Das Auto .... ist mit Blumen geschmückt. (das Brautpaar)

5 Die Geschenke ....haben mir am besten gefallen. (die Freundinnen)

Exercise 2

Change the sentences by putting the spoken German form of the genitive into written German. Note that there is no apostrophe with the genitive of names in German.

1 Das ist die Tochter von Stephanie.

....

2 Das Fahrrad von Frau Glück steht im Keller.

....

3 Was macht der Neffe von Gabi?

....

4 Wo sind die Eltern von Hanna und Lena?

....

Exercise 3

Complete the sentences using the genitive ending of the possessive pronouns.

Zur Familienfeier der Familie Glück sind alle Verwandten gekommen: „Wer ist das kleine Mädchen?", fragt die Großmutter.

„Das ist Amelie, die Nichte .... ", antwortet Frau Glück. (deine Schwiegertochter)

„Zu wem gehört der nette Junge dort drüben?"

„Der gehört zu dem Cousin ...." (dein Mann)

„Den jungen Mann kenne ich auch nicht."

„Das glaube ich dir gerne. Das ist der Freund ...." (deine Enkelin)

„Habe ich diese junge Dame schon einmal gesehen?"

„Das glaube ich kaum. Sie ist heute zum ersten Mal hier. Sie ist die neue Freundin... ." (dein Enkel)

Exercise 4

The bride and groom are writing a thank you letter. Complete the letter using the following words in the correct form: Wohnung, sich freuen, herzlich, Hochzeitsreise, Geschenke, große, kommen, Hochzeit

Liebe Hochzeitsgäste,

wir haben... sehr..., dass Ihr zu unserer... gekommen seid, und wir möchten uns ganz herzlich für die vielen .... bedanken. Ihr habt uns damit eine... Freude bereitet.

Jetzt sind wir schon dabei, die Koffer für unsere .... nach Neuseeland zu packen.

Wenn wir wieder nach Hause... , laden wir Euch gerne in unsere neue... in Zürich ein.

Bis dahin grüßen wir Euch ganz ....!

Hanna und Michael

Vocabulary

Below is a list of vocabulary encountered in this chapter.

aussteigen	*to get off*
behalten	*to keep*
Braut, die, -¨e	*bride*
Bräutigam, der, -e	*(bride)groom*
Brautpaar, das, -e	*bride and groom*
Enkel, der, -	*grandson*
Enkelin, die, -nen	*granddaughter*
entzückend	*lovely*
Erlebnis, das, -e	*experience*
geschmückt	*decorated*
gespannt sein	*to be excited*
Hochzeit, die, -en	*wedding*
Hochzeitsfeier, die, -n	*wedding celebration*
Hochzeitsgast, der, -¨e	*wedding guest*
Hochzeitsgesellschaft, die, -en	*wedding party*
Kostüm, das, -e	*suit*
Neuseeland	*New Zealand*
Reis, der	*rice*
Schwiegereltern *(pl.)*	*parents-in-law*
Standesamt, das, -¨er	*registry office*
Steuer, das, -	*steering wheel*
tragen *in:* **den Namen tragen**	*to be called*
Trauung, die, -en	*wedding ceremony*
in: **etwas weiterhin tun**	*to continue*

day: 24

Hanging out

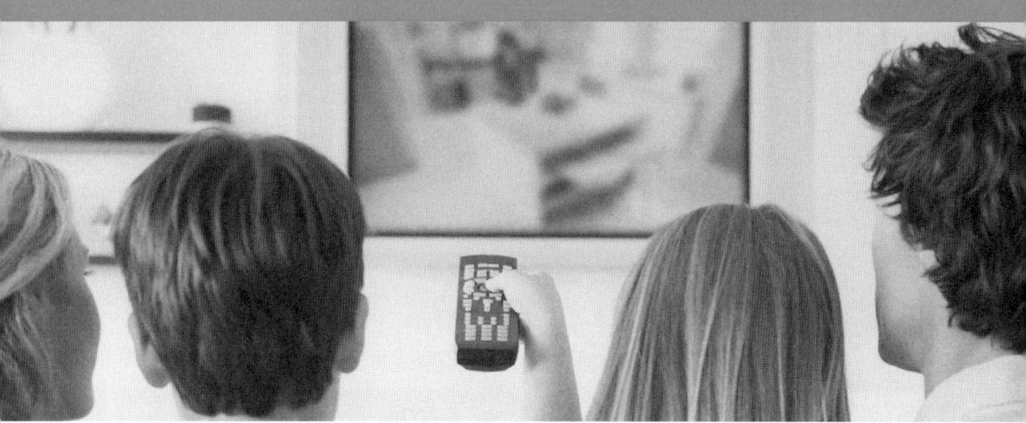

Day 24 discusses what people do in their free time. You will also pick up some more grammar and learn about prepositions that only take the genitive, and how to use *obwohl* (although), *statt* (instead), and *ohne* (without) to suggest an alternate action. You will also discover more about the German people and culture.

TELEVISION...

In Germany, you will be hard pushed to come across a household that does not have a television set, if not several. It is considered impolite by some to call someone when the national news programmes are on (from 7:00 p.m. on ***ZDF*** *and from 8:00 p.m. on* ***ARD****, the two most popular channels for news).*

German conversation: Ein gemütlicher Abend

Eigentlich möchte Yuki heute Abend mit Tobias ins Deutsche Museum gehen.
Aber es regnet. Sie ruft Tobias an.

Yuki: **Hallo Tobias! Sollen wir trotz des Regens ins Museum gehen?**

Tobias: **Hallo Yuki. Ich weiß nicht, wovon du sprichst. Hier scheint die Sonne. Außerhalb der Stadt ist es ganz trocken.**

Yuki: **Hier innerhalb der Stadt regnet es in Strömen.**

Tobias: **Aber Yuki, du hast doch einen Regenschirm. Du kannst doch bis zur U-Bahnhaltestelle laufen, ohne nass zu werden.**

Yuki: **Ich möchte lieber zu Hause bleiben und fernsehen. Ich glaube, heute Abend gibt es ein interessantes Programm.**

Tobias: **Du willst also statt des Museums lieber fernsehen?**

Yuki: **Ja, hast du nicht Lust zu kommen?**

Tobias: **Gut, ich nehme die nächste U-Bahn.**

Yuki: **Fein. Ich mache uns inzwischen etwas zum Essen.**

Nach dreißig Minuten ist Tobias da.

Yuki: **Schön, dass du da bist. Ich habe schon eine Flasche Wein kalt gestellt. Ich hole nur noch die Weingläser aus der Küche.**

Tobias: **Ich habe während der Herfahrt ins Fernsehprogramm geschaut. Es gibt heute Abend im Zweiten eine interessante Diskussion zwischen dem Bundeskanzler und dem Oppositionsführer. Kann ich schon mal einschalten?**

Yuki: **Ja, die Fernbedienung liegt auf dem Tischchen neben dem Fernseher.**

Tobias schaltet das Gerät ein.

Tobias: **Die Sendung beginnt schon. Komm, setz dich.**

Ansagerin: **Sehr geehrte Damen und Herren, eigentlich soll jetzt die Diskussion zwischen dem Bundeskanzler und dem Oppositionsführer stattfinden. Aber wegen eines Wolkenbruchs in Mainz kann der Helikopter des Bundeskanzlers nicht wie vorgesehen landen. Wir senden die Diskussion deshalb zu einem späteren Termin. Wir bitten um Ihr Verständnis. Wir setzen unser Programm mit einer Musiksendung fort.**

Tobias: **So was Dummes. Jetzt bin ich extra wegen dieser politischen Sendung hergekommen, und nun fällt sie aus. Das ist wirklich ärgerlich.**

Yuki: **Schalte mal aufs Erste Programm oder auf einen privaten Sender. Vielleicht finden wir ja da eine politische Sendung.**

Tobias: **Ehrlich gesagt, habe ich jetzt keine Lust mehr auf Fernsehen. Lass**

	uns einen gemütlichen Abend verbringen. Wir können ja auch eine CD hören.
Yuki:	**Ja, die von den Bamberger Symphonikern habe ich schon lange nicht mehr gehört.**

English conversation: A pleasant evening

Yuki would like to go with Tobias to the Deutsches Museum tonight, but it's raining. She phones Tobias.

Yuki:	**Hello, Tobias. Shall we go to the museum in spite of the rain?**
Tobias:	**Hello, Yuki. I don't really know what you're talking about. The sun's shining here. It's quite dry out of town.**
Yuki:	**Here in the centre it's pouring.**
Tobias:	**But Yuki, you've got an umbrella. You can walk to the underground station without getting wet.**
Yuki:	**I'd rather stay at home and watch television. I think there's an interesting programme on this evening.**
Tobias:	**You'd rather watch television than go to the museum?**
Yuki:	**Yes, I would. Don't you feel like coming over here?**
Tobias:	**Yes, okay. I'll come on the next train.**
Yuki:	**Good. In the meantime, I'll make us something to eat.**

Thirty minutes later Tobias arrives.

Yuki:	**Nice to see you. I've put a bottle of wine in the fridge. I'll go and get the wine glasses out of the kitchen.**
Tobias:	**On my way here I had a look at the TV guide. On Channel Two there's an interesting discussion between the Chancellor and the leader of the opposition. Can I switch it on?**
Yuki:	**Yes, go ahead. The remote control is on the table near the television set.**

Tobias switches on the TV set.

Tobias:	**The programme has already started. Come and sit down.**
Presenter:	**Ladies and gentlemen, the discussion between the Chancellor and the leader of the opposition should be taking place now. But due to a downpour in Mainz, the Chancellor's helicopter cannot land as scheduled. We will therefore be broadcasting the discussion at a later date. We apologize for any inconvenience. We will continue our transmission with a music program.**

Tobias:	**How annoying. I came here especially to see this political programme and now it has been cancelled. That's really a nuisance.**
Yuki:	**Put on Channel One or one of the private channels. Perhaps we'll find a political programme.**
Tobias:	**To be honest, I don't feel like watching television any more. Let's just spend a pleasant evening together. We can listen to a CD.**
Yuki:	**Yes, let's do that. I haven't listened to the CD of the Bamberg Symphony Orchestra in quite a while.**

Grammar

Prepositions taking the genitive

Prepositions that take the genitive are: **außerhalb**, **innerhalb**, **statt**, **trotz**, **während**, **wegen.**

Familien mit Kindern wohnen gern außerhalb der Stadt.	Families with children like to live outside the city.
Singles wohnen lieber innerhalb der Stadt.	Single people prefer to live within the city.
Statt der Diskussionsrunde im Fernsehen haben wir uns einen gemütlichen Abend gemacht.	Instead of watching the discussion on television, we spent a pleasant evening together.
Trotz des Regens gehen wir spazieren.	In spite of the rain, we're going for a walk.
Während des Essens klingelte das Telefon.	While we were eating, the telephone rang.
Der Helikopter konnte wegen eines Wolkenbruchs nicht landen.	The helicopter couldn't land due to a cloudburst.

Clauses with *obwohl*

Instead of the preposition **trotz**, a subordinate clause with **obwohl** can be used.

Trotz des Regens gehen wir spazieren.	= **Obwohl** es regnet, gehen wir spazieren.
In spite of the rain, we're going for a walk.	= Although it's raining, we're going for a walk. *subordinate clause* *main clause*

Yuki kauft das Kleid **trotz** des hohen Preises.	= Yuki kauft das Kleid, **obwohl** der Preis hoch ist.
Yuki is buying the dress in spite of the high price.	= Yuki is buying the dress, although it's expensive. *main clause* *subordinate clause*

Like **dass** and **wenn**, **obwohl** introduces a subordinate clause. The main and subordinate clauses are interchangeable, but the sentence construction must be altered. **Obwohl** is used when the activity in the subordinate clause contrasts with the activity in the main clause. There must also be a verb in the subordinate clause. You may have to add a verb.

Obwohl der Preis hoch ist, kauft Yuki das Kleid.	Although the price is high, Yuki is buying the dress.
Wir gehen spazieren, **obwohl** es regnet.	We're going for a walk, although it is raining.

Statt + infinitive with *zu*

Statt fernzusehen, sind wir in die Disko gegangen.

Instead of watching television, we went to the disco.

Statt expresses the idea that something has been done instead of something else. **Statt** is often used with the **infinitive + zu**.

ohne ... zu + infinitive

Du kannst bis zur U-Bahnhaltestelle laufen, ohne nass zu werden.

You can walk to the underground station without getting wet.

Ohne ... zu clauses describe a result or an event which will not occur or should not occur. **Ohne ... zu + infinitive** can be used only when the persons in the main and subordinate clause are the same.

Exercises

Exercise 1

Form sentences following the example below.

1 während – die Hochzeit – hat es geregnet

Während **der Hochzeit** hat es geregnet.

2 außerhalb – Deutschland – spricht man auch Deutsch

....

3 statt – das Auto – nehmen wir die U-Bahn

....

4 trotz – der Regen – gehen wir wandern

....

5 wegen – eine Hochzeitsfeier – ist unser Geschäft geschlossen

....

Exercise 2

Form sentences with obwohl using the verbs given.

1 Trotz des heißen Wetters gehen wir zum Bergsteigen. (sein)

....

....

2 Trotz des Stadtplans findet Yuki den Weg in Bamberg nicht. (haben)

....

....

3 Trotz des koffeinfreien Kaffees kann Yuki nicht schlafen. (trinken)

....

....

Exercise 3

Form sentences with statt + infinitive and zu.

1 nach München fliegen – lieber nach Hamburg fliegen/wir

....

....

2 ins Kino gehen – lieber ins Schwimmbad gehen/sie *(Sg.)*

....

....

3 der Zug fährt nicht um 17.30 Uhr ab – der Zug fährt erst um 18.00 Uhr ab

....

....

4 Das Flugzeug landet nicht 12.15 Uhr – das Flugzeug landet schon um 11.30 Uhr

....

....

Exercise 4

Join the following sentences using ohne ... zu.

1 Die Familie verreist. Sie nimmt die Katze nicht mit.

....

....

2 Die Kinder überqueren die Straße. Sie schauen nicht nach rechts und links.

....

....

3 Die Gäste kommen herein. Sie klingeln nicht an der Tür.

....

....

4 Herr Kawasaki geht nach Hause. Er schaltet den Anrufbeantworter nicht ein.

....

....

5 Sie geht weg. Sie verabschiedet sich nicht.

....

....

6 Er nimmt das Stipendium an. Er überlegt nicht lange.

....

....

Vocabulary

Below is a list of vocabulary encountered in this chapter.

ärgerlich	*annoying*
ausfallen	*to be cancelled*
außerhalb	*out of*
Ausstellung, die, -en	*exhibition*
Bundeskanzler	*Chancellor*
Diskussion, die, -en	*discussion*
Diskussions-runde, die, -n	*discussion group*
dumm	*stupid*
ehrlich gesagt	*to be honest*
eigentlich	*in fact*
es regnet in Strömen	*it's pouring with rain*
fein	*good*
Fernbedie-nung, die, -en	*remote control*
Fernsehpro-gramm, das, -e	*television programme*
fortsetzen	*to continue*
geehrte	*dear*
gemütlich	*pleasant*
Helikopter, der, -	*helicopter*
Herfahrt, die	*way here*
innerhalb	*within*
inzwischen	*in the meantime*
kalt stellen	*to put in the fridge*
landen	*to land*
Lust, die *in:* **Lust haben zu**	*to feel like*
Museum, das, *(pl.)* **Museen**	*museum*
Musiksendung, die, -en	*musical*
nass	*wet*
Oppositions-führer, der, -	*leader of the opposition*
politisch	*political*
Preis, der, -e	*price*
privat	*private*
Regen, der	*rain*
Regenschirm, der, -e	*umbrella*
regnen	*to rain*
schalten	*to turn on*
scheinen	*to shine*
senden	*to broadcast*
Sender, der, -	*TV station*
Sendung, die, -en	*programme*
Sonne, die, -n	*sun*
statt	*instead of*
Tischchen, das, -	*small table*
trocken	*dry*
trotz	*in spite of*
unbedingt	*definitely*
verbringen	*to spend*
verreisen	*to go on holiday*
Verständnis, das	*understanding*
vorgesehen	*if necessary*
während	*during*
wegen	*due to*
Weinglas, das, -¨er	*wine glass*
Wetter, das	*weather*
Wolkenbruch, der, -¨e	*downpour*

day: 25

Daily life

Day 25 introduces you to the world of relative clauses and pronouns, with which you will be able to construct more complex sentences. This chapter also has more vocabulary to broaden your scope of conversation and comprehension. Don't forget to try out the fun Test on page 228 to see how you are progressing!

IN THE NEWS...

In addition to the big daily newspapers such as the ***Süddeutsche Zeitung****, the* ***Frankfurter Allgemeine****,* ***Die Welt*** *or the* ***Züricher Allgemeine Zeitung****, there are many regional newspapers. The best known weekly newspapers with a wide circulation are* ***Die Zeit*** *and the* ***Rheinischer Merkur****. The important political magazines* ***Spiegel*** *and* ***Focus*** *are available on Mondays.*

German conversation: Eine peinliche Situation

Yuki ist auf dem Weg zur Sprachenschule. Am Kiosk kauft sie noch schnell eine Fahrkarte. Jetzt sitzt sie in der Straßenbahn und sieht Beatrice.

Yuki: **Guten Morgen, Beatrice. Wie geht's?**

Beatrice: **Ich bin müde. Ich bin gestern Abend zu spät ins Bett gegangen.**

Yuki: **Ich habe heute Morgen verschlafen.**

An der nächsten Station steigen vier Personen ein. Plötzlich hören Yuki und Beatrice die Stimme eines Mannes: **Fahrscheinkontrolle. Ihre Fahrscheine bitte.**

Beatrice: **Da ist ein Kontrolleur, der unsere Fahrscheine sehen will. Wo habe ich nur meine Fahrkarte? Ach, hier in meinem Geldbeutel. Bitte schön, hier ist meine Fahrkarte.**

Kontrolleur: **Danke.**

Yuki: **Und hier ist meine.**

Kontrolleur: **Ihre Fahrkarte ist nicht gültig.**

Yuki: **Aber ich habe doch eine Fahrkarte gekauft!**

Kontrolleur: **Die Fahrkarte, die Sie gekauft haben, ist in Ordnung. Aber Sie haben sie nicht gestempelt.**

Yuki: **Kann ich die Fahrkarte noch stempeln?**

Kontrolleur: **Nein, das ist jetzt zu spät. Sie müssen eine Strafe von €30 zahlen. Können Sie sich ausweisen?**

Yuki: **Ja, natürlich, hier ist mein Pass.**

Kontrolleur: **Wo wohnen Sie in München?**

Yuki: **Bei Frau Glück, am Rotkreuzplatz 5.**

Kontrolleur: **Wie weit wollen Sie noch fahren?**

Yuki: **Bis zur Universität.**

Kontrolleur: **Ich stelle Ihnen einen Fahrschein aus, mit dem Sie bis zur Universität fahren können. Wollen Sie die €30 sofort zahlen oder lieber überweisen?**

Yuki: **Muss ich die €30 wirklich bezahlen?**

Kontrolleur: **Ja. Ich kann wirklich keine Ausnahme machen. Bitte haben Sie Verständnis. Ich muss mich auch an meine Vorschriften halten.**

Yuki zahlt die 30 Euro. Ihr ist die Situation peinlich.

Kontrolleur: **Hier ist Ihre Quittung. Schauen Sie mal auf das Plakat, das da oben hängt. Da steht ganz deutlich „Fahrscheine vor der Fahrt entwerten". Auf Englisch und Französisch steht es auch noch da. Auf Japanisch allerdings nicht. Aber Sie sprechen ja Deutsch. Auf Wiedersehen!**

English conversation: An embarrassing situation

Yuki is on her way to the language school. At the kiosk she quickly buys a ticket. Now she is sitting on the tram and sees Beatrice.

Yuki: **Good morning, Beatrice. How are you?**

Beatrice: **I'm tired. I went to bed too late last night.**

Yuki: **I overslept this morning.**

At the next station four people get on. Suddenly Yuki and Beatrice hear a man's voice:

Ticket inspection. Your tickets, please.

Beatrice: **The inspector wants to see our tickets. Where did I put my ticket? Oh, here it is in my purse. Here you are. Here's my ticket.**

Inspector: **Thank you.**

Yuki: **And here's mine.**

Inspector: **Your ticket isn't valid.**

Yuki: **But I've just bought it!**

Inspector: **The ticket you bought is all right. But you haven't stamped it.**

Yuki: **Can I still stamp the ticket?**

Inspector: **No, it's too late now. You'll have to pay a fine of 30 euros. Do you have any form of identification?**

Yuki: **Yes, of course. Here's my passport.**

Inspector: **Where do you live in Munich?**

Yuki: **At 5 Rotkreuzplatz, with Mrs. Glück.**

Inspector: **How far do you want to travel?**

Yuki: **As far as the university.**

Inspector: **I'll issue a ticket which will take you as far as the university. Do you want to pay the 30 euros now or would you prefer to transfer the money?**

Yuki: **Do I really have to pay 30 euros?**

Inspector: **Yes, you do. I really can't make an exception. I hope you understand. I have to keep to the regulations.**

Yuki pays 30 euros. She finds the situation very embarrassing.

Inspector: **Here's your receipt. Just look at that notice over there. It states quite clearly "Tickets must be validated before boarding the train". It's also written in English and French. Not in Japanese, though. But you speak German after all. Goodbye.**

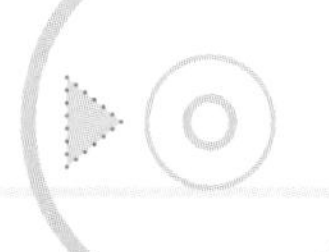

Grammar

Relative clause

Da ist ein Kontrolleur. Der Kontrolleur will unsere Fahrscheine sehen.
There's a ticket inspector. The ticket inspector wants to see our tickets.
Ich stelle Ihnen einen Fahrschein aus. Mit dem Fahrschein können Sie bis zur Universität fahren.
I'll issue a ticket. You can travel as far as the university with the ticket.

The second sentences describe more precisely a person or a thing mentioned in the first sentence. You can form a relative clause and then join the two sentences together. The relative clause always follows the noun or pronoun which it describes more precisely. See below:

Da ist ein Kontrolleur, der unsere Fahrscheine sehen will.
There's an inspector who wants to see our tickets.
Ich stelle Ihnen einen Fahrschein aus, mit dem Sie bis zur Universität fahren können.
I'll issue a ticket, which you can travel with as far as the university.

Relative pronouns

To form a relative clause, you need a relative pronoun. The forms of the relative pronouns correspond to the forms of the definite article with the exception of the dative plural and genitive singular and plural.

	singular			plural
	masculine	*neuter*	*feminine*	
nominative	…, der …	…, das …	…, die …	…, die …
accusative	…, den …	…, das …	…, die …	…, die …
dative	…, dem …	…, dem …	…, der …	…, denen …
genitive	…, dessen …	…, dessen …	…, deren …	…, deren …

Prepositions come before the relative pronouns.
Ich habe gerade mit der Ärztin gesprochen. Sie ist meine Cousine.
I have just spoken to the doctor. She is my cousin.
Die Ärztin, mit der ich gerade gesprochen habe, ist meine Cousine.
The doctor I have just spoken to is my cousin.

Relative clauses

Nominative

singular

masculine

Der Kontrolleur, der jung ist, kommt.

antecedent relative pronoun

neuter

Hier ist das Bier, das gut ist.

antecedent relative pronoun

feminine

Hier ist die Tasche, die neu ist.

antecedent relative pronoun

plural

Hier sind die Kollegen, die aus den USA sind.

antecedent relative pronoun

Accusative

singular

masculine

Der Hornist, den wir gehört haben, wohnt in Bamberg.

antecedent relative pronoun

neuter

Das Gemüse, das Sie gerade essen, ist vom Viktualienmarkt.

antecedent relative pronoun

feminine

Die Dame, die Sie gerade gesehen haben, kommt aus München.

antecedent relative pronoun

plural

Die Touristen, die Sie dort sehen können, sind Japaner.

antecedent relative pronoun

Dative

singular

masculine

Das ist mein Freund, dem das neue Auto gehört.

antecedent relative pronoun

neuter

Das ist das Geburtstagskind, dem die Kinder gratulieren.

antecedent relative pronoun

feminine

Das ist meine Freundin, der ich viel von dir erzählt habe.

antecedent relative pronoun

plural

Das sind meine Nachbarn, denen ich viel geholfen habe.

antecedent relative pronoun

The antecedent that is to be defined more precisely determines the gender (masculine, feminine or neuter) and the number (singular or plural).

The case of the relative pronouns depends on which part of the sentence the relative pronoun replaces. If it replaces the subject, the relative pronoun is in the nominative. If it replaces the object, then it is in the accusative or dative, corresponding to the object. If a genitive attribute or a possessive pronoun is replaced, it is in the genitive.

Genitive

singular

masculine

Siehst du den Hund dort, dessen Herrchen krank ist?

neuter

Magst du das Auto, dessen Farbe ich sehr schön finde?

feminine

Das ist die Frau, deren Fahrrad kaputt ist.

plural

Siehst du die Bamberger Symphoniker, deren Musikinstrumente sehr teuer sind?

Exercises

Exercise 1

Join up the two columns to make complete sentences.

1 Wie heißt das Museum,
2 Das ist Frau Gebhardt,
3 Sind das die Medikamente,
4 Ist das das Restaurant,
5 Hier ist der Blumenstrauß,

a in dem wir so gut gegessen haben?
b das wir in Mainz besucht haben?
c den Frau Gebhardt bekommt.
d die die Ärztin mir verschrieben hat?
e die uns zum Essen eingeladen hat.

1 .... **2** .... **3** .... **4** .... **5** ....

Exercise 2

Complete the sentences using relative pronouns.

1 Das Reisebüro sucht eine junge Frau, ... leichte Büroarbeiten macht.
2 Hier ist ein Herr am Telefon, ... eine Stelle sucht.
3 Frau Glück gibt Yuki einen Brief, ... der Postbote gebracht hat.
4 Yuki hat zwei Freundinnen, ... in die Sprachenschule gehen.
5 Endlich kommen die Gäste, ... ich schon so lange gewartet habe. (warten auf)

Exercise 3

Complete the sentences using the relative pronoun in the genitive.

1 Die Freundin, ... Mann mein Kollege ist, geht mit mir ins Konzert.
2 Der Autofahrer, ... Auto eine Panne hat, ruft den ADAC an.
3 Das Schloss, in .... Räumen Konzerte stattfinden, ist renoviert.
4 Eine Frau, ... Namen ich leider vergessen habe, hat für dich angerufen.

Vocabulary

Below is a list of vocabulary encountered in this chapter.

ADAC, der	*German Automobile Association*
ausstellen	*to write out*
ausweisen (sich)	*to prove one's identity*
Bett *in:* **ins Bett gehen**	*to go to bed*
deutlich	*clearly*
enthalten	*to include*
entwerten	*to stamp/ to validate*
erhöht	*increased*
Fahrschein, der, -e	*ticket*
Fahrschein-kontrolle, die, -n	*ticket inspection*
Fahrt, die, -en *in:* **vor der Fahrt**	*trip, journey before boarding*
Geburtstags-kind, das, -er	*birthday girl/boy*
Geldbeutel, der, -	*purse*
Grammatik, die, -en	*grammar*
gültig	*valid*
halten (sich)	*to keep*
Hand *in:* **in der Hand**	*in one's hand*
Herrchen, das, -	*master (dog owner)*
Hornist, der, -en	*horn player*
Hubschrauber, der, -	*helicopter*
Instrument, das, -e	*instrument*
kaputt	*broken*
Kontrolleur, der, -e	*inspector*
leicht	*easy, simple*
müde	*tired*
Nachbar, der, -n	*neighbour*
Panne, die, -n	*breakdown*
peinlich	*embarrassing*
Plakat, das, -e	*notice, poster*
Quittung, die, -en	*receipt*
renovieren	*to renovate*
Schloss, das, -¨er	*palace, castle*
Situation, die, -en	*situation*
Sprachen-schule, die, -n	*language school*
stattfinden	*to take place*
stempeln	*to stamp*
überweisen	*to transfer (money)*
verschlafen	*to oversleeep*
wegfahren	*to drive away*

Test 4

Work your way around the board. Each correct answer will take you to the next question until you have completed the exercise. Enjoy!

1

Choose one of the two possible solutions. Then go to the square showing the number of the solution you think is correct.

2

Wie geht es deinen Eltern?
... geht es gut.
Denen ▶ 8
Die ▶ 15

3

Wrong!

Go back to number 5.

8

Correct. Continue:
Die Schuhe stehen ... dem Tisch.
zwischen ▶ 6
unter ▶ 25

9

Wrong!

Go back to number 25.

10

Wrong!

Go back to number 14.

11

Wrong!

Go back to number 29.

16

Good. Next one:
Bitte schalten Sie den ... ein, bevor Sie gehen.
Anrufbeantworter ▶ 22
Fax ▶ 18

17

Wrong!

Go back to number 22.

18

Bad luck!

Go back to number 16.

19

Correct!

End of exercise.

24

Wrong!

Go back to number 12.

25

Very good. Continue:
Das ist eine Cousine ... Vaters.
meines ▶ 14
meiner ▶ 9

26

Wrong!

Go back to number 30.

27

Good. Continue:
Ich suche eine Wohnung außerhalb ... Stadt.
die ▶ 23
der ▶ 12

4

Good. Continue:
Der Komposteimer …
auf dem Balkon.
steht ▶ 20
stellt ▶ 7

5

Correct. Next one:
… gehen wir heute
Abend?
Wo ▶ 3
Wohin ▶ 13

6

Wrong!

Go back to number 8.

7

Wrong!

Go back to number 4.

12

Very good. Next one:
Ich hole mir einen
Hamburger. Möchtest
du auch … ?
einen ▶ 16 keinen ▶ 24

13

Correct! Continue:
Ich … am liebsten
bergsteigen.
würden ▶ 21
würde ▶ 29

14

Very good! Continue:
Hat jemand für
mich …
anrufen ▶ 10
angerufen ▶ 30

15

Wrong!

Go back to number 2.

20

Well done! Next one:
Herr Müller bittet
um …
Rückruf ▶ 5
Anruf ▶ 28

21

Wrong!

Go back to number 13.

22

Correct!
Die Geschenke … Gäste
stehen auf dem Tisch.
den ▶ 17
der ▶ 19

23

Sorry!

Go back to number 27.

28

Wrong!

Go back to number 20.

29

Well done! Continue:
Ich kaufe den Pullover,
… er teuer ist.
statt ▶ 11
obwohl ▶ 27

30

Correct. Continue:
Das sind die Nachbarn,
… ich geholfen habe.
deren ▶ 26
denen ▶ 4

day: 26

The accident

Day 26 teaches you how to talk about the past using the preterite and perfect tense for both regular and irregular verbs using *haben* and *sein* (for irregular verbs its best to simply memorize the list!)

BIKES…

In many German cities, cycle paths have been built to make cycling safer. At traffic lights there are often extra lights for cyclists, which are normally synchronized with the lights for pedestrians. Cyclists on cycle paths have right of way. Except during peak periods, passengers may take bicycles on the subway or on local trains but they must have a ticket for the bike. School children are taught road safety regulations at school and take a cycling test at the age of ten.

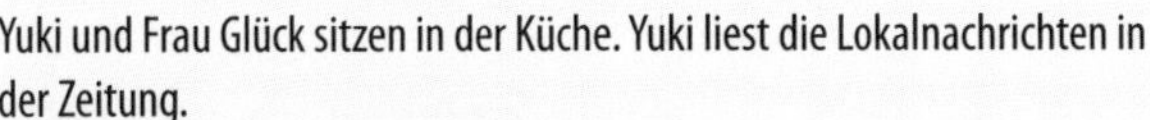

German conversation: Ein Verkehrsunfall

Yuki und Frau Glück sitzen in der Küche. Yuki liest die Lokalnachrichten in der Zeitung.

Schwerer Unfall am Rotkreuzplatz

Gestern Morgen gegen 7.45 Uhr ereignete sich am Rotkreuzplatz ein schwerer Verkehrsunfall, bei dem ein Kind verletzt wurde: Der achtjährige Stefan F. war auf dem Weg zur Schule. Der Schüler fuhr mit seinem Fahrrad auf dem Radweg und wollte die Volkartstraße an der Ampel überqueren. Ein Autofahrer wollte an derselben Stelle rechts abbiegen und übersah den Radfahrer. Es kam zu einem Zusammenstoß, bei dem das Kind vom Fahrrad fiel und sich schwer verletzte. Eine Ambulanz brachte den Schüler ins Krankenhaus. Glücklicherweise trug der Schüler einen Fahrradhelm. Er hatte dadurch keine Kopfverletzungen.

Yuki: **Der Unfall ist ja praktisch vor unserer Haustür passiert. Haben Sie den Unfall gesehen?**

Frau Glück: **Nein, als der Unfall passiert ist, war ich gerade beim Zahnarzt.**

Yuki: **Kennen Sie das Kind?**

Frau Glück: **Ja, das ist der kleine Junge von Frau Freimoser aus dem ersten Stock. Der Bub mit den dunklen Haaren.**

Yuki: **Ach, den meinen Sie? Ja, den kenne ich auch. Er ist wirklich sehr nett und höflich. Er hält mir immer die Tür auf, wenn ich nach Hause komme. Das tut mir leid für den Jungen. Wissen Sie, in welchem Krankenhaus er ist?**

Frau Glück: **Ja, er liegt im Rotkreuz-Krankenhaus, gleich bei uns um die Ecke.**

Yuki: **Vielleicht sollte ich ihn besuchen. Er würde sich bestimmt freuen.**

Frau Glück: **Ja, das glaube ich auch. Lassen Sie uns doch heute Nachmittag gemeinsam hingehen.**

English conversation: A traffic accident

Yuki and Mrs. Glück are sitting in the kitchen. Yuki is reading the local news in the newspaper.

Serious accident at Rotkreuzplatz

A child was injured in a serious accident which happened at Rotkreuzplatz at about 7:45 yesterday morning. 8-year-old Stefan F. was on his way to school. The schoolboy was riding his bike on the cycle path and was about to cross Volkartstraße at the traffic lights. A car driver who was turning right at the same spot did not see the cyclist. The two collided and the child was thrown off his bike and sustained severe injuries. The boy was taken to hospital in an ambulance. Fortunately, the boy was wearing a crash helmet and suffered no head injuries.

Yuki: **The accident happened more or less in front of our house. Did you see the accident?**

Mrs. Glück: **No, I didn't. When the accident happened, I was at the dentist's.**

Yuki:	**Do you know the child?**
Mrs. Glück:	**Yes, I do. He's Mrs. Freimoser's little boy. They live on the first (US 2nd) floor. He's the boy with the dark hair.**
Yuki:	**Oh, do you mean him? Yes, I know him, too. He's really a very nice, polite boy. He holds the door open for me when I come home. I feel so sorry for him. Do you know which hospital he's in?**
Mrs. Glück:	**Yes, he's in Rotkreuz Hospital, just round the corner.**
Yuki:	**Perhaps I should go and see him. I'm sure he'd like that.**
Mrs. Glück:	**Yes, I think he would. Let's visit him together this afternoon.**

Grammar

Preterite and perfect tense

Gegen 7.45 Uhr ereignete sich ein schwerer Verkehrsunfall.
There was a serious traffic accident at about 7:45 a.m.
Stefan F. war auf dem Weg zur Schule.
Stefan F. was on his way to school.
Yuki: Der Unfall ist ja praktisch vor unserer Haustür passiert.
Yuki: The accident more or less happened in front ofour house.

The **preterite** (the past) and the perfect tense are used when the activities or events described are in the past. The **preterite** is used in written language, for example in newspaper reports and written accounts. Apart from a few exceptions, the perfect is normally used in spoken language (more information in Day 27).

Regular verbs

Der Fahrer machte einen Fehler.	The car driver made a mistake.
Am Rotkreuzplatz ereignete sich ein Unfall.	The accident happened at Rotkreuzplatz.

singular			*plural*		
ich	machte	-e	wir	machten	-en
du	machtest	-est	ihr	machtet	-et
Sie	machten	-en	Sie	machten	-en
er/sie/es	machte	-e	sie	machten	-en

singular			*plural*		
ich	antwortete	-e	wir	antworteten	-en
du	antwortetest	-est	ihr	antwortetet	-et
Sie	antworteten	-en	Sie	antworteten	-en
er/sie/es	antwortete	-e	sie	antworteten	-en

The preterite of regular verbs is formed by inserting a -t- or -et- between the stem and the ending. When the stem ends in -d, -t, -m or -n, -et is inserted.

er verabredete sich	he arranged to meet s.o.
sich verabreden:	arrange to meet:
warten: er wartete	wait: he waited
atmen: er atmete	breathe: he breathed
regnen: es regnete	rain: it rained
Ausnahme: wohnen: er wohnte	exception: live: he lived

Irregular verbs

infinitive	*preterite*	*past participle*
beginnen	**begann**	**begonnen**
bitten	**bat**	**gebeten**
bleiben	**blieb**	**ist geblieben**
bringen	**brachte**	**gebracht**
denken	**dachte**	**gedacht**
empfangen	**empfing**	**empfangen**
essen	**aß**	**gegessen**
finden	**fand**	**gefunden**
fliegen	**flog**	**ist geflogen**
frieren	**fror**	**gefroren**
gehen	**ging**	**ist gegangen**
hängen	**hing**	**gehangen**
helfen	**half**	**geholfen**
kennen	**kannte**	**gekannt**
kommen	**kam**	**ist gekommen**
laufen	**lief**	**ist gelaufen**
lesen	**las**	**gelesen**
liegen	**lag**	**gelegen**
misslingen	**misslang**	**ist misslungen**
nehmen	**nahm**	**genommen**
nennen	**nannte**	**genannt**
rufen	**rief**	**gerufen**
schlafen	**schlief**	**geschlafen**
schneiden	**schnitt**	**geschnitten**

schreiben	schrieb	geschrieben
schwimmen	schwamm	ist geschwommen
sitzen	saß	gesessen
sprechen	sprach	gesprochen
trinken	trank	getrunken
verschreiben	verschrieb	verschrieben
werfen	warf	geworfen

Irregular verbs change vowels in the stem of the verb, and the consonants often change too. It's best to learn these forms, as well as the past participles, by heart.

Preterite: haben and sein

haben	**to have**		
singular		*plural*	
ich	hatte	wir	hatten
du	hattest	ihr	hattet
Sie	hatten	Sie	hatten
er/sie/es	hatte	sie	hatten
haben	hatte	hat gehabt	

sein	**to be**		
singular		*plural*	
ich	war	wir	waren
du	warst	ihr	wart
Sie	waren	Sie	waren
er/sie/es	war	sie	waren
sein	w	ar	ist gewesen

Preterite: modal verbs

dürfen	durfte	be allowed to	was allowed to
können	konnte	can, be able to	could
müssen	musste	must, have to	had to
wollen	wollte	want to	wanted to
sollen	sollte	should	should
mögen	mochte	like	liked

Preterite: separable verbs

Der Fahrer bog rechts ab.	The car driver turned right.
Der Zug kam verspätet an.	The train arrived late.

The prefix, as is the case in the present tense, is placed at the end of the sentence.

Exercises

Exercise 1

Put the following verbs into the preterite.

1 achten wir ....

2 bedienen sie *(pl.)* ....

3 bezahlen ich..................

4 fragen ihr ....

5 grüßen wir ....

6 meinen er ....

7 gratulieren du ....

8 lernen sie *(singular)* ....

9 klingeln es ....

10 probieren ich ....

Exercise 2

Form the third person of the preterite of these inseparable verbs (there are four irregular verbs).

1 bekommen ....

2 erklären ....

3 besichtigen ....

4 verdienen ....

5 misslingen ....

6 erzählen ....

7 beginnen ....

8 behandeln ....

9 erwarten ....

10 verschreiben ....

Exercise 3

Complete the sentences by putting the verbs in Exercise 2 into the correct preterite form in the appropriate sentences.

1 Die Touristen .... das Brandenburger Tor.

2 Letztes Jahr .... ich nicht viel Geld.

3 Die Großmutter .... von ihren Enkelkindern.

4 Die Ärztin .... Yuki zwei Medikamente.

5 Gestern .... ich Besuch von meiner Freundin.

6 Das Konzert .... um 20.00 Uhr.

7 Das neue Backrezept .... leider.

8 Die Ärztin .... mich in der neuen Praxis.

9 Die Lehrerin .... die Grammatik.

Exercise 4

Put the following separable verbs into the preterite.

1 ankommen wir ....

2 anprobieren ich ....

3 auflegen ihr ....

4 ausgehen es ....

5 ausfüllen wir ....

6 einladen sie *(Sg.)* ....

7 einkaufen ich ....

8 einpacken wir ....

9 einwerfen ich ....

10 mitbringen er ....

Exercise 5

Complete the following sentences by putting verbs from Exercise 4 into the correct preterite form in the appropriate sentences.

1 Die Hochzeitsgäste .... Geschenke ....

2 Wir .... gestern Abend ....

3 Das Brautpaar .... die Gäste zur Hochzeitsfeier ....

4 Der Zug .... pünktlich in Bamberg ....

5 Wir .... Geschenke für die Hochzeit ....

6 Frau Glück .... den Brief ....

Vocabulary

Below is a list of vocabulary encountered in this chapter.

abbiegen *to turn (off)*
achten *to observe*
achtjährig *8-year-old*
Ambulanz, die, -en *ambulance*
Ampel, die, -n *traffic lights*
anschauen *to look at*
atmen *to breathe*
aufhalten *to hold open*
auflegen *to put down*
ausgehen *to go out*
Autofahrer, der, - *driver*
Autounfall, der, -¨e *car accident*
Backrezept, das, -e *recipe*
begeistert sein *to be enthusiastic*
Besuch, der, -e *visitor*
besuchen *to visit*
bitten *to ask*
Bub, der, -en *boy*
dadurch *for this reason*
dieselbe *the same*
einwerfen *to post*
empfangen *to welcome*
Enkelkind, das, -er *grandchild*
ereignen (sich) *to happen*
erklären *to explain*
erwarten *to expect*
Fahrradhelm, der, -e *crash helmet*
fehlen *to be absent*
frieren *to feel cold*
gemeinsam *together*
glücklicherweise *fortunately*
grüßen *to greet*

Haar, das, -e	*hair*
Haustür, die, -en	*front door*
hingehen	*to go (there)*
höflich	*polite*
klingeln	*to ring*
Kopfverletzung, die, -en	*head injury*
lassen	*to leave*
laufen	*to walk*
leid *in:* **das tut mir leid**	*I'm sorry*
Lokalnachricht, die, -en	*local news*
passieren	*to happen*
Radweg, der, -e	*cycle path*
rennen	*to run*
rufen	*to shout*
Schüler, der, -	*schoolboy*
Stelle, die, -n	*spot*
in: **dieselbe Stelle**	*the same spot*
Tür, die, -en	*door*
üben	*to practise*
übersehen	*to overlook, to fail to see*
Unfall, der, -¨e	*accident*
verabreden (sich)	*to arrange to meet*
Verkehrsunfall, der, -¨e	*traffic accident*
verletzen (sich)	*to injure (oneself)*
verletzt	*injured*
werden	*to become*
werfen	*to throw*
Zusammenstoß, der, -¨e	*collision*

day: 27

At the hospital

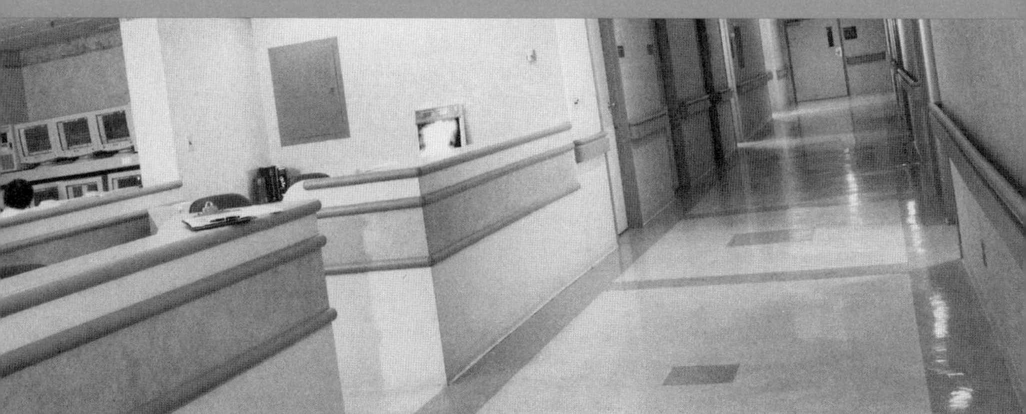

Day 27 delves further into the perfect (past) tense. You will also learn how to write correspondence - both formal and informal. You will expand your vocabulary some more and get to practice everything that you have learnt in this chapter.

DEAR...

When writing a card or letter to a friend, the usual way to open it is with ***Liebe*** *or* ***Hallo****. You can close with* ***Herzlichst, Herzliche Grüße*** *or* ***Liebe Grüße****;* ***deine*** *or* ***dein*** *(informal);* ***eure*** *or* ***euer*** *(plural). All of the above should be followed by your first name. For official correspondence, you should open with* ***Sehr geehrte Damen und Herren****, ... and if you know the addressee you should write, for example,* ***Sehr geehrte Frau Müller,*** *or* ***Sehr geehrter Herr Müller.*** *You can then close with* ***Mit freundlichen Grüßen*** *and sign off with your full name.*

German conversation: Besuch im Krankenhaus

Frau Glück und Yuki besuchen Stefan im Rotkreuz-Krankenhaus. Frau Glück fragt an der Pforte nach der Zimmernummer von Stefan.

Frau Glück: **Wir möchten zu Stefan Freimoser. Er ist seit gestern im Krankenhaus.**

Pförtner: **Freimoser, Stefan ... er liegt auf Station 14, Zimmer 148. Das ist die Kinderstation.**

Frau Glück: **Wie kommen wir zur Kinderstation?**

Pförtner: **Ganz einfach, Sie gehen den Gang entlang. Am Ende des Ganges ist der Aufzug. Mit dem fahren Sie in den vierzehnten Stock. Dort fragen Sie notfalls noch eine Krankenschwester.**

Frau Glück: **Vielen Dank.**

Frau Glück und Yuki sind im Krankenzimmer. Stefan liegt im Bett. Sein rechtes Bein und sein linker Arm sind bandagiert.

Yuki: **Hallo, Stefan!**

Frau Glück: **Grüß dich, Stefan! Wie geht's dir?**

Stefan: **Nicht so gut. Mein Kopf tut mir weh, und bewegen kann ich mich auch nicht richtig.**

Yuki: **Wir haben in der Zeitung gelesen, dass du einen Unfall hattest.**

Stefan: **Steht das in der Zeitung?**

Yuki: **Ja. Wir haben dir die Zeitung mitgebracht. Schau, hier steht's: Schwerer Unfall am Rotkreuzplatz.**

Frau Glück: **Wie ist der Unfall denn passiert?**

Stefan: **Ich bin mit dem Rad in die Schule gefahren, aber ich bin gar nicht bis zur Schule gekommen. Ich wollte an der Ampel bei Grün die Volkartstraße überqueren, doch da war plötzlich ein blaues Auto auf dem Zebrastreifen. Wir sind zusammengestoßen, und ich bin vom Fahrrad gefallen und am Boden liegen geblieben.**

Yuki: **Was ist mit deinem Bein und deinem Arm?**

Stefan: **Ich bin ja auf die Straße gestürzt und habe mir den Arm und das Bein gebrochen.**

Frau Glück: **Was ist mit deinem Fahrrad passiert?**

Stefan: **Das ist ganz kaputt.**

Yuki: **Und was hat der Autofahrer gemacht?**

Stefan: **Der ist mit ins Krankenhaus gefahren und ist bei mir geblieben, bis meine Mutter gekommen ist.**

Yuki: **Hat er sich wenigstens bei dir entschuldigt?**

Stefan: **Ja, er hat mir auch etwas zum Spielen und zum Naschen geschenkt. Er kauft mir auch ein neues Fahrrad. Das hat er mir versprochen. Ich darf es mir sogar aussuchen.**

English conversation: A visit to the hospital

Mrs. Glück and Yuki go to see Stefan in Rotkreuz-Hospital. Mrs. Glück enquires about Stefan's room number at the reception desk.

Mrs. Glück:	**We'd like to see Stefan Freimoser. He has been here since yesterday.**
Porter:	**Freimoser, Stefan … he's in ward 14, room 148. That's the children's ward.**
Mrs. Glück:	**How do we get to the children's ward?**
Porter:	**It's quite easy. You go down the corridor. At the end of the corridor there's a lift/an elevator. Take it to the fourteenth (fifteenth US) floor. If necessary, ask a nurse there to show you the way.**
Mrs. Glück:	**Thank you very much.**

Mrs. Glück and Yuki are in the room. Stefan is in bed. His right leg and his left arm are in bandages.

Yuki:	**Hello, Stefan!**
Mrs. Glück:	**Hello, Stefan! How are you?**
Stefan:	**Not so good. My head hurts and I can't move properly.**
Yuki:	**We read in the paper that you'd had an accident.**
Stefan:	**Is it in the newspaper?**
Yuki:	**Yes. We've brought the paper along for you. Look, here it says: Serious accident at Rotkreuzplatz.**
Mrs. Glück:	**How did the accident happen?**
Stefan:	**I was cycling to school, but I didn't get that far. I was about to cross Volkartstraße. The lights were green, but suddenly there was a blue car on the pedestrian crossing. We collided and I fell off my bike and then I ended up lying on the ground.**
Yuki:	**What have you done to your leg and your arm?**
Stefan:	**Well, I fell on to the road and broke my arm and leg.**
Mrs. Glück:	**What happened to your bike?**
Stefan:	**It's a complete wreck.**
Yuki:	**What did the driver do?**
Stefan:	**He came with me to the hospital and stayed with me until my mother arrived.**
Yuki:	**Did he at least say he was sorry?**
Stefan:	**Yes, he did. He also brought me something to play with and some sweets. He's going to buy me a new bike. He has promised me that. I can even choose it myself.**

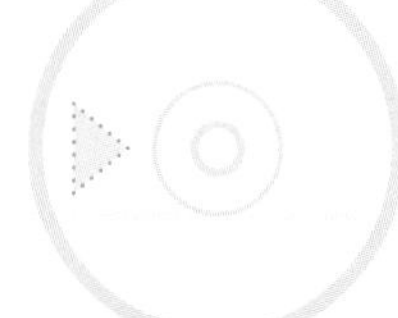

Grammar

Perfect tense

In spoken German the perfect (past) tense is used for activities and events that took place in the past. With **sein**, **haben** and **werden** as well as with modal verbs (**können**, **dürfen**, **müssen**, **wollen**, **mögen**), the preterite is preferred, especially when an adverb of time is at the beginning of the sentence.

Stefan: Ich wollte die Ampel überqueren, doch da war plötzlich ein blaues Auto.

Stefan: I was about to cross at the traffic lights, but suddenly a blue car appeared.

(Rather than: **Ich habe die Ampel überqueren wollen, doch da ist plötzlich ein blaues Auto gewesen.**)

Am Montag hatte ich viel zu tun.

On Monday I had a lot to do.

(Rather than: **Am Montag habe ich viel zu tun gehabt.**)

Both the perfect and preterite are used in questions with **haben** and **sein**:

Warst du schon einmal in Amerika? or **Bist du schon einmal in Amerika gewesen?**

Have you ever been to America?

Hattest du dort eine schöne Zeit? or **Hast du dort eine schöne Zeit gehabt?**

Did you have a nice time there?

Exercises

Exercise 1

The underlined preterite forms are not generally used in spoken language. Replace these forms with the perfect tense.

1 Yuki: Ich <u>rief</u> letzte Woche bei dir an.

....

Tobias: Tut mir leid, aber ich war die ganze Woche in Frankfurt.

2 Beatrice: Was <u>machtest</u> du am Wochenende?

....

Yuki: Ich <u>blieb</u> zu Hause. Ich musste für die Deutschprüfung lernen.

....

3 Yuki: Wo warst du gestern? Warum <u>kamst</u> du nicht zum Deutschunterricht?

....

Maria: Ich war krank.

4 Maria: Warum kamst du nicht zum Wandern mit?

....

Beatrice: Ich wollte einmal ausschlafen.

Exercise 2

Make sentences saying what you did while you were on holiday.

On holiday I ... Im Urlaub ...

e.g. lange schlafen: Im Urlaub habe ich lange geschlafen.

1 spät ins Bett gehen

....

2 gut frühstücken

....

3 ins Schwimmbad gehen

....

4 in die Sauna gehen

....

5 Zeitung lesen

....

Exercise 3

Complete the sentences with bremsen, überholen, Ausfahrt, sperren. Use the correct tense.

1 Die Ampel schaltete auf Gelb und er ....

2 Wir sind gleich da. Bei der nächsten .... musst du von der Autobahn runter.

3 Wegen eines schweren Verkehrsunfalls war die Autobahn . ...

4 Wir sind sehr schnell gefahren, trotzdem .... uns ein Motorradfahrer

....

Vocabulary

Below is a list of vocabulary encountered in this chapter.

Arm, der, -e	*arm*
Aufzug, der, -¨e	*lift / elevator*
Ausfahrt, die, -en	*exit*
Autobahn, die, -en	*motorway/ freeway*
bandagieren	*to bandage*
Bein, das, -e	*leg*
bewegen	*to move*
Boden, der	*ground*
brechen	*to break*
bremsen	*to brake*
entschuldigen (sich)	*to say sorry*
fallen	*to fall*
Gang, der, -¨e	*corridor*
halten	*to stop*
Hausaufgabe, die, -n	*homework*
Kinderstation, die, -en	*children's ward*
langweilig	*boring*
naschen	*to eat sweets*
notfalls	*if necessary*
Pforte, die, -n	*reception*
schalten	*to change to*
sperren	*to close (off)*
stürzen	*to fall over*
überholen	*to overtake*
versprechen	*to promise*
Wandertag, der, -e	*school (hiking) trip*
wehtun	*to hurt*
wenigstens	*at least*
Zebrastreifen, der, -	*pedestrian crossing*
Zimmernummer, die, -n	*room number*
zusammenstoßen	*to collide*

day: 28

Education

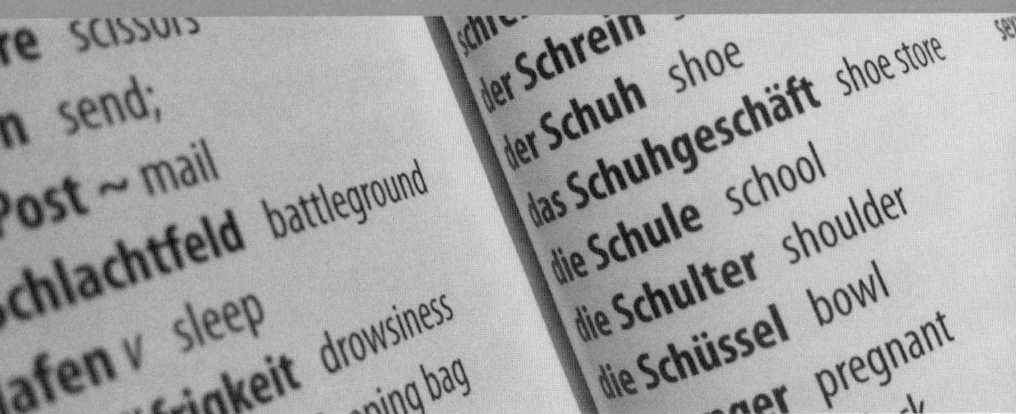

Day 28 discusses education in Germany and exams. It's time to learn your verbs with prepositions and what case they take (don't worry, as you practice and hear German spoken more and more, this will become automatic). You will also learn lots more vocabulary.

THE SCHOOL SYSTEM…

*Children normally start school aged six at the **Grundschule**. After four years, they go on to a **Gymnasium**. After 8 or 9 years, they can do their **Abitur** (final school exams) and go to university. Pupils who do not get the grades to go to a **Gymnasium** attend a **Realschule** and take the **Mittlere Reife** instead of the '**Abi**'. They can then serve an apprenticeship (**Lehre**), or study at a **Fachoberschule**. Those without the option of going to a **Gymnasium** or a **Realschule** go to a secondary school called the **Hauptschule** where the teaching focuses more on practical than academic skills.*

German conversation: Die Abschlussprüfung

Frau Holzer spricht mit den Kursteilnehmern über die Abschlussprüfung.

Frau Holzer:	**Ich möchte mich mit Ihnen über die Abschlussprüfung unterhalten.**
Beatrice:	**Wann findet die Prüfung statt?**
Frau Holzer:	**Die Gruppenprüfung findet am nächsten Mittwoch von 9.00 Uhr bis 12.00 Uhr statt. Für die Einzelprüfungen am Nachmittag hängen wir einen Terminplan aus.**
Maria:	**Können Sie uns bitte noch einmal über die Anforderungen informieren?**
Frau Holzer:	**Natürlich. Die Prüfung besteht aus verschiedenen Prüfungsteilen. Der erste Teil prüft das Leseverstehen. Sie erhalten dazu fünf kurze Texte, zu denen Fragen gestellt werden. Im Prüfungsteil "Schriftlicher Ausdruck" müssen Sie einen Brief mit cirka hundert Wörtern schreiben. Danach machen wir eine Pause. Anschließend gibt es einen Hörverstehenstest und Wortschatzaufgaben. In der Einzelprüfung, die fünfzehn Minuten dauert, stellen wir Ihnen Fragen zu verschiedenen Themen, die wir im Unterricht besprochen haben.**
Yuki:	**Ist das nicht ein bisschen viel?**
Frau Holzer:	**Das glaube ich nicht. Sie haben in den letzten Monaten alle regelmäßig am Kurs teilgenommen. Wir haben alle wichtigen Themen behandelt und uns ausreichend mit der Grammatik beschäftigt. Jetzt können Sie zeigen, was Sie gelernt haben.**
Olivia:	**Müssen wir alle Verben mit Präpositionen kennen?**
Frau Holzer:	**Alle nicht. Sie können sich auf die wichtigsten konzentrieren.**
Yuki:	**Bekommen wir nach der Prüfung ein Zeugnis?**
Frau Holzer:	**Selbstverständlich. Sie brauchen ja einen Nachweis, wenn Sie sich um eine Stelle mit Deutschkenntnissen bewerben wollen. Jetzt habe ich aber noch eine gute Nachricht für Sie: Ich möchte Sie zu unserer Abschlussparty nach der Prüfung ab 19.00 Uhr in der Schule einladen. Vielleicht können wir auf der Terrasse feiern. Das hängt vom Wetter ab. Ich hoffe, Sie kommen alle.**
Klasse:	**Natürlich.**
Yuki:	**Ich freue mich sehr über die Einladung. Aber bis dahin muss ich noch viel lernen.**

English conversation: The final examination

Mrs. Holzer is talking to the course participants about the final examination.

Mrs. Holzer: **I'd like to talk to you about the final exam.**

Beatrice: **When is the exam?**

Mrs. Holzer: **The group exams are on Monday from 9:00 a.m. until 12:00 noon and we'll put up a schedule on the notice board for the one-to-one examinations in the afternoon.**

Maria: **Could you give us some information about the requirements once again please?**

Mrs. Holzer: **Of course. The examination is in several parts. The first part tests reading comprehension. You will be given five short texts followed by questions on the texts. In the section "Written expression" you have to write a letter of about a hundred words. Then there'll be a break. Afterwards there is a listening comprehension test and vocabulary exercises. In the one-to-one examination, which lasts fifteen minutes, we will ask you questions on various topics which we have discussed during the lessons.**

Yuki: **Isn't that rather a lot?**

Mrs. Holzer: **I don't think so. You have all attended the course regularly over the past few months and we have dealt with all the important topics and spent enough time on the grammar. Now you can show what you've learnt.**

Olivia: **Do we have to know all the verbs with prepositions?**

Mrs. Holzer: **Not all of them. You can concentrate on the most important ones.**

Yuki: **Will we be getting a certificate after the exam?**

Mrs. Holzer: **Yes, of course. You will need proof of your knowledge of German when you apply for a job that requires German. But now I've got some good news for you: I'd like to invite you to a party in the school after the exam at 7 p.m. Perhaps we can have the party on the patio. It depends on the weather. I hope you'll all come along.**

Class: **Of course we will.**

Yuki: **I'm very pleased about the invitation. But I've still got a lot to learn before the party.**

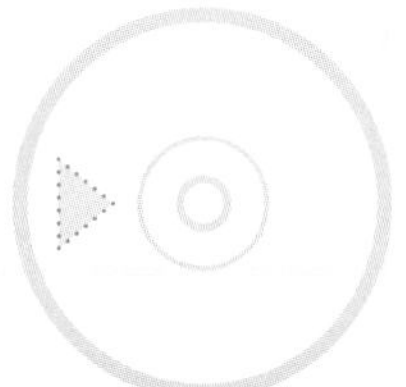

Grammar

Verbs with prepositions

Frau Holzer unterhält sich mit den Kursteilnehmern über die Prüfung.
Mrs. Holzer is talking to the course participants about the examination.
Yuki freut sich über die Einladung.
Yuki is very pleased about the invitation.

There are many verbs which have a specific preposition and take a specific case – usually the dative (D) or the accusative (A).

abhängen von + D	to depend on
sich amüsieren über + A	to be amused at
sich ärgern über + A	to get angry/ annoyed about
aufhören mit + D	to stop it
sich aufregen über + A	to get worked up about
sich bedanken bei + D; **für** + A	to thank for
beginnen mit + D	to start with
berichten über + A	to report on
sich beschäftigen mit + D	to deal with
sich beschränken auf + A	to confine to
bestehen aus + D	to consist of
sich bewerben um + A	to apply for
sich beziehen auf + A	to refer to
bitten um + A	to ask for
brauchen zu + D	to need to
danken für + A	to thank for
denken an + A	to think about
diskutieren über + A	to discuss
einladen zu + D	to invite to
erfahren durch + A	to find out from
sich erinnern an + A	to remember
erzählen von + D	to tell about
fragen nach + D	to ask about
sich freuen über + A	to be pleased about
sich gewöhnen an + A	to get used to
gratulieren zu + D	to congratulate on
sich handeln um + A	to be about
helfen bei + D	to help with
hinweisen auf + A	to refer to
hoffen auf + A	to hope for
informieren über + A	to inform about
sich interessieren für + A	to be interested in
sich konzentrieren auf + A	to concentrate on
sich kümmern um + A	to look after
lachen über + A	to laugh about
nachdenken über + A	to think about
profitieren von + D	to profit from
rechnen mit + D	to reckon with
reden über + A	to talk about
reden von + D	to talk about
schmecken nach + D	to taste of
schreiben an + A	to write to
sich schützen vor + D	to protect o.s. from
sprechen über + A	to speak about
teilnehmen an + D	to take part in
träumen von + D	to dream of
sich unterhalten über + A	to talk about
sich verabreden mit + D	to arrange to meet
verbinden mit + D	to put through to
vergleichen mit + D	to compare to
sich verlassen auf + A	to rely on
sich verlieben in + A	to fall in love with
sich verständigen mit + D	to communicate with
sich verstehen mit + D	to get on (well) with
sich vorbereiten auf + A	to prepare for
warten auf + A	to wait for
sich wenden an + A	to turn to
wissen von + D	to know about

Exercises

Exercise 1

Complete the sentences using the prepositions **um** (2x), **mit** (3x), **über** (2x), **an, aus, nach**.

1 Die Lehrerin informiert die Kursteilnehmer .... den Prüfungstermin.

2 Darf ich .... Ihrem Namen fragen?

3 Die Eltern kümmern sich .... die Kinder.

4 Hast du dich .... deiner Freundin verabredet?

5 Ich muss dich .... Hilfe bitten.

6 Frau Glück versteht sich gut .... Yuki.

7 Ich habe mich .... den Busfahrer geärgert.

8 Bald kann ich mich .... dir auf Deutsch verständigen.

9 Kannst du dich nicht .... diesen Herrn erinnern?

10 Die Abschlussprüfung besteht .... mehreren Teilen.

Exercise 2

Join the halves to make sentences.

1	Wir haben uns über	**a**	mit der Personalabteilung.
2	Vergleichen Sie unsere Reisen	**b**	Tobias verabredet?
3	Wir beziehen uns	**c**	der Übung helfen?
4	Bitte verbinden Sie mich	d	den Deutschen verständigen?
5	Ich warte am Bahnhof	**e**	das deutsche Essen gewöhnt.
6	Wann hat sich Yuki mit	**f**	den Blumenstrauß gefreut.
7	Kannst du mir bei	**g**	den Film amüsiert?
8	Habt ihr euch über	**h**	auf Ihren Brief vom 12. September.
9	Yuki hat sich an	**i**	auf meine Familie.
10	Können Sie sich jetzt mit	**j**	mit den Reisen des Reisebüros Sonnenschein.

1 ..... **2** ..... **3** ..... **4** ..... **5** ..... **6** ..... **7** ..... **8** ..... **9** ..... **10** .....

Vocabulary

Below is a list of vocabulary encountered in this chapter.

abhängen	*to depend on*
Abschlussparty, die, -s	*(end-of-term) party*
Abschlussprüfung, die, -en	*final examination*
Anforderung, die, -en	*requirement*
aufhören	*to stop*
aufregen über (sich)	*get excited about*
aushängen	*to put up on*
behandeln	*to deal with*
berichten	*to report*
beschäftigen mit (sich)	*to deal with*
bestehen aus	*to consist of*
beziehen auf (sich)	*to refer to*
diskutieren	*to discuss*
Einzelprüfung, die, -en	*one-to-one examination*
erfahren	*to find out*
erinnern (sich)	*to remember*
Frage, die, -n	*question*
gewöhnen an (sich)	*to get used to*
Gruppenprüfung, die, -en	*group examination*
handeln um (sich)	*to be about*
aufhinweisen	*to refer to*
hoffen auf	*to hope for*
Hörverstehen, das	*listening comprehension*
informieren	*to inform*
inhaltlich	*text-related*
interessieren für (sich)	*to be interested in*
konzentrieren (sich)	*to concentrate*
kurz	*short*
lachen	*to laugh*
letzte	*last*
nachdenken über	*to think about*
Nachricht, die, -en	*news*
Nachweis, der, -e	*proof*
profitieren	*to profit*
prüfen	*to examine*
Prüfung, die, -en	*examination*
Prüfungsteil, der, -e	*part of the examination*
rechnen	*to reckon*
reden über	*to talk about*
regelmäßig	*regularly*
schützen vor (sich)	*to protect o.s. from*
stellen *in:* **Frage stellen**	*ask*
teilnehmen an	*to take part in*
Terminplan, der, -¨e	*schedule*

Terrasse, die, -n	*patio*
Text, der, -e	*text*
Thema, das, *(pl.)* **Themen**	*topic*
träumen von	*to dream of*
unterhalten über (sich)	*to talk about*
verbinden	*to put through*
vergleichen	*to compare*
verlassen	*to leave*
verlieben in (sich)	*to fall in love with*
verschieden	*different*
verständigen (sich)	*to communicate*
verstehen (sich)	*to get on*
vorbereiten auf (sich)	*to prepare for*
wenden an (sich)	*to turn to*
wichtig	*important*
Wortschatzaufgabe, die, -n	*vocabulary exercise*
Zeugnis, das, -se	*certificate*

day: 29

Surprise!

As you near the end of this course, Day 29 covers subordinate clauses with *weil* (because) and indirect questions using *ob* (whether). You will also be able to put into practice what you have learned and further expand your vocabulary.

CONNECTIONS...

Germany is well connected by train, as you will have already discovered, but it is equally well connected by air. ***Frankfurt am Main*** *is the principal hub for international flights but there are also excellent connections between all the major cities throughout the country.*

German conversation: Eine Überraschung

Heute hatte Yuki ihre Abschlussprüfung. Sie ist müde und kommt nach Hause.
Sie klingelt an der Tür, weil sie ihren Schlüssel vergessen hat.

Yuki: **Entschuldigung, ich habe meinen Schlüssel vergessen.**

Frau Glück: **Das macht nichts. Sie waren heute Morgen sehr in Eile. Wie war die Prüfung?**

Yuki: **Ich hoffe, nicht zu schlecht. Das Leseverständnis war nicht schwierig, weil ich die meisten Wörter kannte. Aber die Wortschatzaufgaben! Ich weiß wirklich nicht, ob ich alle Aufgaben richtig habe. Ich möchte jetzt jedenfalls keine Bücher mehr sehen.**

Frau Glück: **Das glaube ich Ihnen gerne. Aber vielleicht möchten Sie eine Person sehen?**

Yuki: **Eine Person? Wen denn? Ist Tobias da?**

Frau Glück: **Nein. Gehen Sie mal ins Wohnzimmer und schauen Sie, wer dort auf Sie wartet.**

Yuki geht ins Wohnzimmer.

Yuki: **Miki, ich kann es nicht glauben, du bist hier! So eine Überraschung. Wann bist du gekommen?**

Miki: **Heute mit dem Flugzeug, weil du mir doch Geld überwiesen hast. Ich habe einfach einen Tapetenwechsel gebraucht. Immer nur die Familie. Ich musste einfach mal raus.**

Yuki: **Hast du denn schon ein Hotel gebucht?**

Miki: **Nein, aber Frau Glück hat mir schon angeboten, dass ich hier schlafen kann.**

Yuki: **Das ist aber nett. Weißt du was, ich rufe in der Schule an und frage nach, ob du heute Abend an der Abschlussfeier teilnehmen kannst.**

Miki: **Das würde ich gerne machen.**

English conversation: A surprise

Yuki had her final examination today. She is tired and has just come home. She rings the doorbell because she has forgotten her key.

Yuki: **I'm sorry but I've forgotten my key.**

Mrs. Glück: **That doesn't matter. You were in a great hurry this morning. How was the exam?**

Yuki: **I hope that I wasn't too bad. The reading comprehension wasn't difficult because I knew most of the words. But, oh, those vocabulary exercises! I really don't know if I got them all right. At any rate, I don't want to see any more books.**

Mrs. Glück:	I can believe that. But perhaps there is someone you'd like to see?
Yuki:	Someone? Who is it? Is Tobias here?
Mrs. Glück:	No, he isn't. Just go into the living room and see who is waiting for you there.

Yuki goes into the living room.

Yuki:	Miki, I can't believe it, you're here! What a surprise! When did you arrive?
Miki:	Today, by plane. You transferred some money to my account, after all! I needed a change of scene. Just the family all the time. I simply had to get away.
Yuki:	Have you already booked a room in a hotel?
Miki:	No, but Mrs. Glück has already offered to let me sleep here.
Yuki:	That's very kind of her. Do you know what, I'll call the school and ask if you can come to the party this evening.
Miki:	I'd really like that.

Grammar

Subordinate clause with *weil*

main clause	*subordinate clause*
Yuki klingelt an der Tür,	**weil sie ihren Schlüssel vergessen hat.**
Yuki rings the bell	because she has forgotten her key.

The conjunction **weil** is used to give an explanation of something mentioned in the main clause. It answers the question Why? **Warum? Wieso? Weshalb?**

The subordinate clause can come first , in which case the word order is inverted in the main clause.

subordinate clause	*main clause*
Weil du mir Geld überwiesen hast,	**bin ich mit dem Flugzeug gekommen.**
Weil sie ihren Schlüssel vergessen hat,	**klingelt Yuki an der Tür.**
Because she has forgotten her key	Yuki rings the bell.

Indirect questions with *ob*

Darfst du heute Abend an der Abschlussfeier teilnehmen?	Ich frage nach, ob du heute Abend an der Abschlussfeier teilnehmen darfst.
Can you go to the party tonight?	I'll ask whether you can go to the party tonight.
direct question without an interrogative pronoun	*indirect question*

main clause	*subordinate clause*
Ich weiß nicht,	ob ich alle Aufgaben richtig habe.

I don't know whether I got all the exercises right.

The conjunction ob is used in indirect interrogative clauses without an interrogative pronoun. In the subordinate clause, the verb, as in all subordinate clauses, is found at the end of the sentence.

Exercises

Exercise 1

Join these sentences using a subordinate clause with weil.

Yuki geht ins Bett. Sie ist müde.

Yuki geht ins Bett, weil sie müde ist.

1 Stefan liegt im Krankenhaus. Er hatte einen Unfall.

....

2 Ich komme zu spät. Ich habe den Bus Verpasst.

....

3 Yuki geht zur Post. Sie will Briefmarken kaufen.

....

4 Mir tun die Augen weh. Ich habe zu lange gelesen.

....

5 Ich bin nass. Ich hatte keinen Regenschirm.

....

Exercise 2

Make indirect questions from direct questions beginning with Weißt du, ….

Kommt Miki zur Abschlussfeier? Weißt du, ob Miki zur Abschlußfeier kommt?

1 Findet morgen die Prüfung statt?

....

2 Fährt dieser Zug nach Berlin?

....

3 Beginnt das Konzert um 19.30 Uhr?

....

4 Gibt es hier eine Toilette?

....

Exercise 3

Complete the sentences using ob or weil.

1 Sie ist mit dem Auto gefahren, ... es geregnet hat.

2 Yuki möchte wissen, ... Tobias heute Abend kommt.

3 Weißt du, ... es morgen Abend ein Fußballspiel im Fernsehen gibt?

4 Ich habe das Telefon nicht gehört, ... ich im Bad war.

Exercise 4

Complete the sentences using: Bordkarte **(boarding pass),** Fenster **(window),** landen **(land),** Flug **(flight),** alle elektronischen Geräte **(all electronic devices),** Gepäck **(luggage),** Gang **(aisle),** sich anschnallen **(fasten seatbelts),** Einsteigen **(boarding).**

1 Wir .... in wenigen Minuten auf dem Flughafen Köln/Bonn. Wir bitten Sie, ... auszuschalten. Bitte begeben Sie sich auf Ihren Sitzplatz zurück und .... Sie ....

2 Begeben Sie sich bitte sofort zum Check-in und geben Sie Ihr .... auf.

3 Kapitän Müller und seine Besatzung wünschen Ihnen einen angenehmen ....

4 Möchten Sie einen Platz am? .... oder am...?

5 Hier ist Ihre .... Das .... beginnt um 13.15 Uhr am Ausgang A8.

Vocabulary

Below is a list of vocabulary encountered in this chapter.

alle angenehm	*all pleasant*
anschnallen	*to fasten your seatbelt*
Aufgabe, die, -n	*exercise*
ausschalten	*to switch off*
begeben (sich)	*to proceed to*
bestehen	*to pass (an exam)*
Besatzung, die	*crew*
Bordkarte, die, -n	*boarding pass*
Check-in, der	*check-in counter*
Eile, die	*hurry*
einsteigen	*to board*
elektronisch	*electronic*
Gang, der, -¨e	*aisle*
Gepäck, das	*luggage*
jedenfalls	*at any rate*
Kapitän, der, -e	*captain*
ob	*whether*
rausmüssen	*to have to get away*
schwierig	*difficult*
Tapetenwechsel, der, -	*change of scene*
Toilette, die, -n	*toilet*
weil	*because*
Weshalb?	*Why?*

day: 30

Goodbye

Congratulations, you've reached the final chapter of this course. Day 30 marks the end of your trip to Germany. By now, you should be quite confident understanding, speaking, and writing German in a variety of situations. You should have acquired a comprehensive vocabulary, and be comfortable with German grammar. Well done!

SAYING GOODBYE...

Auf Wiedersehen! *is the normal way of saying goodbye, and you usually shake hands. It is also common for friends and relatives to give each other a hug or a kiss on the cheek when saying goodbye.* ***Ciao! (Tschau!)*** *is also used to say bye, in addition to the common informal* ***Tschüs!***

German conversation: Die Heimreise

Der letzte Tag von Yukis und Mikis Deutschlandaufenthalt ist gekommen. Sie haben ihre Koffer gepackt und sind ein bisschen traurig. Frau Glück und Tobias bringen die beiden zum Flughafen.

Frau Glück:	**Haben Sie auch nichts vergessen, Yuki?**
Yuki:	**Nein, ich denke, ich habe alles eingepackt. Aber mein Koffer ist so schwer. Diese vielen Souvenirs. Der Bierkrug ist am schwersten. Aber den musste ich einfach mitnehmen.**
Tobias:	**Wo hast du denn dein Abschlusszeugnis?**
Yuki:	**Hier im Handgepäck. Das Zeugnis behalte ich bei mir, damit ich es meinen Freunden gleich zeigen kann. Ich bin so froh, dass ich die Prüfung so gut bestanden habe.**
Tobias:	**Ich bin wirklich erstaunt, was du in so kurzer Zeit alles gelernt hast.**
Yuki:	**Ja, als ich vor sechs Monaten nach Deutschland kam, konnte ich kaum ein Wort Deutsch sprechen.**
Tobias:	**Du musst unbedingt wiederkommen. Vielleicht im nächsten Sommer?**
Yuki:	**Wenn ich es mir leisten kann, komme ich gern wieder.**
Frau Glück:	**Yuki, Ihr Flug nach Sapporo ist soeben aufgerufen worden. Ich glaube, Sie müssen zur Passkontrolle.**
Yuki:	**Wo ist Miki?**
Frau Glück:	**Gerade war sie noch da.**
Tobias:	**Sie steht da drüben am Kiosk. Jetzt kommt sie.**
Miki:	**Ich wollte nur noch schnell einen Bildband über München kaufen, damit meine Familie sehen kann, wo ich war.**
Frau Glück:	**Wir müssen zur Passkontrolle.**

An der Passkontrolle.

Tobias:	**Es tut mir wirklich leid, dass du zurückfliegen musst, Yuki.**
Yuki:	**Mir auch, Tobias.**
Tobias:	**Ich habe noch ein kleines Abschiedsgeschenk für dich.**
Yuki:	**Was ist denn das?**
Tobias:	**Ein Herzerl fürs Herzerl.**
Yuki:	**Herzlichen Dank. Das ist lieb von dir!**

Tobias und Yuki umarmen sich. Nun sind auch Frau Glück und Miki an der Passkontrolle.

Yuki:	**Vielen Dank für alles, was Sie für mich getan haben, Frau Glück. Es hat mir sehr gut bei Ihnen gefallen.**
Frau Glück:	**Sie waren mir eine angenehme Mitbewohnerin. Ich wünsche Ihnen einen guten Rückflug, Yuki, und Ihnen einen guten Flug nach Amerika, Miki. Grüßen Sie Ihre Familie von mir.**
Miki:	**Vielen Dank noch mal, dass ich bei Ihnen wohnen durfte.**
Yuki und Miki:	**Auf Wiedersehen!**

English conversation: Going back home

It's the last day of Yuki's and Miki's stay in Germany. They have packed their suitcases and are a little sad. Mrs. Glück and Tobias are taking them to the airport.

Mrs. Glück:	**Are you sure you haven't forgotten anything, Yuki?**
Yuki:	**Yes, I think I've packed everything. But my case is so heavy. All these souvenirs. The beer mug is the heaviest. But I really had to take it with me.**
Tobias:	**Where have you got your examination certificate?**
Yuki:	**Here in my hand luggage. I'll carry it with me, so that I can show it to my friends as soon as I arrive. I'm so glad that I did so well on the exam.**
Tobias:	**I'm quite astonished that you've learnt so much in such a short time.**
Yuki:	**Yes. When I came to Germany six months ago, I could hardly speak a word of German.**
Tobias:	**You really must come back again. Perhaps next summer?**
Yuki:	**If I can afford it, I'd love to come back.**
Mrs. Glück:	**Yuki, they've just called out the flight to Sapporo. I think you have to go to passport control.**
Yuki:	**Where's Miki?**
Mrs. Glück:	**She was here a moment ago.**
Tobias:	**There she is, over there at the kiosk. She's coming now.**
Miki:	**I just wanted to buy an illustrated book about Munich so that I can show my family where I have been.**
Mrs. Glück:	**We've got to go to passport control.**

At passport control.

Tobias:	**I'm so sorry that you have to fly back home, Yuki.**
Yuki:	**So am I, Tobias.**
Tobias:	**I've got a little farewell present for you.**
Yuki:	**What is it?**
Tobias:	**A little heart for a sweetheart.**
Yuki:	**Thank you so much. That's very sweet of you!**

Tobias and Yuki give each other a hug. Mrs. Glück and Miki are now also at passport control.

Yuki:	**Thank you so much for everything you have done for me, Mrs. Glück. I did enjoy staying with you.**
Mrs. Glück:	**You were a very pleasant flat mate/roommate. I hope you have a pleasant flight back, Yuki. And Miki, I hope you have a pleasant flight to the States, too. Give your family my kindest regards.**
Miki:	**Thank you once again for letting me stay with you.**
Yuki and Miki:	**Goodbye!**

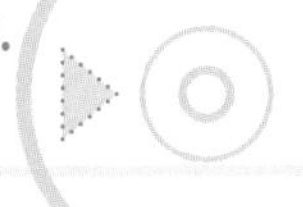

Grammar

Subordinate clauses with *als*

Ich war nicht zu Hause, als der Unfall passierte.
I wasn't at home when the accident happened.
Als der Unfall passierte, war ich nicht zu Hause.
When the accident happened, I was not at home.

Als is used for a unique event or a unique situation in the past. **Als** introduces a subordinate clause in the past. The activities or situations described in both the main and subordinate clauses happen at the same time. Either the main or the subordinate clause can come first. If the main clause comes second, the verb and subject are inverted in the main clause.

Subordinate clauses with *damit*

Das Zeugnis behalte ich bei mir, damit ich es meinen Freunden gleich zeigen kann.
I'll carry the certificate with me so that I can show it to my friends immediately.

Subordinate clauses with **damit** describe a purpose, an objective, an aim or an intention.

Exercises

Exercise 1

Complete the following sentences, putting the verbs in brackets into the preterite.

1 Als es an der Tür .... , ... Frau Glück die Tür. (klingeln/öffnen)

2 Ich .... am Flughafen, als das Flugzeug .... (sein/landen)

3 Wo .... ihr, als es .... ? (sein/regnen)

4 Als der Fußgänger die Straße .... , ... es zu einem Unfall. (überqueren/kommen)

Exercise 2

Complete the sentences using modal verbs. Begin all the sentences with "Als ich ein Kind war".

Als ich ein Kind war, musste ich um 19.00 Uhr ins Bett gehen. (müssen)

1 ich nicht immer fernsehen. (dürfen)

....

2 ich nie mit meinem Bruder spielen. (wollen)

....

3 ich Karotten essen. (müssen)

....

4 ich nicht in den Kindergarten gehen. (wollen)

....

Exercise 3

Make sentences by joining the two clauses with damit.

Ich gehe heute Abend früh ins Bett.

Ich will morgen ausgeschlafen sein.

Ich gehe heute Abend früh ins Bett, damit ich morgen ausgeschlafen bin.

1 Ich schicke dir eine E-Mail. Es geht schneller.

....

2 Ich mache die Tür zu. Du kannst dich auf deine Arbeit konzentrieren.

....

3 Yuki lernt Deutsch. Sie kann sich um eine interessante Stelle bewerben.

....

4 Maria muss früh aufstehen. Sie will den Zug nicht verpassen.

....

Exercise 4

Complete the sentences using the following words: Abflug **(departure/take-off),** Visum **(visa),** Abreise **(departure),** stornieren **(cancel),** kontrollieren **(check),** abholen **(collect),** Einreise **(entry),** starten **(take off),** Grenze **(frontier).**

1 Zwei Tage vor der .... kann ich die Tickets im Reisebüro ....

2 Da sie krank war, musste sie ihren Flug ....

3 An der Grenze wurde ich nicht ....

4 Das Flugzeug .... um 9.45 Uhr. Wir müssen zwei Stunden vor dem .... am Flughafen sein.

5 Vor einer Reise nach Vietnam muss man ein .... beantragen.

6 Wir sind mit dem Auto gefahren. Bei der .... nach Frankreich mussten wir zwei Stunden an der .... warten.

Vocabulary

Below is a list of vocabulary encountered in this chapter.

Abflug, der, -¨e	*take-off / departure*
Abreise, die, -n	*departure*
Abschiedsgeschenk, das, -e	*farewell present*
Abschlusszeugnis, das, -se	*examination certificate*
aufrufen	*to call out*
bestehen	*to pass (an exam)*
Bierkrug, der, -¨e	*beer mug*
Bildband, der, -¨e	*illustrated book*
drüben	*over there*
Einreise, die, -n	*entry*
erstaunt sein	*to be astonished*
Flug, der, -¨e	*flight*
Flughafen, der, -¨	*airport*
Grenze, die, -n	*frontier, border*
Handgepäck, das	*hand luggage*
Heimreise, die, -n	*journey home*
Herzerl, das	*little heart, sweetheart*
kontrollieren	*to check*
leisten (sich)	*to afford*
Mitbewohner, der *(Pl)*	*flat mate/ roommate*
mitnehmen	*to take along*
packen	*to pack*
Passkontrolle, die, -n	*passport control*
rechtzeitig	*in time*
Rückflug, der, -¨e	*return flight*
soeben	*just now*
Souvenir, das, -s	*souvenir*
starten	*to take off*
stornieren	*to cancel*
umarmen (sich)	*to hug one another*
unbedingt	*really*
Visum, das, *(Pl)* **Visa**	*visa*
vorbereiten (sich)	*to get ready*
zurückfliegen	*to fly back*

Key to exercises

Day 1

Exercise 1: 1. Sie 2. Du 3. Sie/Wir 4. Er 5. Sie
Exercise 2: 1. lernt 2. wohnen 3. kommt 4. trinkt 5. lerne
Exercise 3: 1. bist 2. seid 3. sind 4. sind
Exercise 4: 1. hat/haben 2. haben 3. habe 4. hat
Exercise 5: 1. b 2. d 3. c 4. a

Day 2

Exercise 1: 1. Der 2. Das 3. Das 4. Das 5. Der
Exercise 2: 1. eine Frau. Die 2. ein Hund. Der 3. eine Katze. Die
Exercise 3: 1. einen Tee und ein Wasser 2. einen Kaffee 3. eine Cola 4. einen Hund 5. eine Katze 6. ein Auto
Exercise 4: 1. Wer 2. Was 3. Wen 4. Was 5. Wen
Exercise 5: 1. Was möchtest du trinken? 2. Wir dürfen hier nicht parken. 3. Yuki kann im Wohnzimmer fernsehen. 4. Ihr könnt im Bad duschen. 5. Du darfst hier rauchen.

Day 3

Exercise 1: 1. Was möchten Sie trinken? 2. Wohin wollen Sie fahren? 3. Wohin fahren Sie? 4. Was nehmen Sie?
Exercise 2: 1. Das Kind will Schokolade. 2. Wir wollen in die Stadt fahren. 3. Yuki will eine Fahrkarte kaufen. 4. Frau Glück und Yuki wollen Kaffee trinken. 5. Du willst Deutsch lernen.
Exercise 3: 1. Yuki kann Deutsch sprechen. 2. Yuki will in die Stadt fahren. 3. Sie muss eine Fahrkarte kaufen. 4. Sie muss die Fahrkarte stempeln.
Exercise 4: 1. Darf/kann/soll ich Ihnen das Zimmer zeigen? 2. Du kannst/darfst die Schokolade essen. 3. Yuki muss zwei Streifen stempeln. 4. Ihr sollt nicht streiten.
Exercise 5: 1. Hier kann/darf/soll man parken. 2. Hier darf man nicht parken. 3. Hier muss man rechts abbiegen. 4. Hier darf man nicht rauchen. 5. Hier kann man Kaffee trinken.
Exercise 6: 1. Ich gehe nicht in die Stadt. 2. Wir fahren nicht nach Paris. 3. Ich möchte nicht fernsehen. 4. Die U-Bahn fährt nicht ins Zentrum.
Exercise 7: 1. Was lernt Yuki? 2. Wo kann Yuki eine Fahrkarte kaufen? 3. Wo ist die Haltestelle? 4. Wohin will Yuki fahren? 5. Wo wohnt Yuki? 6. Wie viele Streifen muss Yuki stempeln? 7. Wohin fährt die U-Bahn?
Exercise 8: 1. in/durch 2. durch/in 3. ohne 4. bis 5. für 6. um 7. gegen

Day 4

Exercise 1: 1. das Stadtzentrum 2. der Bücherschrank 3. die Briefmarke 4. der Briefumschlag 5. das Abendessen
Exercise 2: 1. 37 2. 42 3. 99 4. 867 10. 1200
Exercise 3: 1. Viertel nach neun/neun Uhr fünfzehn 2. halb eins/zwölf Uhr dreißig 3. Viertel vor fünf/vier Uhr

fünfundvierzig 4. zehn nach acht/acht Uhr zehn 5. fünf vor halb sieben/sechs Uhr fünfundzwanzig
Exercise 4: 1. Morgens/Samstags 2. Mittags 3. abends 4. nachts 5. Samstags
Exercise 5: 1. Amerikanerin 2. Franzose 3. Polin 4. Türke
Exercise 6: 1. Agne kommt aus Schweden und fährt in die USA. 2. Carlos kommt aus Spanien und fährt nach Polen. 3. John kommt aus England und fährt in die Schweiz. 4. David kommt aus Israel und fährt nach Portugal.
Exercise 7: 1. Koffer 2. Bücher 3. Streifenkarten 4. Äpfel 5. Städte

Day 5

Exercise 1: 1. Ich möchte diesen Käse. Was kostet dieser Käse? 2. Ich möchte diese Wurst. Was kostet diese Wurst? 3. Ich möchte diese Milch. Was kostet diese Milch? 4. Ich möchte dieses Bier.
Was kostet dieses Bier? 5. Ich möchte diesen Honig. Was kostet dieser Honig?
Exercise 2: 1. Ich möchte ihn. 2. Wohin geht sie? 3. Yuki trifft ihn. 4. Yuki trifft sie. 5. Wo wohnt er?
Exercise 3: 1. vier Euro achtundsechzig Cent 2. achtzehn Euro siebzehn Cent 3. einhundertsiebenundzwanzig Euro fünfzehn Cent 4. eintausenddreihundertfünfundvierzig Euro elf Cent 5. zehntausendsechshundertneunundneunzig Euro dreißig Cent
6. zweihundertsechzehntausendzweihundertzweiundzwanzig Euro neunundneunzig Cent
Exercise 4: 1. b/c – 2. a – 3. a/b
Exercise 5: 1. Poskarte 2. Telefon 3. Briefträger 4. Paket 5. Briefkasten 6. Briefmarke 7. Adresse 8. Briefumschlag

Day 6

Exercise 1: 1. Das Zimmer ist hell, hübsch, groß, günstig. 2. Das Kaufhaus ist groß, hell, hübsch, hell, groß, schwer, günstig. 3. Der Mantel ist hübsch. 4. Der Brief ist schwer/groß.
Exercise 2: 1. ein neues Buch 2. ein günstiges Fahrrad 3. eine weiße Bluse 4. eine gute Idee 5. eine neue Zeitung
Exercise 3: Women's Clothing 1. das Hemd 2. die Krawatte 3. der Regenschirm 4. die Hose 5. die Schuhe 6. das Jackett
Men's clothing 1. das Hemd 2. die Krawatte 3. der Regenschirm 4. die Hose 5. die Schuhe 6. das Jackett
Exercise 4: 1. c 2. d 3. e 4. a 5. b

Day 7

Exercise 1: 1. Yuki geht heute Abend aus. 2. Sie müssen diesen Antrag ausfüllen./ Diesen Antrag müssen Sie ausfüllen. 3. Was ziehe ich heute Abend an? 4. Was darf ich Ihnen anbieten?
5. Ich nehme den Regenschirm mit. 6. Yuki nimmt die Einladung an.
Exercise 2: 1. sich 2. mich 3. uns 4. sich 5. sich
Exercise 3: 1. die Beratung 2. die Einzahlung 3. die Sitzung 4. die Wohnung

Day 8

Exercise 1: 1. noch; gerne 2. mitten 3. hinein; heraus 4. auch, gerne, heute, noch, hier. 5. Heute; Danach 6. Dort oben/ hier 7. zweimal; hier; da/hier/dort
Exercise 2: 1. Setzen Sie sich! Setzt euch! Setz dich! 2. Kommen Sie her! Kommt her! Komm her! 3. Kommen Sie herein! Kommt herein! Komm herein!
Exercise 3: 1. z.B. Äpfel, Orangen, Bananen, Kiwis, Aprikosen 2. Lammfleisch, Rindfleisch, Kalbfleisch, Geflügel 3. Vollkornbrot, Weißbrot, Pumpernickel

Exercise 4: 1. die Köchin 2. die Französin 3. die Lehrerin 4. das Mädchen 5. die Dame
Exercise 5: 1. Gute Nacht! 2. Herbst 3. Winter 4. links 5. unten 6. der Abend 7. heraus 8. Pech

Day 9

Exercise 1: 1. dem 2. den 3. der 4. dem 5. den 6. den 7. dem
Exercise 2: 1. der Freundin 2. den Kindern 3. dem Gastgeber 4. den Touristen 5. den Gästen 6. dem Mann 7. den Kindern
Exercise 3: 1. mit den Kollegen 2. bei Frau Glück 3. aus den USA 4. seit einem Monat 5. Nach dem Abendessen 6. gegenüber dem Rathaus 7. mit der U-Bahn 8. nach dem Konzert
Exercise 4: 1. Die Kinder spielen vor dem Haus. 2. Wir zahlen den Hut an der Sammelkasse. 3. Wir kaufen ein Kleid im Kaufhaus. 4. Die Haltestelle ist neben der Straße.

Day 10

Exercise 1: 1. ihre 2. ihr 3. ihr 4. ihr 5. sein 6. sein 7. seine 8. ihre
Exercise 2: 1. Ich suche meinen Pass. 2. Er sucht seine Fahrkarte. 3. Wir suchen unser Klassenzimmer. 4. Sie sucht ihre Brille. 5. Ich suche meinen Schlüssel.
Exercise 3: 1. Ihre/ihrer 2. ihrem 3. meinen 4. meinem 5. meiner
Exercise 4: 1. mir 2. dir; mir 3. ihm 4. uns 5. uns; euch

Day 11

Exercise 1: 1. Yuki kennt Tobias seit drei Wochen. 2. Ich bin seit fünf Monaten in Deutschland. 3. Ich arbeite seit drei Stunden am Computer. 4. Die Kinder spielen seit 30 Minuten Fußball. 5. Ich lese das Buch seit fünf Tagen.
Exercise 2: 1. verdienen 2. bewirbt sich 3. die Stellenangebote 4. Englischkenntnisse 5. buchstabiert 6. Computer 7. stellt sich im Reisebüro vor
Exercise 3: 1. c – 2. e – 3. d – 4. a – 5. b
Exercise 4: 1. Ärztin 2. Sekretärin 3. Schreiner 4. Mechaniker 5. Lehrerin 6. Bauer

Day 12

Exercise 1: 1. Ich muss mich beeilen, ich möchte nämlich bald zu Hause sein. 2. Wie geht es dir? Mir geht es nämlich nicht gut. 3. Wann kommen Sie? Wir wollen nämlich weggehen. 4. Ich habe leider heute Abend keine Zeit. Ich gehe nämlich ins Konzert.
Exercise 2: 1. Guten Tag! Mein Name ist Natsumura. Ich möchte mich bei Ihnen vorstellen. 2. Guten Tag! Mein Name ist Würtz. Bitte nehmen Sie Platz! Möchten Sie etwas zu trinken? 3. Wie gut sprechen Sie Englisch und Deutsch? 4. Welche Computerprogramme können Sie anwenden? 5. Ich kann zwei Computerprogramme, nämlich Word und Excel. 6. Wie viele Stunden muss ich am Abend arbeiten? 7. Wie viel verdiene ich an einem Abend? 8. Wir zahlen 10 Euro die Stunde.
Exercise 3: 1. c 2. c 3. a

Day 13

Exercise 1: 1. bin 2. hast 3. seid 4. haben 5. haben 6. bist 7. habe 8. habt

Exercise 2: 1. Um 8.30 Uhr bin ich in die Stadt gefahren. 2. Danach habe ich den Sprachunterricht besucht. 3. Um 12.00 Uhr habe ich Mittagspause gemacht. 4. Um 13.00 Uhr bin ich zurück zur Schule gekommen. 5. Ab 15.00 Uhr habe ich in der Bibliothek Zeitung gelesen. 6. Danach habe ich meine Freundinnen abgeholt. 7. Anschließend haben wir Kuchen gegessen und Kaffee getrunken. 8. Um 18.00 Uhr haben mich meine Freundinnen nach Hause gebracht. 9. Am Abend habe ich Deutsch gelernt. 10. Nachts habe ich gut geschlafen.
Exercise 3: 1. Haben Sie Geld umgetauscht? 2. Sind Sie nach Frankfurt geflogen? 3. Sind Sie U-Bahn gefahren? 4. Sind Sie ins Konzert gegangen? 5. Haben Sie Wiener Schnitzel gegessen?
Exercise 4: 1. gefahren, geflogen, gegeben, gegangen, hingefahren, gekommen, gelaufen, gelesen 2. abgesagt, gebracht, eingekauft, gekauft, gemacht, gesucht, gewusst, gezahlt 3. anprobiert, bedient, besucht, erledigt, eröffnet, versucht
Exercise 5: 1. Ich habe die Gebhardts gestern besucht. 2. Ich bin vor zwei Tagen nach Hamburg geflogen. 3. Ich habe um 7.00 Uhr gefrühstückt. 4. Yuki hat heute Morgen Tobias angerufen. 5. Ich habe am Montag Geld umgetauscht.

Day 14

Exercise 1: 1. Sonntags gehen die Freundinnen spazieren. 2. Leider ist Tobias nicht zu Hause. 3. Heute lädt Yuki Maria und Beatrice ins Café ein. 4. Gestern haben wir Kuchen gegessen. 5. Gerne nehmen wir eure Einladung an.
Exercise 2: 1. gewonnen, gegessen, getrunken 2. gehabt, geschmeckt, gekauft, gewählt, gefrühstückt 3. probiert, studiert
Exercise 3: 1. gegessen, getrunken 2. bestellt 3. geschmeckt 4. gefunden 5. gewesen
Exercise 4: 1. Wir möchten bestellen (bitte). 2. Guten Tag! Möchten Sie bestellen? or Haben Sie schon gewählt? 3. (Entschuldigung) Wir möchten bitte bezahlen. 4. Was haben Sie gehabt? or Alles zusammen?

Day 15

Exercise 1: 1. Hans ist fleißig, Tobias ist fleißiger, und Franz ist am fleißigsten. 2. Das Rathaus ist hoch, der Olympiaturm ist höher, und die Alpen sind am höchsten. 3. Das Fahrrad ist schnell, die U-Bahn ist schneller, und das Flugzeug ist am schnellsten.
Exercise 2: 1. viel, mehr, am meisten 2. klein, kleiner, am kleinsten 3. groß, größer, am größten 4. gut, besser, am besten 5. teuer, teurer, am teuersten
Exercise 3: 1. Äpfel sind größer als Kirschen. 2. Roggenbrot ist dunkler als Weißbrot. 3. Das rote Kleid ist schöner als das weiße Kleid. 4. Die schwarze Schuhe sind schicker als die grüne Schuhe.
Exercise 4: 1. Wir freuen uns, dass du uns zum Geburtstag einlädst. 2. Ich hoffe, dass wir am Wochenende die Alpen sehen. 3. Frau Glück meint, dass Yuki eine ruhige Mitbewohnerin ist. 4. Frau Gebhardt hofft, dass ihr Mann Wein gekauft hat. 5. Tobias geht davon aus, dass er einen neuen Job bekommt.

Day 16

Exercise 1: 1. Wo ist die Wärmflasche? Ich finde sie nicht. 2. Haben Sie einen Termin? Nein, ich habe keinen Termin. 3. Haben Sie Husten? Nein, ich habe keinen Husten. 4. Ich habe die Apotheke nicht gleich gefunden. 5. Frau Glück hat keine Zahnschmerzen.
Exercise 2: 1. d 2. a 3. b 4. e 5. c
Exercise 3: 1. Tobias spricht nicht nur Deutsch, sondern auch Englisch. 2. Frau Glück kauft nicht nur Obst, sondern auch Gemüse. 3. Der Bäcker backt nicht nur Brot, sondern auch Brötchen. 4. Wir essen nicht nur Kuchen, sondern trinken auch Kaffee. 5. Du liest nicht nur Bücher, sondern hörst auch Konzerte.
Exercise 4: Eine Maus geht in der Stadt spazieren. Sie heißt Mona.

Sie hat seit Tagen nichts gegessen und nur Wasser getrunken. Sie ist hungrig und traurig. Sie sieht nicht gut aus. Da trifft sie eine Katze. Sie heißt Lisa. Sie hat gegessen. Sie ist satt und glücklich.
Die Katze sagt zur Maus: "Was ist los mit dir, Mona? Du siehst nicht gut aus." Die Maus antwortet: "Ich habe seit Tagen nichts gegessen und nichts getrunken. Ich habe keine Wohnung, keine Kleider, keine Freunde und kein Geld. Ich bin unglücklich."
Lisa sagt zu Mona: "Komm doch mit zu mir. Ich lade dich ein.
Die Maus kann das nicht glauben. Sie fragt vorsichtig: "Darf ich wirklich zu dir kommen?" "Warum glaubst du mir nicht?", fragt die Katze. "Noch nie ist eine Katze so freundlich zu mir gewesen", antwortet die Maus. Katzen und Mäuse können nie und nimmer Freundinnen werden." "Wir probieren es einfach", antwortet die Katze. Dann hat sie die Maus mit nach Hause genommen. Sie hat ihr zu essen und zu trinken gegeben, sie hat ihre Freundinnen kennengelernt und sie hat bei ihr gewohnt.
Nach einigen Wochen sagt die Maus zur Katze: "Du hast mir nicht nur zu essen und zu trinken gegeben, sondern mir auch Kleider und deine Wohnung gegeben. Was kann ich für dich tun? Ich möchte dir etwas schenken."
"Schenk mir einfach dein Herz", antwortete die Katze. Seitdem heißen sie Mona-Lisa.

Day 17

Exercise 1: 1. Die Hose ist so teuer wie die Jacke. 2. Frau Gebhardt ist so alt wie Frau Glück. 3. Nelken sind so schön wie Rosen. 4. Vollkornbrot ist so gesund wie Pumpernickel.
Exercise 2: 1. d 2. c 3. a 4. b
Exercise 3: 1. a b c d e 2. a c f
Exercise 4: 1. die Krankenversicherung 2. das Versicherungskärtchen 3. die Kopfschmerzen 4. die Sprechstundenhilfe 5. das Geburtstagsgeschenk 6. die Brausetabletten 7. das Krankenhaus 8. die Hausärztin

Day 18

Exercise 1: 1. c 2. g 3. f 4. h 5. a 6. e 7. b 8. d
Exercise 2: 1. Wenn ich die U-Bahn verpasst habe, nehme ich den Bus. 2. Wenn der Bäcker kein Brot mehr hat, kaufe ich Brötchen. 3. Wenn mein Magen übersäuert ist, esse ich nichts, sondern trinke nur Tee. 4. Wenn ich kein Geld mehr habe, hole ich Geld am Automaten. 5. Wenn mein Hausarzt keine Sprechstunde hat, suche ich einen anderen Arzt.
Exercise 3: 1. Yuki fährt mit dem Zug, und zwar mit dem ICE. 2. Sie geht gern einkaufen, und zwar am Abend. 3. Tobias isst gern Käse, und zwar Emmentaler. 4. Frau Glück hört gern Musik, und zwar Mozart.

Day 19

Exercise 1: 1. Yuki arbeitet abends, um Geld zu verdienen. 2. Sie geht abends ins Konzert, um die Bamberger Symphoniker zu hören. 3. Sie fährt mit dem ICE, um schneller in Bamberg zu sein. 4. Sie geht zu Fuß, um die Stadt kennenzulernen.
Exercise 2: 1. denen 2. Das 3. Der 4. Denen
Exercise 3: 1. d 2. e 3. f 4. c 5. g 6. b 7. h 8. a

Day 20

Exercise 1: 1. stehen 2. stellt 3. hängt 4. gelegt 5. liegen 6. setzt
Exercise 2: 1. Ich habe an der Bushaltestelle auf dich gewartet. 2. Bist du in der Küche? 3. Kannst du den Blumenstrauß auf das Fensterbrett stellen? 4. Die Kinder gehen in den Kindergarten. 5. Tobias setzt sich neben

Yuki und Frau Glück.
Exercise 3: 1. Ja, auf meinem Schreibtisch, oben rechts, liegen welche. 2. Ja, da vorne steht einer. 3. Auf dem Tisch liegen auch noch welche. 4. Möchtest du auch einen?

Day 21

Exercise 1: 1. das Schwarzbrot 2. das Schlafzimmer 3. die Sprechstunde 4. das Grünglas
Exercise 2: 1. Das Joggen / Das Wandern im Wald ist gesund. 2. Das Zahlen mit der Kreditkarte geht ganz einfach. 3. Beim Wandern kann man nette Leute kennenlernen. 4. Das Wohnen in einer Großstadt ist oft teuer.
Exercise 3: 1. Ich würde am liebsten in die Disko gehen. 2. Ich würde am liebsten einen Kuchen backen. 3. Ich würde am liebsten die Zeitung lesen. 4. Ich würde am liebsten ins Schwimmbad gehen.
Exercise 4: 1. Hast du dich schon entschieden, wohin du fahren möchtest? 2. Sie erkundigt sich, wann der Zug fährt. 3. Die Deutschen haben sich daran gewöhnt, Müll zu sortieren. 4. Wir treffen uns um 6.00 Uhr am Bahnhof. 5. Kennen Sie sich in der Altstadt aus?

Day 22

Exercise 1:
Frau Dietl kommt ins Büro.

Frau Dietl	Hat jemand für mich angerufen?
Herr Wagner	Ja. Herr Schmölder bittet um Rückruf.
Frau Dietl	Hat er seine Nummer hinterlassen?
Herr Wagner	Nein.
Frau Dietl	Ich glaube, ich habe seine Nummer.
Herr Wagner	Sie haben auch ein Fax erhalten. Ich habe es auf Ihren Schreibtisch gelegt.
Frau Dietl	Haben Sie die E-Mail nach Amerika geschickt?
Herr Wagner	Ja. Sie ist schon angekommen.
Frau Dietl	Bitte schalten Sie den Anrufbeantworter ein, bevor Sie gehen.

Exercise 2: 1. Wir spielen entweder Tennis oder wir gehen in die Disko. 2. Wir gehen entweder ins Theater oder ins Kino. 3. Wir fahren entweder nach München oder nach Berlin. 4. Wir gehen entweder ins Restaurant oder wir kochen zu Hause.
Exercise 3: 1. Das Kind packt das große Geschenk als erstes aus. 2. Yuki tauscht auf der Post Geld um. 3. Yuki gibt den Brief an ihre Schwester auf der Hauptpost auf. 4. Ich gebe den Mantel an der Garderobe ab. 5. Frau Dietl nimmt das Telefonat an und leitet es weiter. 6. Yuki schaut nach, ob die Reiseunterlagen fertig sind. 7. Herr Wagner schaltet den Anrufbeantworter ein. 8. Der Lieferant kommt durch die Hintertür herein.

Day 23

Exercise 1: 1. Die Tante des Bräutigams ist auch gekommen. 2. Das Kleid der Braut ist am schönsten. 3. Die Geschenke der Hochzeitsgäste sind fantastisch. 4. Das Auto des Brautpaar(e)s ist mit Blumen geschmückt. 5. Die Geschenke der Freundinnen haben mir am besten gefallen.
Exercise 2: 1. Das ist Stephanies Tochter. 2. Frau Glücks Fahrrad steht im Keller. 3. Was macht Gabis Neffe? 4. Wo sind Hannas und Lenas Eltern?
Exercise 3: Zur Familienfeier der Familie Glück sind alle Verwandten gekommen. "Wer ist das kleine Mädchen?", fragt die Großmutter. "Das ist Amelie, die Nichte deiner Schwiegertochter", antwortet Frau Glück. "Zu wem gehört der nette Junge dort drüben?" "Der gehört zu dem Cousin deines Mannes." "Den jungen Mann kenne ich auch nicht." "Das glaube

ich dir gerne. Das ist der Freund deiner Enkelin.""Habe ich diese junge Dame schon einmal gesehen?""Das glaube ich kaum. Sie ist heute zum ersten Mal hier. Sie ist die neue Freundin deines Enkels."
Exercise 4: Liebe Hochzeitsgäste, wir haben uns sehr gefreut, dass Ihr zu unserer Hochzeit gekommen seid und wir möchten uns ganz herzlich für die vielen Geschenke bedanken. Ihr habt uns damit eine große Freude bereitet. Jetzt sind wir schon dabei, die Koffer für unsere Hochzeitsreise nach Neuseeland zu packen. Wenn wir wieder nach Hause gekommen sind, laden wir Euch gerne in unsere neue Wohnung in Zürich ein. Bis dahin grüßen wir euch ganz herzlich!
Hanna und Michael

Day 24

Exercise 1: 1. Während der Hochzeit hat es geregnet. 2. Außerhalb Deutschlands spricht man auch Deutsch. 3. Statt des Autos nehmen wir die U-Bahn. 4. Trotz des Regens gehen wir wandern. 5. Wegen einer Hochzeitsfeier ist unser Geschäft geschlossen.
Exercise 2: 1. Obwohl das Wetter heiß ist, gehen wir zum Bergsteigen. 2. Obwohl Yuki einen Stadtplan hat, findet sie den Weg in Bamberg nicht. 3. Obwohl Yuki koffeinfreien Kaffee getrunken hat, kann sie nicht schlafen.
Exercise 3: 1. Statt nach München zu fliegen, fliegen wir lieber nach Hamburg. 2. Statt ins Kino zu gehen, geht sie lieber ins Schwimmbad. 3. Statt um 17.30 Uhr abzufahren, fährt der Zug erst um 18.00 Uhr ab. 4. Statt um 12.15 Uhr zu landen, landet das Flugzeug schon um 11.30 Uhr.
Exercise 4: 1. Die Familie verreist, ohne die Katze mitzunehmen. 2. Die Kinder überqueren die Straße, ohne nach rechts und links zu schauen. 3. Die Gäste kommen herein, ohne an der Tür zu klingeln. 4. Herr Kawasaki geht nach Hause, ohne den Anrufbeantworter einzuschalten. 5. Sie geht weg, ohne sich zu verabschieden. 6. Er nimmt das Stipendium an, ohne lange zu überlegen.

Day 25

Exercise 1: 1. b 2. e 3. d 4. a 5. c
Exercise 2: 1. ...junge Frau, die... 2. ...ein Herr am Telefon, der ... 3. ...einen Brief, den... 4. ...zwei Freundinnen, die... 5. ...die Gäste, auf die...
Exercise 3: 1. Die Freundin, deren Mann... 2. Der Autofahrer, dessen Auto... 3. Das Schloss, in dessen Räumen... 4. Eine Frau, deren Namen...

Day 26

Exercise 1: 1. wir achteten 2. sie bedienten 3. ich bezahlte 4. ihr fragtet 5. wir grüßten 6. er meinte 7. du gratuliertest 8. sie lernte 9. es klingelte 10. ich probierte
Exercise 2: 1. bekam 2. erklärte 3. besichtigte 4. verdiente 5. misslang 6. erzählte 7. begann 8. behandelte 9. erwartete 10. verschrieb
Exercise 3: 1. besichtigten 2. verdiente 3. erzählte 4. verschrieb 5. bekam 6. begann 7. misslang 8. behandelte 9. erklärte
Exercise 4: 1. wir kamen an 2. ich probierte an 3. ihr legtet auf 4. es ging aus 5. wir füllten aus 6. sie lud ein 7. ich kaufte ein 8. wir packten ein 9. ich warf ein 10. er brachte mit
Exercise 5: 1. Die Hochzeitsgäste brachten Geschenke mit. 2. Wir gingen gestern Abend aus. 3. Das Brautpaar lud die Gäste zur Hochzeitsfeier ein. 4. Der Zug kam pünktlich in Bamberg an. 5. Wir kauften Geschenke für die Hochzeit ein. 6. Frau Glück warf den Brief ein.

Day 27

Exercise 1: 1. Ich habe letzte Woche bei dir angerufen. 2. Was hast du am Wochenende gemacht? Ich bin zu Hause geblieben. 3. Warum bist du nicht zum Deutschunterricht gekommen? 4. Warum bist du nicht zum Wandern mitgekommen?
Exercise 2: 1. Im Urlaub bin ich spät ins Bett gegangen. 2. Im Urlaub habe ich gut gefrühstückt. 3. Im Urlaub bin ich ins Schwimmbad gegangen. 4. Im Urlaub bin ich in die Sauna gegangen. 5. Im Urlaub habe ich Zeitung gelesen.
Exercise 3: 1. bremste 2. Ausfahrt 3. gesperrt 4. hat … überholt

Day 28

Exercise 1: 1. Die Lehrerin informiert die Kursteilnehmer über den Prüfungstermin. 2. Darf ich nach Ihrem Namen fragen? 3. Die Eltern kümmern sich um die Kinder. 4. Hast du dich mit deiner Freundin verabredet? 5. Ich muss dich um Hilfe bitten. 6. Frau Glück versteht sich gut mit Yuki. 7. Ich habe mich über den Busfahrer geärgert. 8. Bald kann ich mich mit dir auf Deutsch verständigen. 9. Kannst du dich nicht an diesen Herrn erinnern? 10. Die Abschlussprüfung besteht aus mehreren Teilen.
Exercise 2: 1. f 2. j 3. h 4. a 5. i 6. b 7. c 8. g 9. e 10. d

Day 29

Exercise 1: 1. Stefan liegt im Krankenhaus, weil er einen Unfall hatte. 2. Ich komme zu spät, weil ich den Bus verpasst habe. 3. Yuki geht zur Post, weil sie Briefmarken kaufen will. 4. Mir tun die Augen weh, weil ich zu lange gelesen habe. 5. Ich bin nass, weil ich keinen Regenschirm hatte.
Exercise 2: 1. Weißt du, ob die Prüfung morgen stattfindet? 2. Weißt du, ob dieser Zug nach Berlin fährt? 3. Weißt du, ob das Konzert um 19.30 Uhr beginnt? 4. Weißt du, ob es hier eine Toilette gibt?
Exercise 3: 1. Sie ist mit dem Auto gefahren, weil es geregnet hat. 2. Yuki möchte wissen, ob Tobias heute Abend kommt. 3. Weißt du, ob es morgen Abend ein Fußballspiel im Fernsehen gibt? 4. Ich habe das Telefon nicht gehört, weil ich im Bad war.
Exercise 4: 1. Wir landen in wenigen Minuten auf dem Flughafen Köln/Bonn. Wir bitten Sie, alle elektronischen Geräte auszuschalten. Bitte begeben Sie sich auf Ihren Sitzplatz zurück und schnallen Sie sich an. 2. Begeben Sie sich bitte sofort zum Check-in und geben Sie Ihr Gepäck auf. 3. Kapitän Müller und seine Besatzung wünschen Ihnen einen angenehmen Flug. 4. Möchten Sie einen Platz am? Fenster/Gang oder am Gang/Fenster? 5. Hier ist Ihre Bordkarte. Das Einsteigen beginnt um 13.15 Uhr am Ausgang A8.

Day 30

Exercise 1: 1. Als es an der Tür klingelte, öffnete Frau Glück die Tür. 2. Ich war am Flughafen, als das Flugzeug landete. 3. Wo wart ihr, als es regnete? 4. Als der Fußgänger die Straße überquerte, kam es zu einem Unfall.
Exercise 2: 1. Als ich ein Kind war, durfte ich nicht immer fernsehen. 2. Als ich ein Kind war, wollte ich nie mit meinem Bruder spielen. 3. Als ich ein Kind war, musste ich Karotten essen. 4. Als ich ein Kind war, wollte nicht in den Kindergarten gehen.
Exercise 3: 1. Ich schicke dir eine E-Mail, damit es schneller geht. 2. Ich mache die Tür zu, damit du dich auf deine Arbeit konzentrieren kannst. 3. Yuki lernt Deutsch, damit sie sich um eine interessante Stelle bewerben kann. 4. Maria muss früh aufstehen, damit sie den Zug nicht verpasst.
Exercise 4: 1. Zwei Tage vor der Abreise kann ich die Tickets im Reisebüro abholen. 2. Da sie krank war, musste sie ihren Flug stornieren. 3. An der Grenze wurde ich nicht kontrolliert. 4. Das Flugzeug startet um 9.45 Uhr. Wir müssen zwei Stunden vor dem Abflug am Flughafen sein. 5. Vor einer Reise nach Vietnam muss man ein Visum beantragen. 6. Wir sind mit dem Auto gefahren. Bei der Einreise nach Frankreich mussten wir zwei Stunden an der Grenze warten.

Vocabulary

A

abbiegen *turn; to turn (off)*
Abend, der, -e *evening*
Abendessen, das, - *evening meal*
Abendstunde *in:* in den Abendstunden *in the evening(s)*
aber *in:* Sie haben aber Glück! *really*
abfahren *to leave*
Abfall, der, -¨e *waste*
Abflug, der, -¨e *take-off/departure*
abgeben *in:* an der Garderobe abgeben *to leave*
abhängen *to depend on*
abholen *to pick up; to collect*
abhören *to listen to*
Abreise, die, -n *departure*
Abschiedsgeschenk, das, -e *farewell present*
Abschlussparty, die, -s *(end-of-term) party*
Abschlussprüfung, die, -en *final examination*
Abschlusszeugnis, das, -se *certificate of completion*
Absender, der, - *sender*
Abteil, das, -e *compartment*
Abteilung, die, -en *department*
abtropfen *to drip (off)*
achten *to observe*
achtjährig *8-year-old*
ADAC, der *German Automobile Association*
Adresse, die, -n *address*
Aktenkoffer, der, - *briefcase*
alle *all*
alles *everything*
alles zusammen *all together; just one bill*
Alpen, die *(pl.)* *Alps*
also *therefore*
also dann bis morgen *See you tomorrow*
also gut *okay then*
Alufolie, die, -n *aluminium/aluminum foil*
am (= an dem) *in:* am Kiosk *at (the)*
am Apparat *on phone (speaking)*
am besten *the best thing*
am Computer *on the computer*
am *in:* am Samstag *on Saturday*
am liebsten *most of all*
am meisten the *most*
Ambulanz, die, -en *ambulance*
Amerika *America*
Amerikareise, die, -n *trip to the States*
Ampel, die, -n *traffic lights*
amüsieren (sich) *to enjoy oneself*
an *at*
Anästhesist, der, -en *anaesthetist*
anbieten *to offer*
andere *other*
Anforderung, die, -en *requirement*
anfragen *to ask*
Angebot, das, -e *offer*
angenehm *pleasant*
ankommen *to arrive*
Ankunft, die *arrival*
Anmeldung, die, -en *in:* ohne vorherige Anmeldung *appointment*
annehmen *to accept*
anprobieren *to try on*
Anruf, der, -e *call*
Anrufbeantworter, der, - *answering machine*
anrufen *to ring, to telephone*
anschauen *to have a look at; to look at*
anschließend *afterwards*
anschnallen *to fasten seatbelts*
anstrengend *tiring*
Antrag, der, -¨e *application form*
antreffen *to find*
antworten *to answer*
anzahlen *to make a down payment/ to put down a deposit*
anziehen *to wear*
Aperitif, der, -s *aperitif*
Apfel, der, -¨ *apple*
Apotheke, die, -n *chemist, chemist's, pharmacy*
Apotheker, der, - *chemist*
Apparat, der, -e *telephone*
Aprikosenkonfitüre, die, -n *apricot jam*
April *April*
Arbeit, die, -en *work, job*
arbeiten *to work*
Arbeitstag, der, -e *working day*
Arbeitszeit, die, -en *working hours*
Architekt, der, -en *architect*
Architektin, die, -nen *architect*
ärgerlich *annoying*
ärgern (sich) *to get angry; to be annoyed*
Arm, der, -e *arm*
Arzt, der, -¨e *doctor*

Ärztin, die, -nen *(woman) doctor*
atmen *to breathe*
auch *too, also*
auf *on*
auf Wiederhören ***(am Telefon)*** *goodbye (phone)*
auf Wiedersehen *goodbye*
Aufenthalt, der, -e *stay*
Aufgabe, die, -n *exercise*
aufgeben ***in:*** eine Postkarte aufgeben *to send*
aufhalten *to hold open*
aufhören *to stop*
auflegen *to put down, to hang up*
aufmachen *to open*
aufregen (sich) *to get excited*
aufrufen *to call out*
aufstehen *to get up*
aufwachen *to wake up*
Aufzug, der, -¨e *lift, elevator*
Auge, das, -n *eye*
August, der, -e *August*
aus *from*
Ausfahrt, die, -en *exit*
ausfallen *to be cancelled*
ausfüllen *to fill in*
ausgehen *to go out*
ausgezeichnet *excellent*
aushängen *to put up on*
auskennen (sich) *to know one's way around*
Auskunft, die, -¨e *information*
auspacken *to open*
ausrichten ***in:*** Kann ich ihm/ihr etwas ausrichten? *Can I give him/her a message?*
ausschalten *to switch off*
aussehen *to look*
außer *except*
außerdem *as well*
außerhalb *out of*
Aussichtsturm, der, -¨e *observation tower*
aussteigen *to get out of, to get off*
ausstellen *to write out, to issue*
Ausstellung, die, -en *exhibition*
aussuchen *to choose; to pick out*
Auswahl, die *selection*
ausweisen (sich) *to prove one's identity*
Auto, das, -s *car*
Autobahn, die, -en *motorway, freeway*
Autofahrer, der, - *driver*
Autounfall, der, -¨e *car accident*
Automat, der, -en *ticket machine*
Autor, der, -en *author*

B

Baby, das, -s *baby*
backen *to fry; to bake (in oil)*
Backrezept, das, -e *baking; recipe*
Bad, das, -¨er *bathroom*
Bahnangestellte, der ***or*** die, -n *booking clerk*
Bahnhof, der, -¨e *train station*
bald *soon*
Balkon, der, -e *balcony*
Banane, die, -n *banana*
bandagieren *to bandage*
Bank, die, -¨e ***in:*** *(for sitting on) bench*
Bank, die, -en *bank*
bar ***in:*** in bar *in cash*
bar auf die Hand *all in cash*
Basilikum, das *basil*
Bauer, der, -n *farmer*
Bäuerin, die, -nen *farmer*
Baum, der, -¨e *tree*
bayerisch *Bavarian*
Becher, der, - *mug*
bedanken (sich) *to say thank you*
bedienen *to serve*
bedienen (sich) *to help oneself*
Bedienung, die, -en *waiter/waitress*
beeilen (sich) *to hurry*
befinden (sich) *to be*
begeben (sich) *to proceed to*
begeistert sein *to be enthusiastic; to be thrilled*
beginnen *to start*
begrüßen *to greet*
Begrüßung, die, -en *greeting*
Begrüßungsparty, die, -s *(welcoming) party*
behalten *to remember; to keep*
Behälter, der, - *container*
behandeln *to deal with; to treat*
bei ***in:*** bei Frau Glück *at*
Bein, das, -e *leg*
bekommen *to get;*
benutzen *to use*
bereits *already*
Berg, der, -e *mountain*
Bergsteigen, das *mountain climbing*
berichten *to report*
Beruf, der, -e *profession*
beruflich *on business*
berühmt *famous*
Besatzung, die, -en *crew*
beschäftigen mit (sich) *to deal with*
besichtigen *to tour; to look at*

besorgen *to go and get*
bestehen *to pass (an exam)*
bestehen aus *to consist of*
bestellen *to order*
Besuch, der, -e *visitor*
besuchen *to visit*; *to go and see*
Bett, das, -en *bed*;
in: ins Bett gehen *to go to bed*
bewegen *to move*
bewegen (sich) *to get some exercise*
bewerben (sich) *to apply*
Bewerber, der, - *applicant*
bezahlen *to pay for*
Bezahlung, die, -en *pay*
beziehen auf (sich) *to refer to*
Bibliothek, die, -en *library*
biegen *to turn*
Bier, das, -e *beer*
Bierkrug, der, -¨e *beer mug*
Bierschinken, der *ham sausage*
Bild, das, -er *picture*
billig *cheap*
Birne, die, -n *pear*
bis *in:* bis ins Zentrum *to the center*
bis dahin *until then*
bis nach oben *up to the top*
Biskuit, der, -s *sponge cake*
bisschen *a little : in: ein bisschen*
bitte *please*
bitte schön! *here you are*
bitten *to ask*
bitten *in:* um Rückruf bitten *to ask s.o. to call back*
blass *pale*
blau *blue*
Blech, das, -e *tin*
bleiben *to stay*
Blick, der, -e *view*
Blume, die, -n *flower*
Blumengeschäft, das, -e *flower shop*
Blumenkohl, der *cauliflower*
Blumenstrauß, der, -¨e *bunch of flowers*
Blümlein, das, - *little flower*
Bluse, die, -n *blouse*
Boden, der *ground*
Bordkarte, die, -n *boarding pass*
brauchen *to need*
Brauchen Sie sonst noch etwas? *Anything else?*
braun *brown*
Braunglas, das *brown glass*
Brausetablette, die, -en *soluble tablet*
Braut, die, -¨e *bride*
Bräutigam, der, -e *(bride)groom*
Brautpaar, das, -e *bride and groom*
brechen *to break*
breit *wide*
bremsen *to brake*
Brezel, die, -n *pretzel*
Brief, der, -e *letter*
Briefkasten, der, -¨ *letter box*
Briefmarke, die, -n *stamp*
Briefträger, der, - *postman*
Briefumschlag, der, -¨e *envelope*
Brille, die, -n *glasses*
bringen *to bring*
Brot, das, -e *bread*
Brötchen, das, - *roll*
Brücke, die, -n *bridge*
Bruder, der, -¨ *brother*
Bub, der, -en *boy*
Buch, das, -¨er *book*
Bücherschrank, der, -¨e *bookcase*
Buchhaltungsprogramm, das, -e *book-keeping program*
buchstabieren *to spell*
Bund Petersilie, der, - *sprig of parsley*
Bundeskanzler, der, - *Chancellor*
bunt *colored*
Büro, das, -s *office*
Büroarbeit, die, -en *office work*
Bus, der, -se *bus*
Bushaltestelle, die, -n *bus stop*

C

Cafeteria, die, -s *cafeteria*
Champagner, der, - *champagne*
Check-in, der *check-in desk*
Cola, die, - or -s *coke*
Computer, der, - *computer*
Container, der, - *container*
Cousin, der, -s *cousin (male)*
Cousine, die, -n *cousin*

D

da *then*; *there*
da drüben *over there*
dabei sein *in:* wir sind gerade dabei *we're just thinking about it*
dadurch *for this reason*
Dame, die, -n *lady*
Damenbekleidung, die *ladies' fashions*
damit *with that*

Dampfschiff, das, -e *steamer*
danach *after, afterwards*
Däne, der, -n *Dane*
danke *thank you*
danken *to thank*
dann *then*
Darf ich dir alles Gute zum Geburtstag wünschen? *I'd like to wish you a very happy birthday*
das kommt darauf an *that depends*
das macht *that makes*
dass *that*
dauern *to last*
davon ausgehen *to assume*
Dein (Briefschluss) *yours (at the end of a letter or email)*
denken *to think*
denn *then*
deshalb *therefore*
deutlich *clearly*
Deutsch *German*
Deutschland *Germany*
Deutschunterricht, der *German lesson/class*
Dezember, der, - *December*
dich *(Akk) you*
Dienstag, der, -e *Tuesday*
diese *(pl.) these*
dieselbe *the same*
dieser *this*
dir *(Dat) you*
direkt *directly; in:* direkt ins Zentrum *right*
Dirndl, das, - *dirndl*
Disko, die, -s *disco*
Diskussion, die, -en *discussion*
Diskussionsrunde, die, -n *discussion group*
diskutieren *to discuss*
doch *then; instead; after all*
Dom, der, -e *cathedral*
Donnerstag, der, -e *Thursday*
dort *there*
dort oben *up there*
Dose, die, -n *tin, can*
draußen *outside*
drehen (sich) *to turn*
dringend *urgently*
drüben *over there*
dumm *stupid*
dunkel *dark*
dünn *thin*
durch *through*
dürfen *to be allowed to*
Durst *in:* Durst haben *to be thirsty*
durstig *thirsty*
duschen (sich) *to have/take a shower*

E

EC-Karte, die, -n *EC card*
E-Mail, die, -s *e-mail*
Ecke, die, -n *corner*
Edamer, der *Edam*
Ehepaar, das, -e *married couple*
ehrlich gesagt *to be honest*
Eierschale, die, -n *eggshell*
Eigelb, das, -e *egg yolk*
Eiffelturm, der *Eiffel Tower*
eigentlich *really*
Eile, die *hurry*
ein/e *a/an*
eine Postkarte aufgeben *to send a postcard*
einfach super! *simply marvellous*
Einfahrt, die, -en *drive*
einkaufen *to buy*; *to go shopping*
Einkaufsbummel, der, - *look around the shops*
einladen *to invite*, *to treat*
Einladung, die, -en *invitation*
einleitend *introductory*
einmal *once*
einpacken *to wrap*; *to pack*
Einreise, die, -n *entry*
einschalten *to switch on*
einschenken *to pour out*
einsteigen *to board*
einwerfen *to post*
Einzelprüfung, die, -en *one-to-one examination*
Eis, das ice *cream*
elektronisch *electronic*
Eltern, die *(pl.)* *parents*
Emmentaler, der *Emmentaler*
empfangen *to welcome*
empfehlen *to recommend*
Ende, das, -en *end*
enden *to finish*
endlich *at long last*
eng *tight*
England *England*
Englischkenntnisse, die (pl.) *knowledge of English*
Enkel, der, - *grandson*
Enkelin, die, -nen *granddaughter*
Enkelkind, das, -er *grandchild*
enthalten *to contain*; *to include*
entlang *along*

entscheiden (sich) *to decide*
entschuldigen (sich) *to say sorry*
Entschuldigung! *excuse me!*
entsprechend *proper, appropriate*
entweder *either*
entweder... oder *either...or*
entwerten *to stamp*, *to validate*
entzückend *lovely*
Erbse, die, -n *pea*
Erdbeere *strawberry*
Erdgeschoss, das, -e *ground floor*
ereignen *to happen*
erfahren *to find out*
erfinden *to inven*
erforderlich *required*
erhalten *to receive*
erheben *to raise*
erinnern an *to remember*
erklären *to explain*
erkunden *to explore*
erkundigen (sich) *to make enquiries*
Erlebnis, das, -e *experience*
Ermäßigung, die, -en *reduction*
Ermäßigungskarte, die, -n *a card which entitles you to a reduction*
eröffnen *to open*
erst *not until*
erst einmal *first of all*; *in:* wir sammeln erst *first of all*
erstaunt sein *to be astonished*
erster Stock *first floor, second floor (US)*
erwarten *to expect*
erwünscht *desirable*
erzählen *to talk about*; *to tell*
es (Akk.) *it*
es gibt *there is/there are*
es regnet in Strömen *to pour with rain*
essen *to eat*
Essen, das, - *in:* das Abendessen *meal*
Esslöffel, der, - *tablespoon*
Essig, der *vinegar*
etwas *something*
euch *you*
euer *your*

F

fahren *to go*
Fahrkarte *in:* einfache Fahrkarte *single/one way ticket*
Fahrkarte, die, -n *ticket*
Fahrschein, der, -e *ticket*
Fahrscheinkontrolle, die, -n *ticket inspection*
Fahrrad, das, -¨er *bike*
Fahrradhelm, der, -e *crash helmet*
Fahrt, die *in:* vor der Fahrt *before boarding*
Fall, der, -¨e *fall*
fallen *to fall*
Familie, die, -n *family*
fantastisch *wonderful; fantastic*
Farbe, die, -n *color*
Fax, das, -e *fax*
Februar, der, -e *February*
fehlen *to be missing; to be absent*
in: Was fehlt Ihnen denn? *What's wrong with you?*
feiern *to celebrate*; *in:* Party feiern *to give a party*
Feiertag, der, -e *holiday*
fein *good*
Fenster, das, - *window*
Fensterbrett, das, -er *window sill*
Fernbedienung, die, -en *remote control*
fernsehen *to watch TV*
Fernseher, der, - *television set*
Fernsehprogramm, das, -e *television programme*
fertig *ready*
Fieber, das *temperature*
Fieberthermometer, das, - *thermometer*
Film, der, -e *film*
Filtertüte, die, -n *paper filter*
finanzieren *to pay for*
finden *to find*; *in:* wie findest du *to like*
Fitness-Gymnastik, die *workouts*
Flasche, die, -n *bottle*
Fleisch, das *meat*
Fleischbrühe, die, -n *stock*
fleißig *hard, diligent(ly)*
fliegen *to fly*
Flug, der, -¨e *flight*
Flugbegleiter, der, - *flight attendant*
Flugbegleiterin, die, -nen *flight attendant*
Flughafen, der, -¨ *airport*
Flugzeug, das, -e *plane*
Fluss, der, -¨e *river*
fortsetzen *to continue*
Foto, das, -s *photo*
Frage, die, -n *question*
fragen *to ask*
Franken *Franconia*
Frankreich *France*
Französisch *French*
Frau, die, -en *woman*
frei *free*

Freitag, der, -e *Friday*
Fremdenverkehrsamt, das, -¨er *Tourist Information*
Fremdsprachenkenntnis, die, -se *knowledge of a foreign language*
Freude bereiten *to give pleasure*
freuen (sich) *to be pleased*
freundlich *kind*
frieren *to feel cold*
frisch *fresh*
Frischkäse, der *cream cheese*
Friseur, der, -e *hairdresser*
Friseurin, die, -nen *hairdresser*
früh *early*
Frühling, der, -e *spring*
Frühstück, das *breakfast*
frühstücken *to have breakfast*
Führung, die, -en *tour*
füllen *to fill*
Fünfziger, der, - *50-euro note*
für *for*
Fuß *in:* zu Fuß sein *on foot*
Fußballsieg, der, -e *football/soccer victory*

G

Gang, der, -¨e *corridor; aisle*
ganz *whole*
gar nicht *really*
in: ich weiß gar nicht *I really don't know*
Garderobe, die, -n *cloakroom, hook; stand*
garnieren *to garnish*
Gast, der, -¨e *guest*
Gastgeber, der, - *host*
Gastgeberin, die, -nen *hostess*
Gebäude, das, - *building*
geben *to give*
Geburtstag, der, -e *birthday*
Geburtstagsfeier, die, -n *birthday party*
Geburtstagskind, das, -er *birthday girl/boy*
geehrte *dear*
gefallen *in:* mir gefällt's *I like*
Geflügel, das *poultry*
gegen *in:* gegen den Baum *into*
gegenüber *opposite*
gehen *to go*
in: es geht mir besser *I feel better*
gekocht *boiled*
Geld, das, -er *money*
Geld zurückbekommen *to get money back*
gemeinsam *together*
Gemüse, das *vegetables*
Gemüserest, der, -e *vegetable peelings*
gemütlich *pleasant*
genau *exact*
geöffnet *open*
Gepäck, das *luggage*
gerade *just*
geradeaus *straight ahead*
Gerät, das, -e *device*
gerne *in:* ja gerne *yes, thanks*
gerne mitbringen *if you like*
Geschäft, das, -e *shop*
Geschenk, das, -e *present*
Geschichte, die, -n *story*
geschmückt *decorated*
Geschwister, die *(pl.)* *brothers and sisters*
gespannt sein *to be excited*
gestern *yesterday*
gesund *healthy*
gewinnen *to win*
gewöhnen an (sich) *to get used to 20*
Gewürz, das, -e *spice*
Glas, das, -¨er *glass*
Glascontainer, der, - *bottle bank,glass container*
glauben *to think, to believe*
gleich *just*
gleichzeitig *at the same time*
Glockenspiel, das, - *glockenspiel*
Glück, das *in:* Glück haben *luck; to be lucky*
glücklich *happy*
glücklicherweise *fortunately*
Gramm, das, - *gramme*
Grammatik, die *grammar*
gratulieren *to congratulate*
Grenze, die, -n *frontier, border*
groß *big*
Großeltern, die *(pl.)* *grandparents*
Großmutter, die, -¨ *grandmother*
Großvater, der, -¨ *grandfather*
Großstadt, die, -¨e *city*
Größe, die, -n *size*
grün *green*
Grünglas, das *green glass*
Gruppe, die, -n *group*
Gruppenprüfung, die, -en *group examination*
Grüß Gott *good morning, good afternoon or good evening*
Gruß, der, -¨e *regards, greetings*
grüßen *to greet, to say hello*
gültig *valid*
günstig *reasonably priced*

gut *good*
Gute *in:* Was gibt's denn Gutes? *what's on the menu?*
guten Morgen! *good morning*
guten Tag! *hello*

H

Haar, das, -e *hair*
Haarschnitt, der, -e *haircut*
haben *to have*
Hälfte, die, -n *half*
Halstuch, das, -¨er *scarf*
halten *to stop*
halten (sich) *to keep*
Haltestelle, die, -n *(U-Bahn, Zug) stop*
Halteverbot, das, -e *no stopping*
Hand *in:* in der Hand *in one's hand*
Handgepäck, das *hand luggage*
Handtasche, die, -n *handbag*
handeln um (sich) *to be about*
hängen *to hang*
Haufen, der, - *pile*
Hauptpost, die *main post office*
Haus, das, -¨er *house*
Hausarzt, der, -¨e *general practitioner*
Hausaufgabe, die, -n *homework*
Haustür, die, -en *front door*
Heimreise, die, -n *journey home*
heißen *in:* Wie heißen Sie? *to be called*
helfen *to help*
Helikopter, der, - *helicopter*
hell *light*
Hemd, das, -en *shirt*
heraus *out of*
herauskommen *to come out*
Herbst, der *autumn, fall*
herein *in:* kommen Sie herein! *in*
hereinkommen *to come in*
Herfahrt, die *way here*
herkommen *to come here*
Herrchen, das, - *master (dog owner)*
herrlich *wonderful*
Herz, das, -en *heart*
Herzerl, das, - *little heart; sweetheart*
herzliche Grüße *best regards*
Herzlichen Glückwunsch zum Geburtstag! *happy birthday!*
heute *today*
hier *here*; hier vorne *over there*
Hilfe, die *help*
Himbeere, die, -n *raspberry*
himmlisch *absolutely wonderful*
hinauf *up*
hinaufkommen *to get/to come up*
hinausgehen *to go out*
hinein *into*
hineingehen *to go into*
hinfahren *to drive (to)*
hingehen *to go (there)*
hinterlassen *to leave*
hinunter *down*
hinweisen auf *to refer to*
hoch *high*
Hochzeit, die, -en *wedding*
Hochzeitsfeier, die, -n *wedding celebration*
Hochzeitsgast, der, -¨e *wedding guest*
Hochzeitsgesellschaft, die, -en *wedding party*
hoffen auf *to hope for*
hoffentlich *I hope, hopefully*
höflich *polite*
holen *to go and get*
Honig, der *honey*
hören *to hear*
Hornist, der, -en *horn player*
Hörverstehen, das *listening comprehension*
Hose, die, -n *trousers, pants*
hübsch *pretty*
Hubschrauber, der, - *helicopter*
Hund, der, -e *dog*
Hunderter, der, - *100-euro note*
Hunger, der *in:* Hunger haben *to be hungry*
hurra *hurrah*
Husten, der *cough*
Hut, der, -¨e *hat*

I

IC (InterCity), der, -s *intercity*
IC-Zuschlag, der, -¨e *IC surcharge*
ICE (InterCityExpress), der, -s *intercity express*
ich *I*
Idee, die, -n *idea*
ihm *(to) him*
ihn *him*
ihnen *(to) them*
ihr *(to) her*
ihr (showing possession) *her*
im (= in dem) *in the*
in *in*
in der Nähe *near here*

Information, die, -en *in:* Informationen unter *information on*
informieren *to inform*
Ingenieur, der, -e *engineer*
Ingenieurin, die, -nen *engineer*
inhaltlich *text-related*
Innenstadt, die, -¨e *town/city centre*
innerhalb in, *within*
ins (= in das) *into the*
Instrument, das, -e *instrument*
interessant *interesting*
interessieren für (sich) *to be interested in*
inzwischen *in the meantime*
Italien *Italy*

J

ja *yes*
ja, gerne *yes, thanks*
Jackett, das, -s *jacket*
Jahr, das, -e *year*
Jahreszahl, die, -en *year*
Januar, der, _e *January*
jeden *every*
jedenfalls *certainly; at any rate*
jemand *someone*
jetzt *now*
Job, der, -s *job*
Jobsuche, die *looking for a job*
joggen *to go jogging*
Joghurt, der, -s *yogurt*
Juli, der, -s *July*
jung *young*
Juni, der, -s *June*

K

Kaffee, der, -s *coffee*
Kaffeemaschine, die, -n *coffee machine*
Kalbfleisch, das *veal*
kalt *cold*
kalt stellen *to put in the fridge, to chill*
Kamillentee, der, -s *chamomile tea*
Kännchen, das, - *small pot*
Kapitän, der, -e *captain*
kaputt *broken*
Karotte, die, -n *carrot*
Karte, die, -n *card* ; *in:* Konzertkarte *ticket*
Kartoffel, die, -n *potato*
Kartoffelsalat, der, -e *potato salad*
Karton, der, -s *cardboard*
Käse, der *cheese*
Käsesahnetorte, die, -n *cream cheese cake*
Kasse, die , -n *in:* Krankenkasse *health insurance (provider)*
Kassenpatient, der, -en *non-private patient*
Kater, der, - *tomcat*
Kätzchen, das, - *kitten*
Katze, die, -n *cat*
kaufen *to buy*
Kaufhaus, das, -¨er *department store*
Kaufmann, der, *(pl.)* Kaufleute *salesperson*
kaum *hardly*
kein *no*
Keller, der, - *cellar*
Kellner, der, - *waiter*
Kellnerin, die, -nen *waitress*
kennen *to know*
kennenlernen *to get to know*
Kenntnis, die, -se *knowledge*
Kind, das,-er *child*
Kindergarten, der, -¨ *kindergarten*
Kinderstation, die, -en *children's ward*
Kino, das, -s *cinema, movie theater*
Kiosk, der, -e *kiosk*
Kirche, die, -n *church*
Kirsche, die, -n *cherry*
Klassenzimmer, das, - *classroom*
Kleid, das, -er *dress*
Kleider, die *(pl.) clothes*
Kleidung, die *clothes*
klein *small*
Kleinstadt, die, -¨e *small town*
klingeln *to ring*
klingen *to sound*
Knoblauch, der *garlic*
knusprig *crisp*
kochen *to cook*
Köchin, die, -nen *cook*
koffeinfrei *decaffeinated*
Koffer, der, - *suitcase*
Kollege, der, -n *colleague*
Kollegin, die, -nen *colleague*
kommen *to come*
Kompliment, das, -e *compliment*
kompliziert *complicated*
Komposteimer, der, - *compost bin*
können can, *to be able to*
Kontrolleur, der, -e *inspector*
kontrollieren *to check*

konzentrieren (sich) *to concentrate*
Konzert, das, -e *concert*
Kopfschmerztablette, die, -n *headache tablet*
Kopfverletzung, die, -en *head injury*
kosten *to cost*
köstlich *tasty*
Kostüm, das, -e *suit (for women)*
krank *ill*
Krankenhaus, das -¨er *hospital*
Krankenkasse, die, -en *health insurance*
Krankenpfleger, der, - *male nurse*
Krankenschwester, die, -n *nurse*
krankenversichert sein *to be medically insured*
Krankenversicherung, die, -en *health insurance*
Kräuter, die *(pl.)* *herbs*
Krawatte, die, -n *tie*
kreativ *creative*
Kreditkarte, die, -n *credit card*
Küche, die, -n *kitchen*
Kuchen, der, - *cake*
Kursteilnehmer, der, - *course participant*
kurz *short*
Kuss, der, -¨e *kiss*

L

lachen *to laugh*
Lammfleisch, das *lamb*
Land, das, -¨er *country*
landen *to land*
lang *long*
langweilig *boring*
lassen *to leave*
Lastwagen, der, - *lorry, truck*
laufen *to walk; to run*
Leberwurst, die, -¨e *liver sausage*
lecker *delicious, tasty*
legen *to put*
Lehrer, der, - *teacher*
Lehrerin, die, -nen *teacher*
leicht *light*; *easy*
leid *in:* das tut mir leid *I'm sorry*
leider *I'm afraid*; *unfortunately*
leisten (sich) *to afford*
lernen *to learn*, *to study*
lesen *to read*
letzte *last*
Leute, die *(pl.)* *people*
lieb *sweet, nice*
lieben *to like*
lieber *in:* sollen wir lieber? *is it better to?*
Lieferant, der, -en *supplier*
liegen *to lie*
liegen lassen *to leave behind*
links *left*
lohnen (sich) *to be worthwhile*
Lokalnachricht, die, -en *local news*
los sein *in:* etwas ist mit mir los *something is wrong with me*
Los, das, -e *lottery ticket*
Losverkäufer, der, - *lottery seller*
Luft, die, -¨e *air*
Lust, die *in:* Lust haben zu *feel like*

M

machen *to make*; Machen Sie sich schick! *Wear something smart!*
Mädchen, das, - *girl*
Magen, der -¨ *stomach*
Mai, der, -e *May*
mal *in:* lesen Sie mal *you should read*
man *one*
manchmal *sometimes*
Mann, der, -¨er *man*
Mantel, der, -¨ *coat*
Märchen, das, - *story, fairy tale*
Markt, der, -¨e *market*
Marktstand, der, -¨e *market stall*
März, der, -e *March*
Maus, die, -¨e *mouse*
Mechaniker, der, - *mechanic*
Mechanikerin, die, -nen *mechanic*
Medikament, das, -e *medicine*
Mehl, das *flour*
mehr *more*
mein *my*; mein Name ist *my name is*
meinen *to think*
meistens *usually*
messen *to measure*
Mexiko *Mexico*
mich *(Akk)* *me*
Milch, die *milk*
Mineralwasser, das *mineral water*
mir *(Dat)* *me*
mischen *to mix*
misslingen *to fail*
mit *with*
Mitbewohnerin, die, -nen *flatmate/roommate*
mitbringen *to bring (along)*
miteinander *with each other*

mitkommen *to come too*
mitnehmen *to take with; to take along*
Mittagspause, die, -n *lunch break*
Mitte, die *middle*
mitten *in the middle of*
Mittwoch, der, -e *Wednesday*
mögen *to like*
Moment, der, -e *moment*
Montag, der, -e *Monday*
Morgen, der, - *morning*
morgens *every morning*
müde *tired*
Mülltonne, die, -n *dustbin, garbage can*
München *Munich*
Museum, das, *(pl.)* **Museen** *museum*
Musiksendung, die, -en *music programme*
Muskatnuss, die, -¨e *nutmeg*
müssen *must, to have to*
Mutter, die, -¨er *mother*
Muttersprache, die, -n *native language*

N

nach *in:* **nach Paris** *to*
nach links *to the left*
nach oben *to the top*
nach rechts *to the right*
Nachbar, der, -n *neighbour*
nachdenken über *to think about*
nachfragen *to enquire*
Nachmittag, der, -e *afternoon*
nachmittags *every afternoon*
Nachricht, die, -en *message; news*
nachschauen *to have a look*
nachsehen *to have a look*
nächste *nearest;* **nächste Woche** *next week*
Nacht, die, -¨e *night*
nachträglich *belated*
nachts *every night*
Nachweis, der, -e *proof*
nah *near*
Nähe *in:* **in der Nähe** *near here*
Name, der, -n *name*
naschen *to eat sweets*
nass *wet*
natürlich! *of course*
neben *next to*
Neffe, der, -n *nephew*
nehmen *to take*
nehmen Sie Platz! *take a seat*
nein *no*
Nelke, die, -n *(flower) carnation*
Nelken, die *(pl.) (spice) cloves*
nett *nice*
neu *new*
neulich *the other day*
Neuseeland *New Zealand*
nicht *not*
nicht nur… sondern auch *not only… but also*
Nichte, die, -n *niece*
nie *never*
nie und nimmer *never ever*
niemals *never*
niemand *nobody*
nirgends *nowhere*
nirgendwo *nowhere at all*
noch *in:* **noch Zeit haben** *still*
noch einmal *once again*
Norden, der *north*
Nordpol, der *North Pole*
normalerweise *normally*
Normalpreis, der, -e *normal price*
notfalls *if necessary*
November, der, - *November*
Nummer, die, -n *number*
nun *now*
nur *only*

O

ob *whether*
oben *up*
Obst, das *fruit*
Obstsalat, der, -e *fruit salad*
Obstschale, die, -n *fruit peel*
oder *or*
offen *open*
öffnen *to open*
ohne *without*
Öl, das, -e *oil*
Olympiamedaille, die, -n *Olympic medal*
Oma, die, -s *grandma*
Onkel, der, - *uncle*
Opa, der, -s *grandpa*
Oppositionsführer, der, - *leader of the opposition*
Orchester, das, - *orchestra*
Ordnung, die *in:* **in Ordung** *in order; okay*
organisch *organic*
Osten, der *east*
Österreich *Austria*

P

Paar, das, -e *pair*
Päckchen, das, - *small parcel/packet*
packen *to pack*
Packung, die, -en *package*
Paket, das, -e *parcel*
Paniermehl, das *breadcrumbs*
Panne, die, -n *breakdown*
Papier, das, -e *paper*
Papierkorb, der, -¨e *wastepaper basket*
Papierserviette, die, -n *serviette, napkin*
Papiertaschentücher, die *(pl.) tissues*
Paprika, das *(spice) paprika*
Paprika, der, -s *pepper*
parken *to park*
Parkplatz, der, -¨e *car park*
Party feiern *to throw a party*
Pass, der, -¨e *passport*
Passkontrolle, die, -n *passport control*
passen *to fit*; *in:* das passt mir *to suit*
passieren *to happen*
Patient, der, -en *patient*
Pause, die, -n *break*
Pech, das *in:* Pech haben *to be unlucky*
peinlich *embarrassing*
per Luftpost *by airmail*
Person, die, -en *person*
Personalbüro, das, -s *personnel department*
Petersilie, die *parsley*
Pfeffer, der *pepper*
Pflaster, das, - *plaster*
Pflaume, die, -n *plum*
Pforte, die, -n *reception*
phantastisch *just wonderful*; *fantastic*
Plakat, das, -e *notice, poster, sign*
Plastik, das *plastic*
Platz, -¨e *seat; room*
Platz nehmen *to take a seat*
Platzreservierung, die, -en *seat reservation*
Polen *Poland*
politisch *political*
Polizist, der, -en *policeman*
Polizistin, die, -nen *policewoman*
Porto, das, -s *postage*
Post, die *post*
Postamt, das, -¨er *post office*
Postbote, der, -n *postman/mailman*
Postkarte, die, -n *post card*
Postleitzahl, die, -en *post/zip code*
Preis, der, -e *price*
privat *private*
Privatpatient, der, -en *private patient*
Probe fahren *to test-drive*
probieren *to try; to taste*
profitieren von *to profit from*
Programm, das, -e *programme*
Prospekt, der, -e *brochure*
Prost! *Cheers!*
Prozent, das, -e *per cent/ percent*
prüfen *to examine, to test*
Prüfung, die, -en *examination*
Prüfungsteil, der, -e *part of the examination*
Pumpernickel, der, - *pumpernickel*
pünktlich *punctual*

Q

Quittung, die, -en *receipt*

R

Rabatt, der, -e *discount*
Rad fahren *to go cycling*
Radweg, der, -e *cycle path*
Radieschen, das, - *radish*
Radio, das, -s *radio*
Rathaus, das, -¨er *town hall*
rauchen *to smoke*
Raucher *smoker/smoking*
Raum, der, -¨e *room*
raus *get away*
rebellieren *to rebel*
rechnen *to reckon*
rechts *right*
rechtzeitig *in time*
reden über *to talk about*
regelmäßig *regularly*
Regen, der *rain*
Regenmantel, der, -¨ *raincoat*
Regenschirm, der, -e *umbrella*
Regional-Express, der, -e *regional express*
regnen *to rain*
Reihe, die, -n *row*
Reis, der *rice*
Reise, die, -n *trip*
Reisebüro, das, -s *travel agency*
reisen *to travel*
Reiseunterlagen, die *(pl.)* *travel documents*
Reiter, der, - *rider*
rennen *to run*

renovieren *to renovate*
rentieren (sich) *to be worthwhile*
reservieren *to reserve*
Restaurant, das, -s *restaurant*
Restbetrag, der, -¨e *outstanding sum*
Rezept, das, -e *recipe; prescription*
Rindfleisch, das *beef*
Ring, der, -e *ring*
Rock, der, -¨e *skirt*
Roggenbrot, das *rye bread*
romantisch *romantic*
Rose, die, -n *rose*
rot *red*
Rotkohl, der *red cabbage*
Rückfahrkarte, die, -n *return/round trip ticket*
Rückflug, der, -¨e *return flight*
Rückruf, der, -e *return call*
rufen *to shout*
ruhig *in:* ruhig streicheln *if you want*

S

Sachertorte, die, -n *Sachertorte*
sagen *to say*
Sahne, die *cream*
Salbei, der *sage*
Salz, das *salt*
Sammelkasse, die, - *main cash desk*
sammeln *to collect*
Sammlung, die, -en *collection*
Samstag, der, -e *Saturday*
satt *in:* satt sein *to be full*
schade! *what a pity*
schälen *to peel*
schalten *to turn on*, *to switch (to)*
schauen *to look*
schauen *in:* dann schauen wir halt *let's see*
Scheibe, die, -n *slice*
Schein, der, -e *bank note, money bill*
scheinen *to shine*
schenken *to give a present*
schick *smart, nice*
schicken *to send*
Schimmelkäse, der *blue cheese*
Schinken, der *ham*
schlafen *to sleep*
Schlafzimmer, das, - *bedroom*
schlecht *bad*
schließen *to close*
schließlich *after all*
Schloss, das, -¨er *castle*
Schlüssel, der, - *key*
schmecken *to taste*
schneiden *to cut*
schnell *quick(ly)*
Schnittlauch, der *chives*
Schnitzel, das, - *escalope*
Schokolade, die, -n *chocolate*
Schokoladenglasur, die, -n *chocolate icing*
schön *nice*
Schrank, der, -¨e *cupboard*
schreiben *to write*
schreien *to cry*
Schreiner, der, - *carpenter*
Schreinerin, die, -nen *carpenter*
Schuh, der, -e *shoe*
Schuhabteilung, die, -en *shoe department*
Schule, die, -n *school*
Schüler, der, - *schoolboy; student*
Schürze, die, -n *apron*
schützen vor (sich) *to protect o.s. from*
Schwager, der, - *brother-in-law*
Schwägerin, die, -nen *sister-in-law*
schwarz *black*
Schwarzwälder Kirschtorte, die, -n *Black Forest Gateau*
Schweinefleisch, das *pork*
schwer *heavy*
Schwester, die, -n *sister*
Schwiegereltern *(pl.) parents-in-law*
schwierig *difficult*
schwimmen *to swim*
Schwimmbad, das, -¨er *swimming pool*
sehen *to see*
sehr *very*
sein *to be*; *his*
sein (showing possession) *his*
seit *in:* seit drei Jahren *for three years*
seit wann? *how long?*
seitdem *since*
Sekretär, der, -e *secretary*
Sekretärin, die, -nen *secretary*
selbstverständlich *of course*
selten *seldom*
senden *to send*; *to broadcast*
Sender, der, - *broadcast station*
Sendung, die, -en *programme*
Senf, der *mustard*
September, der, - *September*
setzen (sich) *to sit down*
sicher *sure*

Sie *you (formal)*
sie *(Akk. Sg.)* *her*
sie *(Akk. Pl.)* *them*
Sie wünschen, bitte? *can I help you?*
Situation, die, -en *situation*
sitzen *to sit*
Sitzplatz, der, -¨e *seat*
so... wie *as... as*
So eine Überrraschung! *What a surprise!*
soeben *just*
sogar *even*
Sohn, der, -¨e *son*
sollen *should*
Sommer, der, - *summer*
Sommerkleid, das, -er *summer dress*
Sommermantel, der, ¨ *summer coat*
Sondermarke, die, -n *commemorative stamp*
Sonne, die, -n *sun*
Sonnenblume, die, -n *sunflower*
Sonnenmilch, die *sun(tan) lotion*
Sonnenschein, der *sunshine*
Sonntag, der, -e *Sunday*
sonst *otherwise* ; *in:* sonst noch etwas *anything else*
sortieren *to sort (through, out)*
Souvenir, das, -s *souvenir*
Sozialversicherungsbeitrag, der, -¨e *social insurance contribution*
Spanien *Spain*
spannend *exciting*
Sparpreis, der, -e *discount price*
Spaß, der, -¨e *fun*
später *later*
spazieren gehen *to go for a walk*
sperren *to close*
spielen *to play*
Sport treiben *to play sport*
Sportart, die, -en *sport*
Sprache, die, -n *language*
Sprachenschule, die, -n *language school*
sprechen *to speak*
Sprechstunde, die, -n *surgery, doctor's office hours*
Sprechstundenhilfe, die, -n *receptionist*
Sprechzeit, die, -en *surgery, office hours*
Stadt, die, -¨e *town*
Stadtbesichtigung, die, -en *guided tour of the city*
Stadtführerin, die, -nen *tour guide*
Stadtplan, der, -¨e *city map*
Stadtzentrum, das, *(pl.)* Stadtzentren *city center*
Standesamt, das, -¨er *registry office*
starten *to take off*
Station, die, -en *stop*
statt *instead of*
stattfinden *to take place*
stehen *to be*
Stelle, die, -n *job*; *in:* dieselbe Stelle *the same spot*
Stellenangebot, das, -e *job ad*
stellen *to put*
stellen *in:* eine Frage stellen *to ask*
stempeln *to stamp; to validate*
Steuer, das, - *steering wheel*
Steuer, die, -n *tax*
Stock, der, - *floor*
stornieren *to cancel*
Straße, die, -n *street*
Straßenbahn, die, -en *tram*
streicheln *to stroke*
Streifen, der, - *strip*
Streifenkarte, die, -n *strip ticket*
streiten *to quarrel*
Strumpfhose, die, -n *tights*
Stück, das, -e *piece*
Student, der, -en *student*
studieren *to study*
Stufe, die, -n *step*
Stuhl, der, -¨e *chair*
Stunde, die, -n *hour*
Stundenplan, der, -¨e *timetable; schedule*
stürzen *to fall*
suchen *to look for*
Süden, der *south*
Supermarkt, der, -¨e *supermarket*

T

Tafel, die, -n *in:* Tafel Schokolade *bar of chocolate*
täglich *daily*
Tante, die, -n *aunt*
tanzen *to dance*
Tapetenwechsel, der, - *change of scene*
Tasse, die, -n *cup*
Taxi, das, -s *taxi*
Taxifahrer, der, - *taxi driver*
Tee, der, -s *tea*
teilnehmen an *to take part in*
Teilnehmer, der, - *participant*
Telefon, das, -e *telephone*
Telefonhörer, der, - *receiver*
telefonieren *to ring, to call*
Telefonnummer, die, -n *telephone number*
Telefonzelle, die, -n *telephone box/booth*

Tennis spielen *to play tennis*
Termin, der, -e *appointment*
Terminplan, der, -¨e *(time) schedule*
Terrasse, die, -n *terrace, patio*
teuer *expensive*
Text, die, -e *text*
Theater, das, - *theatre*
Thema, das, *(pl.)* **Themen** *topic*
Tier, das, -e *animal*
Tisch, der, -e *table*
Tochter, die, -¨ *daughter*
Toilette, die, -n *toilet*
Tokio *Tokyo*
toll! *great!*
Tomate, die -n *tomato*
Torte, die, -n *gateau, cake*
Tourist, der, -en *tourist*
Trachtengeschäft, das, -¨e *traditional costume shop*
tragen (Kleidung) *to wear* ; in: **den Namen tragen** *to be called*
träumen von *to dream of*
traurig *sad*
Trauung, die, -en *wedding ceremony*
treffen (sich) *to see each other; to meet*
Treffpunkt, der, -e *meeting place*
trennen *to separate*
Trennung, die, -en *separation*
trinken *to drink*
trocken *dry*
Tropfen, der, - *drop*
trotz *in spite of*
trotzdem *nevertheless*
Tulpe, die, -n *tulip*
tun *to do*
Tunnel, der, - *tunnel*
Tür, die, -en *door*
Turm, der, -¨e *tower*
tut mir leid *I'm sorry*
Tütchen, das, - *small carrier/plastic bag*
Tüte, die, -n *bag*

U

U-Bahn, die, -en *underground, subway*
U-Bahn-Fahrer, der, - *underground/ subway driver*
U.A.w.g. = Um Antwort wird gebeten *Please reply, R.S.V.P.*
übel *sick; ill*
üben *to practise*
über *over*
überhaupt nicht *not at all*
überholen *to overtake*
überlegen *to think about*
übermorgen *the day after tomorrow*
übernehmen *to do, to take over*
überqueren *to cross*
Überraschung, die, -en *surprise*
übersäuern *to become too acidic;* **übersäuerte Magen, der** *overacidified stomach*
übersehen *to overlook*
überweisen *to transfer*
übrig *left*
übrigens *incidentally, by the way*
Uhr, die, -en *clock*
um *around*
um... zu *in order to*
um *in:* **um ... Uhr** *at... (o'clock)*
umarmen (sich) *to hug one another*
Umkleidekabine, die, -n *changing cubicle/room*
Umschlag, der, -¨e *envelope*
umständlich *complicated; lot of trouble*
umtauschen *to change*
unbedingt *absolutely; definitely; really*
und *and*
und zwar *namely*
Unfall, der, -¨e *accident*
ungefähr *about*
Universität, die, -en *university*
uns *us*
unser *our*
unten *down*
unter *under*
unterhalten über (sich) *to talk about*
Unterricht, der *lessons*
Unterschied, der, -e *difference*
unterschreiben *to sign*

V

Vanilleeis, das, - *vanilla icecream*
Vater, der, -¨er *father*
verabreden (sich) *to arrange to meet*
Veranstaltung, die, -en *event*
verbinden *to put through, to connect*
verbringen *to spend*
verdienen *to earn*
vergessen *to forget*
vergleichen mit *to compare with*
verheiratet sein *to be married*
Verkäufer, der, - *shop assistant*

Verkäuferin, die, -nen *shop assistant*
Verkehrsunfall, der, -¨e *traffic accident*
verlassen *to leave*
verletzen (sich) *to injure (oneself)*
verletzt *injured*
verlieben in (sich) *to fall in love with*
vermeiden *to avoid*
verpassen *to miss*
verreisen *to go on holiday/vacation*
verschicken *to send*
verschieden *different*
verschlafen *to oversleep*
verschreiben *to prescribe*
Versicherungskärtchen, das, - *medical insurance card*
versprechen *to promise*
verständigen mit (sich) *to communicate with*
Verständnis, das *understanding*
verstehen *to understand*; (sich) *to get on/along*
versuchen *to try*
Verwandte, die *(pl.) relatives*
viel *a lot of*
vielen Dank *thank you very much*
vielleicht *possibly* ; *perhaps*
vier *four*
viermal *four times*
Viertel, das, - *quarter*
Visum, das, *(pl.),* Visa or Visum *visa*
voll *full*
Vollkornbrot, das, -e *wholemeal bread*
von *from; in:* von… bis *from… until*
vor *in front of*
vorbeikommen *to come by; in:* einfach vorbeikommen *just come and see*
vorbeilaufen *to walk past*
vorbereiten *to prepare*
vorbereiten auf (sich) *to prepare for; to get ready for*
vorgesehen *in:* falls *if necessary*
vorherig *previous*
Vormittag, der, -e *morning*
vormittags *every morning*
Vorschlag, der, -¨e *in:* einen Vorschlag machen *to make a suggestion*
vorschlagen *suggest*
Vorschrift, die, -en *regulation*
vorsichtig *careful(ly)*
vorstellen (sich) *to introduce oneself*
Vorstellungsgespräch, das, -e *job interview*
Vorstellungstermin, der, -e *interview*
Vorteil, der, -e *advantage*
vorzüglich *exquisite, excellent*

W

wählen *to choose*; *to dial (telephone)*
während *during*
Wahrzeichen, das, - *landmark*
Wald, der, -¨er *forest*
Wand, die, -¨e *wall*
wandern *to hike, to walk*
wann? *when?*
warm *warm*
Wärmflasche, die, -n *hot water bottle*
warten *to wait*
was? *what?*; Was gibt es Neues? *What's new?*
Was kann ich für Sie tun? *What can I do for you?*
Wasser, das, - *water*
Weg, der, -e *way*
wegen *due to*
wegfahren *to drive away*
weggehen *to go away*
wegkommen *in:* günstig wegkommen *to be better off*
wehtun *to ache*; *to hurt*
weil *because*
Wein, der, -e *wine*
Weinglas, das, -¨er *wine glass*
Weinlokal, das, -e *wine bar*
weiß *white*
Weißbrot, das, -e *white bread*
Weißglas, das *clear glass*
Weißkraut, das *white cabbage*
Weißwein, der, -e *white wine*
Weißwurst, die, -¨e *white sausage*
weiter *in:* weiter zur *as far as*
weitergehen *to continue walking; to go ahead*
weiterhin *continue* in: etwas weiterhin tun *to continue to do something*
weiterleiten *to put through, to forward*
weitermachen *to carry on*
welche? *which?*
Welt, die, -en *world*
wem? *(Dat) who?, (to) whom?*
wen? *(Akk) who?, whom?*
wenden an (sich) *to turn to*
wenigstens *at least*
wer? *who?*
werden *to become*
werfen *to throw*
werfen *in:* einen Blick werfen *to take a look*
Werktag, der, -e *working day*
werktags *during the week*
weshalb? *why?*
Westen, der *west*

Wetter, das *weather*
wichtig *important*
widersprechen *to contradict*
wie? *how?;* Wie ist Ihr Name? *What's your name?*
wie lange? *how long?*
wie oft? *how often?*
Wie spät ist es? *What time is it?*
Wie viel Uhr ist es? *What time is it?*
wie viele? *how many?*
wieder *again*
wiederkommen *to come back*
wiegen *to weigh*
willkommen *welcome*
Windbeutel, der, - *cream puff*
Winter, der, - *winter*
wir *we*
wirklich *really*
wissen *to know*
wo? *where?*
Woche, die, -n *week*
Wochenende, das, -n *weekend*
woher? *where from?*
wohin? *where to?*
wohnen *to live*
Wohnzimmer, das, - *living room*
Wolkenbruch, der, -¨e *downpour*
wollen *to want*
Wort, das, -¨er *word*
Wörterbuch, das, -¨er *dictionary*
Wortschatzaufgabe, die, -n *vocabulary exercise*
Wunder, das, - *in:* kein Wunder *no wonder, it's not surprising*
wunderschön *beautiful*
wünschen *to wish*
Wurst, die, -¨e *cold meat/cut*
würzen *to season*

Y

Yen, der, - *yen*
Ypsilon *y*

Z

zahlen *to pay*
Zahnschmerzen, die *(pl.)* *toothache*
Zäpfchen, das, - *suppository*
Zebrastreifen, der, - *zebra crossing/pedestrian crossing*
Zehner, der, - *10-euro note/bill*
Zehn-Euro-Schein, der, -e *10-euro note/bill*
zeichnen *to draw*
zeigen *to show*
Zeit, die, -en *time*
Zeitung, die, -en *newspaper*
Zentrum, das, *(pl.)* Zentren *centre*
zerstören *to destroy*
Zeugnis, das, -se *certificate*
ziehen lassen *to let something stand*
Zimmer, das, - *room*
Zimmernummer, die, -n *room number*
Zitrone, die, -n *lemon*
Zitronenscheibe, die, -n *slice of lemon*
zu *to; in*
zu Hause *at home*
zu viel *too much*
Zucker, der *sugar*
zuerst *first*
Zug, der, -¨e *train*
zugeben *to add*
zuhören *to listen to*
zuletzt *finally*
zum = zu dem *to the*
zum Beispiel *for example*
zum Wohl! *to your health!*
zurück *back*
zurückbekommen *to get back*
Geld zurückbekommen *to get money back*
zurückfliegen *to fly back*
zurückkommen *to come back*
zurückrufen *to ring/call back*
zusagen *accept*
zusammen *altogether, together*
zusammenkommen *to meet*
Zusammenstoß, der, -¨e *collision*
zusammenstoßen *to collide*
zuschauen *to watch*
Zutat, die, -en *ingredient*
zuzahlen *in:* Sie müssen dazuzahlen *you have to pay a contribution*
zwei *two*
zweimal *twice*
zweite *second*
Zwiebel, die, -n *onion*
zwischen *between*